U-188

U-188

A German Submariner's Account
of the War at Sea 1941–1945

As told to Klaus Willmann
by Anton Staller

Translated by Geoffrey Brooks

Frontline Books, London

Original German-language edition titled *Das Boot U 188*, first published by
Rosenheimer Verlagshaus in 2008

This English edition first published in 2015 by Frontline Books

an imprint of Pen & Sword Books Ltd,
47 Church Street, Barnsley, S. Yorkshire, S70 2AS
www.frontline-books.com

Copyright © 2008 Rosenheimer Verlagshaus GmbH & Co. KG, Rosenheim,
Germany

Translation copyright © Frontline Books, 2015

ISBN: 978-1-84832-760-3

CIP data records for this title are available from the British Library

For more information on our books, please visit
www.frontline-books.com, email info@frontline-books.com
or write to us at the above address.

Printed and bound by CPI Group (UK) Ltd, Croydon, CR0 4YY

Typeset and designed by M.A.T.S. Leigh-on-Sea, Essex

Contents

List of Plates

Note on Credits.
The photographs on the cover and in the plate section are from private sources. The original copyright in the photographs could not be determined in every case.

This book is dedicated to the memory of Anton Staller,
organ-maker of Grafing, died 6 February 2008, to his shipmates
aboard *U-188* and to all U-boat men of his time.

Preface

The Second World War, to those that fought and lived through it, was a very personal experience. All have their own memories, all their own stories to tell. Many had a 'good' war, finding lucrative posts far from the fields of conflict. For some it was the most memorable time of their lives, full of adventure and excitement. To others, though, the war was a terrible and sickening episode, a period that was so traumatic they could never relate its events and many veterans went to their graves with their stories untold.

It is also true that many who fought side-by-side, even shoulder-to-shoulder, saw their experiences differently. Within households, a decorated war hero might have a pacifist brother; parents who still bore the scars of the First World War sought desperately to restrain their children from rushing to arms just two decades later.

However different the experiences of individuals were, and however divergent their opinions, all are equally valid. Indeed, it is not for others to decry the words of those survivors of that awful conflict. We were not there; we do not know.

This is why Anton Staller's memoir is so important, particularly as his condemnation of his wartime service differs from the more positive recollections of many of the young men of his generation. It may be that with the passage of time, Staller's views have hardened. It is also a fact that time colours our perspective of past events. Some memories fade whilst other details become entrenched within our personal monologue and then embellished each time they are repeated.

In this book, Anton Staller looks back a long way, and it is inevitable that as the fog of war mingles with the mists of the past, his ability to see clearly may, at times, have become somewhat obscured.

The consequence of this is that some of the rich detail, which is the distinguishing feature of this book, is at times at odds with other, more established accounts. It is in the full knowledge of this that this book has been published.

Some of Anton Staller's recollections of the war at sea with the Kriegsmarine may be in part at variance with those of others, but they are his memories of that time. The Second World War was, to those that fought and lived through it, a very personal experience, and *U-188* is Anton Staller's very personal story.

Introduction

I was born in 1934, one of the people to whom Federal Chancellor Kohl referred to as 'being blessed with a late birth'. My experience of the war is seeing US Forces arriving in my home village in the Bayerischer Wald. Only by hearing their very impressive accounts did I came to know the almost indescribable anxiety, tension and sufferings of my fellow countrymen just a few years older than myself who fought in the Second World War. Therefore I considered at length whether I was competent to relate the experience of one of the few U-boat men to have survived to the date of writing.

It was not until Toni Staller showed me the *U-188* War Diary, in which the watchkeeping officers and *Kapitänleutnant* ('*Kaleu*') Lüdden had set down all important and non-routine events in terse military phraseology, that I began to cast aside my doubts. This War Diary fell into the hands of the French Resistance in 1944 and was passed by them to British naval authorities who evaluated it in the minutest detail. Years after the war it arrived in Germany.

At the time of writing in 2007, there are few surviving members of the U-boat fraternity who by virtue of fortunate circumstances returned home. They are the eye-witnesses of a merciless naval war. One of them, Anton Staller, began his naval career as an ordinary seaman aboard *U-188*.

When he introduced me to electrical-engine room Petty Officer Baumann, who had sailed with him on three voyages aboard *U-188* and confirmed what Toni Staller told me, my last doubts disappeared. Following my reading of former Waffen-SS

Rottenführer Herbert Maeger's book *Verlorene Ehre, Verratene Treue,*[1] also published by Rosenheimer, I decided to relate Staller's story in the first person, convinced that only in that way is it possible to show readers how the Third Reich misused its young men and sent them to their deaths.

Klaus Willmann
Grafing, December 2007

---

1. Also published in English by Frontline Books as *Lost Honour, Betrayed Loyalty: The Memoir of a Waffen-SS Soldier* (2015).

Author's Foreword

The storm had raged around us for days. Our boat *U-188* pitched and rolled through the wild seas and could barely hold her course. We were to meet up here in the North Atlantic with other U-boats. All had orders to attack a heavily protected convoy bringing war materials from the United States to Britain.

Clad in leather suit and oilskins, I was the last man of the relief lookouts up onto the bridge. The howling of the storm and the raging of the grey-green waves was so loud that I could hardly understand what was shouted to me and had to guess. Quickly I fastened the snap hook at the end of a thick steel wire into the loop of my chest harness. Now I was safely secured to the breast-high steel coaming surrounding the conning tower. Without this safeguard, the breakers, ceaselessly crashing against our boat and sometimes sweeping over it, would have had us overboard like bundles of straw.

No matter how hard *U-188* tried to make headway against the raging seas, it seemed to us all the time that we were standing still. Over the next hour the strength of the wind increased. More and more often my companion Rötters and I, watching astern, would catch the warning shouts from Korn, the officer of the watch, or of Steimer at our backs, facing into the direction of travel: 'Watch out!' We would take a deep breath, knowing that in the next few seconds a breaker would sweep across the boat.

We could see the waves, capped with spindrift and up to ten metres high, moving towards us. They were faster than the boat, buried the stern and now Rötters or I would call out the warning loud and at the right moment: 'Watch out!' My footing would be swept away. In the sudden darkness the seconds became minutes, and my numbed hands inside the soaking gloves would seek desperately for a

3

handhold on the coaming edges. I would feel the ice-cold water enter my oilskins. The towel wrapped around my throat to prevent water getting in proved useless. No part of our bodies remained dry.

When we were relieved after four long hours our eyes burned with the strain and we tumbled, just like the bridge watch before us, half drunk and numb with cold, into the control room. Water entered the boat by the ton through the tower hatch, the voice tubes and the diesel ventilation mast and washed around threateningly in bilges under our feet. The bilge pumps worked ceaselessly to return it overboard.

The weather forced 'Kaleu' Lüdden to submerge. As we dived, the violent pitching and tossing of the boat gradually calmed into a gentle rocking. As this was going on I stood in the electric-motor or E-room desperately trying to peel off my protective clothing. Colleagues eventually gave me a hand and rubbed me dry with towels. Dressed in my thick blue roll-neck sweater, dry underwear and trousers, I hurried off to join the others at the cook's small galley and after emptying a steaming beaker of tea I felt a pleasant warmth stream through my body. I recovered quickly and was overcome by the almost irresistible urge to sleep.

I heaved myself up from the longitudinal flooring into my narrow bunk located between a maze of piping close above my head and a torpedo below it. Shortly before I fell asleep, images and memories of recent days raced through my head. How had it come about that I was here in this U-boat, a tiny cog in a clock mechanism, having to function as a part of the whole, a helpless sacrifice to the events of the era?

Chapter One

I Volunteer for the Kriegsmarine

On 9 September 1941, fourteen days before my eighteenth birthday, I received my summons for conscription from the military district commander for Rosenheim. It was just a short letter resplendent with the Reich eagle and swastika. Naturally like myself all my friends and acquaintances of my age had been in the Hitler Youth, for since 1939 by virtue of amendments to the Reich Youth Law all German children depending on sex had been obliged to be members of either the Hitlerjugend or the *Bund Deutscher Mädchen*, the League of German Girls. It would be wrong of me to protest nowadays that the comradeship, communal singing around camp fires and rambles from a campsite did not afford me a pleasurable feeling of community. It only occurred to me later that these pre-military activities in the countryside and suchlike trained us all for unconditional obedience.

During the short journey from Grafing to Rosenheim – the stretch of railway track between Munich and Salzburg was already electrified by then – I thought of the approximately 300 workers doing their obligatory six-month Reich Work Service (Reichsarbeitdienst – RAD) whom I had often observed being drilled on the meadow near the Urtelbach stream right behind the gymnastic hall in Grafing. They were housed in three large, simple barrack huts where the high school stands today. Naturally, I also knew that they did not just do military drill, but were primarily engaged in draining the swampy meadows in our surrounding countryside, straightening streams and carrying out useful work at other camps elsewhere throughout the Reich. I was used to a day's work, from early morning to late in the evening, but I found the RAD drill repugnant. Neither songs such as *Es ist so schön Soldat zu sein* (It's so fine to be a soldier) or *Oh du schöner Westerwald*, or seeing the ruler-straight columns of brown-uniformed men marching with shining spades at the shoulder filled me with the enthusiasm which the Reich leadership desired one to develop for these State institutions. Quite the contrary: when the old journeyman Lohhauser at my workplace, the organ-builder firm of Siemann at Munich, happened to mention that his son had volunteered for the Kriegsmarine and therefore did not have to do the obligatory RAD service, I spent several weeks reflecting on whether I should do the same in order to avoid RAD, the idea of which I found so unpleasant. Additionally I considered that my apprenticed trade as an organ-builder had few future prospects. Therefore I volunteered for the Kriegsmarine. As a child I had dreamed of far-distant places, and I had always been somehow attracted to the water. Furthermore, I thought, there was no barrack square on a ship where one could be subjected to military drill like those pitiable RAD servants. It was thoughts like these that kept my mind busy as I sat in that train going to Rosenheim.

In my quiet joy at having escaped the RAD was mixed a drop of bitter sorrow, for none of my companions of equal age came with me. They were all mustered at Wasserburg am Inn, where the Army made its choice, and most of them were probably taken into the Gebirg-jäger [mountain troops].

The building which housed the Rosenheim Military District Command was not far from the Loretowiese where Rosenheim's fun-fairs were held. An hour later I found myself in a spacious room standing in a long queue with countless other naked young men. Everything went ahead without much delay. One after another we were given a cursory examination by a doctor: blood pressure taken, a few knee bends, blood pressure taken again, stethoscope listened to heart and lungs, 'Bend over' (as I did this I would dearly have loved to let one rip), 'Mouth open!' and so on. Naturally I was written up 'kv' (fit for the front), I had expected nothing less, for I felt as fit as a fiddle and I was.

Two days later I celebrated my conscription together with the other eighteen-year-olds at Grafing. On 22 June 1941 the Führer had ordered the attack against the Soviet Union, and now the German Army was heading victoriously and apparently unstoppably eastwards. Almost daily special radio bulletins reported new gains of territory in Russia, of divisions of 'Communist sub-humans' wiped out. It was said that they had been planning to attack us and the German attack had pre-empted it. German U-boats were sinking large numbers of 'enemy ships' and seemed supreme at sea. France had been subdued and occupied by German troops. The German Luftwaffe flew operations against England. We fresh recruits felt like the Chosen, for soon we would also be numbered amongst those who contributed to 'Endsieg'.

In the market town of Grafing near Munich obituaries had continued to appear since the beginning of the Polish campaign; but what did that signify for us? The Reich Propaganda Ministry was insistent that it was an honour for a German man to die for Führer, Volk and Fatherland and that Germany would never forget its fallen heroes. Furthermore probably each one of us thought: Why should I worry about it? Nothing is going to happen to me!

On 22 June 1941, when the offensive against the Soviet Union began, my father had cast a damper on my euphoria. It was evening, my mother and three sisters had already gone to bed and the two of us sat alone in the kitchen of our small flat in Gries-Strasse. Father opened up an atlas before me on the table and reminded me of Napoleon's campaign in Russia. 'My boy! I don't want to discourage you but this Austrian has learnt nothing. First he gave the British their reason to declare war on us when he invaded Poland. The British, of all people, with their many connections and possessions around the world. And now this enormous Russia too? Nothing good will ever come of it.'

When I gave him a concerned look he put an arm around my shoulder and added, 'I can tell you that because I know that you won't tell the Nazis about me and have me hauled off by the Gestapo. I also know that you will soon be a soldier. Your one and only aim should be to come back home safely.' In a low voice he added, 'I am an old *Frontschwein* from the First World War. Perhaps at the end when they start running short of people they will come for me too.'

It was early afternoon when I shook the hands of my schoolfriends and friends of my own age at the rendezvous for our call-up celebration in front of Grafing railway station. We laughed and joked freely and, despite my secret doubts, I let myself be infected by their certainty of victory. Fritz Meier carried a white cardboard plaque fitted to a wooden frame inscribed with 'Vintage 1923' in large letters. We marched down Bahnhof-Strasse and crowded into the Grandauer inn on the market square. The innkeeper provided plenty of free beer, and because the autumn evening promised to be very mild, we went on from there to the 'Beim Wildbräu' beer-garden opposite. All the celebrants knew that they would soon be doing their RAD service and afterwards join the Gebirgsjäger or other branches of the Wehrmacht to perform their service for the Fatherland. I alone was still waiting for my call-up to the Kriegsmarine. Without exception we all felt ourselves to be grown men, wanted to be treated as such and therefore here too, untroubled at a series of tables pushed together in front of the beer-garden, we drank the free beer which the innkeeper and some of the other guests had placed on our tables.

Only a very keen observer might have noticed some faces amongst the loud-mouthed tipplers which seemed more reserved and reflective. Yet nobody could or wanted to stand aside from it, and so all were revellers.

Towards six that evening we heard loud singing:

'Es zittern die morschen Knochen der Welt vor dem Grossen Krieg:
Wir haben den Schrecken gebrochen, für uns war's ein grosser Sieg:
Wir werden weiter marschieren, wenn alles in Scherben fällt,
Denn heute da hört uns Deutschland
Und morgen die ganze Welt.'
('The shaky knees of the world still tremble at the Great War:
We have overcome the horror of it, for us it was a great victory.
We shall keep on marching, even if everything falls apart,
For today Germany listens to us, and tomorrow the whole world.')

A Hitler-Youth standard-bearer was marching across the market square. Julius Scheuer jumped up from his bench and ran to the semi-circular ornate stone parapet which divided the raised beer-garden from the market place. Laughing he bent forward over the grey granite structure, his powerful voice shouting louder than the singer: 'What do you want then, you lousy kid? You can't even march properly!' Schorsch Sauer stood up beside him and called out, 'And you'll have to learn singing too!' Max Kreitmeier joined the pair of them and roared; 'Obviously we can't win the war with you little stinging-nettle soldiers! So we'll have to get it over with before any of you gets hurt!'

We all rose just in time to see how an HJ-boy in the last rank turned, stuck out his tongue, bent over and – without breaking step – pointed with one finger to his rectum. Everybody roared with laughter. Julius Scheuer had stood beside me on the bench to get a better view. He was supporting himself with one hand on my shoulder and wiping the tears from his cheeks with the other. 'Those kids seem to have a sense of humour,' Konrad Trindl said.

Fired up by the alcohol, now they were all showing off and some-one promised, 'By the time these toy soldiers get to our age we will have already shown the enemy what for.'

'Obviously, we are going to win! You can almost hear the bulletins announcing victory!'

'And the Führer has said that the Russian campaign will soon have a glorious end!' Here I thought of my father and preferred to keep quiet. Then I heard from the other end of the benches, 'One shouldn't want to slip away when others have long been fighting at the foremost front.' Hans Weber, sitting opposite me called back, 'Schorsch, If you can let me know how to get away before call-up I'll buy you all the beer you want!'

Loud laughter broke out at this for a few seconds before Max Kreitmeier intervened angrily: 'What rubbish! As if any of us can disappear before his call-up! Everyone knows what happens to a shirker! Without further ado he is put up against a wall and shot as a coward and dishonourable traitor to his people!'

Not only I shrank back in horror when an unknown man at one of the neighbouring tables commented: 'That's right! And so it should be! My son has already been in Russia for some time. So hurry up and help him win for us!'

There was an embarrassed silence for a few seconds, and Hans Weber hastened to add: 'Well, you can see we're on our way!' Julius Scheuer ended the awkward moment: 'Hans, let this old cabbage grower say what he likes – everybody can!' With that we turned back to ourselves and soon our carefree youthfulness won the upper hand.

Later that evening, just before curfew, the innkeeper invited us into the saloon: 'Inside you can celebrate as long as you like. The next time you all meet up you won't be as young as this, and the local police will turn a blind eye today to our future defenders of the Fatherland.'

Few left. I remained behind, and when I stepped out into the market place on very unsteady legs, it was not long before morning dawned over the roofs of Grafing.

On the evening of 28 September 1941, five days after my eighteenth birthday, it was with very mixed feelings that I entered a Kriegs-marine barracks. It was surrounded by a high wire-mesh fence and lay in open country not far from the town of Buxtehude. The first impression of my future residence was more than sobering. The clean, grey barrack huts were an unpleasant reminder of those of the RAD at home, and when an ill-humoured petty officer in the office described how to get to my room, I felt quite down, and not only because of the long train journey I had just had. As the twelfth and last arrival in my room I had naturally the bed farthest from the only window in the musty room.

Next morning it all started: the shrill bosun's whistle tore us from sleep. After early morning exercises in our underwear, and a by-no-means delightful breakfast in the canteen hut, we fell in for roll-call on the spacious parade ground. There were about 300 recruits. A petty officer ordered us, in an impressively loud voice, to form three groups of equal size in an open square facing him. Now we saw what the pre-military training of the Hitler Youth had been about, and a few instructors, keen to show their importance, roared into action as the ordered ranks of threes began to form relatively quickly.

A impeccably-uniformed full lieutenant came out from one of the offices. The petty officer approached him with a couple of steps, came to attention, saluted and reported. The lieutenant said, 'You will not be issued uniforms here, but at the competent training unit at Bergen op Zoom. Your transport to Holland leaves in a few days!' At this point he paused to scrutinise our ruler-straight ranks. 'Before you leave us here, we must try to make useful naval soldiers of you! The Führer expects from every man unconditional obedience and total personal commitment to the realisation of our great aims!'

Over the next few days I asked myself again and again if I had done the right thing in volunteering for the Kriegsmarine. We were split up into groups, and wild raging instructors of the barracks permanent staff, able seamen, leading seamen and petty officers, hounded us with indescribable harshness across the parade ground in our civilian clothing.

Stillgestanden! Attention! *Die Augen links*! Eyes left! *Volle Deckung!* Lie flat!' *Sprung auf!* On your feet! *Marsch, marsch!*

We spent every evening washing our clothes and sweaty under-wear, our main hope being that in the damp cool of autumn they would be dry by morning. We often slept naked, for nobody had expected to spend such a long time in civilian dress. Every day we had room inspection, and woe betide the unfortunate inmate whose bed-pack was not made as per regulations or in whose locker the duty petty officer found a speck of dirt. Some of us began to have nightmares and I earnestly hoped that it would be better for us in Holland.

Finally, seven days later, the instructors led us to railway coaches reserved for the Kriegsmarine and handed us over at Bergen op Zoom to naval soldiers in field-grey. Naturally we had been aware for some time that as from today our infantry training began, and would last three months. The mild, warm rays of the autumn sun bathed the Dutch plain in light as carrying our small suitcases in the right hand we passed by the guards at the barracks gate singing loudly. The cared-for reddish-brown clinker planking of the former Dutch barracks shone with cleanliness within. This was how I had imagined a Kriegsmarine barracks would be, and I was probably not the only one to heave a sigh of relief when I entered our appointed squad-room with eleven other recruits.

Next morning our rather exaggerated expectations were nipped in the bud. The 'squad-room bulls' supervised our uniform issue and stifled our protests. Objections such as 'These boots are too big for me' or 'These dungarees are too small,' were answered by 'Change the boots with someone else, you blockhead,' or 'That jacket is fine, you Mummy's darling. Your stomach is too fat! That will soon change!'

After barely three hours without any helpful instructions we were all busy clearing out our tall lockers according to Army regulations. An able seaman of the permanent staff went through the long hut, and as he reached the door of our room roared: 'You are to pack your civilian clothing in impeccable condition into your suitcase or cartons at once! Every item of luggage must be labelled with your home address in legible script! That must be done as quick as you can. By tomorrow there will be no time for it, not even if you want to add a little note to Mummy. Tomorrow you will be sworn in to our Führer Adolf Hitler, to Volk and Fatherland. Then we shall make fine naval soldiers out of you effeminate sissies!' At that he shut the door again.

Heinz Lücker had his locker next to mine. He winked and murmured softly, 'That little braggart will sooner or later explode with his own importance, but the fishes will never get to eat him. That type always stays safely ashore.' At Buxtehude I had wondered once or twice at how candidly and trustingly Heinz confided in me. I also told him more than I did the others.

Next morning, dressed in our field-grey uniforms, highly polished jackboots and steel helmets we paraded in an open-sided square to be sworn in. In the afternoon following the declaration sworn before a Commander, our company commander and a number of naval officers, some of our instructors were unmasked as imaginative sadists.

Heinz Lücker and I were assigned to the same squad and seemed to have had a stroke of luck with our platoon leader. Petty Officer Maiwald shouted just as loudly as the others, but under his rough exterior we thought we saw from the beginning his good-natured, perhaps even indulgent core. We guessed that he would be three or four years older than ourselves. He wore the Black Wound Badge, the ribbon of the Iron Cross Second Class on his breast and limped a bit, which told us that he must already have been in action before he landed up here as an instructor.

Even our infantry instructors had to follow the training programme, however, for Lt-Commander Wolters saw everything. After a couple of days we gave our strict and unforbearing company commander the nickname 'The North Sea Terror'. He had the unpleasant habit of suddenly turning up unexpectedly alongside a platoon, looking over every man closely and then demanding: 'Do you not want to, or can't you? Don't pretend to be tired, or I shall personally keep you at it until you hear the angels singing!'

One day when threatening autumn clouds hung over the Netherlands, we saw the 'North Sea Terror' strutting through the training grounds behind the barrack blocks. I feared the worst when I saw him head directly for our squad. We were practising the correct way to pass senior officers when marching rigidly. Lt-Commander Wolters was only a few metres away when he shouted, 'Everybody listen out for my command!'

After a couple of minutes I felt the sweat running down my forehead, making my eyes burn. In our grey dungarees we now had to crawl through the wet autumn grass carrying the carbine and wearing our gas masks. The idea was to move forwards as quickly as possible hugging the ground. There was hardly enough air coming through the filter of my gas mask when the company commander called out, 'Go faster! Some of you lame ducks probably think you're on convalescence here! Stand up! March! March! It can be more difficult to breathe aboard warships than here. Therefore learn to breathe sparingly!'

Heinz Lücker told me later that 'this arse' had pressed down his buttocks with a boot and asked him quietly, 'Are you hoping for a wound to bring you home? With your hindquarters stuck up like that, are you hoping to be shot there and brought back to the Homeland?' Finally, after half an eternity, the 'North Sea Terror' made off after pausing to give some of us a blinding look. I had the impression that his steely blue eyes rested longer on me than on my comrades.

'Gas masks off!' The voice of Petty Officer Maiwald came as a relief. Heinz Lücker was standing beside me as we tore them off. He looked towards the officer in a rage and whispered half loud in my ear: 'Now he's going to bestow his charm on Schmidt's squad. Does that wandering scarecrow think we're going to land in England next and march with our jackboots and carbines on London?'

Before I could answer I noticed Petty Officer Maiwald standing close behind us. 'I should like to have overheard that, Lücker' he said.

Then he turned to us all, each still breathing heavily and trying to pack the gas mask in its long cylindrical metal container; 'You can form a semi-circle and sit down.' I was just about to obey this very welcome order when a wave by Maiwald stopped me. 'Herr Lt-Commander Wolters seems to have taken you to his fatherly heart. I am supposed to ask you if you would like to be his valet.' Speaking quietly enough to ensure that the others did not hear him he added, 'Woe betide you if you dare to turn down this generous offer. That would mean hell on earth for you here in future.' Raising his voice again he asked, 'What shall I report to the Herr Lt-Commander?'

In a couple of seconds I weighed up the pro's and con's which would arise by being in the immediate presence of the 'North Sea Terror'. Then I came to attention and reported: 'I am happy to accept the assignment, Herr Petty Officer.'

Maiwald gave me a nod. 'This and nothing else was expected of you, Ordinary Seaman Staller.'

Next day after my squad-room colleagues had completed the barracks drill and were engaged cleaning all rooms, floors, showers and toilets before the duty petty officer arrived to inspect them, I had to report to Lt-Commander Wolters. Privately I wondered if my duties with him as his valet would enable me to escape future punishment measures inflicted on the squad. If the duty petty officer found dirt or dust in some obscure corner of our room he would have us up half the night chasing round the parade ground.

Following Maiwald's advice I went with highly-polished field boots, spotless fingernails and clean dungarees to the first floor of the barracks block and with foreboding knocked on the door behind which the all-powerful 'North Sea Terror' lived.

The door was thrown open: I came to attention, saluted and reported myself. To my surprise the base commander greeted me in the most friendly manner. He invited me into his room courteously, showed me his uniforms hanging in a large wardrobe, the brushes for their care, his boots, the elegant shoes to go with his walking-out uniform and other personal belongings to which I would have to direct my attentions over the coming few months. Maiwald had told me what special value the commander placed on shiny footwear and also mentioned some other peculiarities I would do well to bear in mind. At the end of our infantry training in Holland I was surprised at how successful I had been serving the 'North Sea Terror' almost to his complete satisfaction.

A few days before Christmas 1941 – that harsh winter was also unusually cold in the Netherlands – we were subjected to a very thorough examination by a Kriegsmarine medical team. Clad only in underwear, I was one of the last in line in the moderately heated barracks gymnasium. The senior surgeon handed me a certificate with a nod of the head. It concluded with the note 'GFU'.

At attention I enquired, 'Request permission to ask the Senior Surgeon a question. What does GFU mean?'

'Man! You can be proud of it! This result is achieved by only a few. With your strange calling naturally you cannot serve in an engine room or on electrical machinery. But from the medical point of view you are outstandingly suitable for the seaman branch of the U-boat Arm. GFU means "Gun captain U-boat!"'

In horror I replied, 'But I wanted to be a surface sailor. Underwater I will definitely become claustrophobic and endanger my shipmates. I consider myself completely unsuitable for the U-boat Arm.'

The doctor's friendly face for show vanished. 'Silence!' he shouted. This drew the attention of everybody to us. 'Where you are sent to serve Führer, Volk and Fatherland is not for you to decide! The Kriegsmarine does not have jurisdiction to take into account special wishes. We all have our duty to fulfil where we are sent. Dismiss!'

Next morning we were put aboard a train at Bergen op Zoom. None of us had got to see much of the Dutch town for an outbreak of scarlet fever in one of the barrack blocks had resulted in all of us being confined to camp. As our railway coaches were now being coupled up there was a blizzard which obscured the view of the outside like a white curtain at every window.

During the halting journey eastwards it cleared up and towards evening one of the recruits called out, 'We're crossing the Ems! Boys, we're almost back home!'

Soon after, the train stopped at Leer in East Frisia where we got out and paraded in the station forecourt before being marched off behind the blue-uniformed petty officers to the Kriegsmarine holding camp. This consisted of some unpretentious barrack huts surrounded by wire mesh fencing in open country outside the town. After supper we were assigned rooms. Heinz Lücker was in the bed next to me and everybody speculated until late in the night: When and where would we be trained finally for the front at sea? I was the squad-room senior and towards midnight received an evil rebuke from an able seaman, for even our room had to observe silence at night, 'Your loud twaddle can be heard everywhere! Shut up!'

Next morning a petty officer stamped through the barrack hut blowing his bosun's whistle and shouting: 'Boys! Be glad that you were able to slumber so peacefully with us here! Our infantry in Russia has frozen limbs. Everybody outside! After breakfast bring your greys in impeccable condition. You are to receive a new issue of clothing!'

By midday we were admiring each other in our smart blue walking-out uniforms. Leave at last! Finally seeing friendly civilians again . . . laughing with and chatting up girls . . . In small groups we gathered at the camp gate. Beforehand, however, each of us had to be inspected in a booth near the guardroom by a couple of grinning petty officers and senior grade seamen. A petty officer of 22 or 23 years with an ugly, fresh-looking scar on his chin explained: 'Before we let you rutting stags loose on civilized humanity, we must look at each of you under the microscope. You have learnt respect and how to salute per regulations. We do not want to get to hear any complaints in this regard.'

In front of me in the queue was the Viennese Franz Plaschok. The petty officer ordered: 'Show your fingernails! Take off your shoes and socks!' Then he began to sniff loudly. 'Now look at this type. The showers were given extra heat for you all, and this little piglet still wants to go out with stinky feet. Have you ever smelt anything like it?' He gave Plaschok a reproachful look. 'Wash your feet and put on clean socks! Today we shall be lenient. I will hold your leave pass here. You can apply to me for it later, but as a German sailor. Dismiss!' He turned to me at once. 'Produce your comb!'

As everybody else before me had done, I had to open the trouser fly of my walking-out uniform and drop them to allow my underpants to be inspected for cleanliness. Then we had to produce the issue condom. 'We cannot hand you over to our patroness in the town

16

unprotected! Woe be to him who gets infected with something. That is self-mutilation and will be severely punished! Nobody will be happy about it. Therefore: unconditional cleanliness and hygiene in every situation of your life!'

For the third Christmas of the war at the naval transit camp at Leer every room received a pitiful little tree. Heinz Lücker told us that on one of his long walks he had discovered a forestry school with marvellous small fir trees. 'They have a really big choice!' Our squad decided at once: 'If we cannot celebrate Christmas at home because these Heinis still don't know where they want to send us, then we should at least have a decent tree!' Lücker added: 'If somebody is prepared to go there, then we can all club together and buy one.'

There was nobody to be found at this forestry school and as squad-room senior an hour later I began sawing a very carefully chosen little fir tree. It was the only time I had ever committed theft.

Next morning an ordinary seaman from a neighbouring hut threw open our door and warned us: 'They are coming to you next, looking for a stolen Christmas tree.' Like lightning Lücker whipped the little tree off its plinth and rushed out of the room with it. 'I'll hide it in the neighbouring room's rafters. Put the original tree in its place!' At that he disappeared but soon returned. 'They'll never find it. What a decent East Prussian gardener hides remains undiscovered.' Horst Krause and I had just finished replacing the meagre tree on the plinth between the two rows of beds in our room when the door was thrown open. Senior Boatswain Heinisch and a gentleman in a green jacket looked around our room as if searching for something. We all stood at attention and gave them questioning looks, since we had no idea what this could possibly be about. Nevertheless I was relieved when the boatswain said to his companion, 'Well, Herr Manser, this is the last of the occupied rooms. The others are all locked up. Our sailors don't go round sawing down fir trees that don't belong to them! I was sure of that before we started.'

On 9 January 1942, together with Heinz Lücker and four other comrades from Bergen op Zoom, I went aboard the *Wilhelm Gustloff* at Gotenhafen near Danzig. We all knew that with this cruise ship the National Socialist organisation 'Kraft durch Freude' (Strength through Joy) had conveyed deserving compatriots into the

Norwegian fjords, to sightsee along interesting European coasts and even farther-flung destinations. Now it served the 2nd U-boat Training Division as a floating barracks. To me she looked gigantic.

As a church organ builder I had no technical qualifications and so with Lücker had been selected for the seaman branch aboard U-boats. Because of our unusually good health and excellent vision as confirmed by medical testing, we were to be trained as conning-tower lookouts, for other bridge-watch tasks and to familiarise ourselves with the deck guns.

Our lodgings were in one of the lower decks just below the waterline in a two-bunk outer cabin. Our training company had its quarters here. We emptied out sea-bags and stowed everything in the locker exactly as per regulations. Lücker finished first, checked his work critically and then said, 'Toni, the two of probably can't be collared here by the duty NCO. Let's hope we don't have that unpleasant mate, the one with the square, flat face we had to salute.'

I agreed with him, adding, 'It's all the same, Heinz. The main thing is, we're here together and can help each other get through it.'

For some days the confusion of longitudinal and transverse corridors seemed like a labyrinth. We often mixed up the 'tween decks, found the training rooms only with difficulty and once even got lost trying to find the dining hall.

From now on we drilled until we were sick of it, learnt to tie nautical knots in record time, to throw lines accurately, at a glance recognise German and enemy warships, and recite the armament and fighting power of each. We also had to know aircraft types and their range off pat, which often brought out the worst impatience in instructors. We were also trained to exhaustion in ship-to-ship visual signalling by flag and morse lamp, in short everything that was necessary on a U-boat conning tower. Here too on the *Wilhelm Gustloff* every instructor was a king, but nearly all of them prepared us for what lay ahead in a thoroughly impressive and easily remembered way, if in rough colloquial tones. 'On a U-boat, every man depends on the ability and reliability of his shipmates no matter at what station he is on the boat!'

Punctually at six every morning we were awoken by the shrill of the bosun's pipe. 'Up and out of your shit-baskets!' We had to stand at attention at the foot of the bed wearing our knee-length white nightshirts. Woe betide the unfortunate man who failed to do this quickly enough. 'You sleepy Mummy's boy. Thirty press-ups!' The mate with the flat, square face liked to demonstrate his power.

I knew from our conversations at Bergen op Zoom that Lücker came as I did from a family whose members were not convinced National Socialists. We had become close friends and spoke frankly between ourselves. Provided we were not too tired we would continue whispered conversations after the official time for sleep, he from the bunk above mine.

Often we exchanged memories of our childhood and youth. I told him that in March 1932 my father had taken my seven-year-old sister Lisa and myself, then aged nine, in the car of an SPD friend for a drive in the country. It was not intended to be a pleasure trip although we children had great fun tossing SPD handbills opposing the election of Hitler out of the car windows. In 1933 my father spent some time in 'protective custody' and I told Lücker that afterwards I found it inexplicable that my father had allowed himself to be persuaded, as a convinced Social Democrat, to join the Nazi Party. Heinz related that his parents at Allenstein had been friendly with a Jewish medical family. When they disappeared suddenly one night his father, a Catholic, experienced similar difficulties for talking out of turn about the Jews.

Nevertheless we both believed that Germany would win the war. The daily bulletins of successes, not only from the U-boat Arm, strengthened us in this belief and also that the war was justified, for the Versailles Treaty of 1919, often called 'the peace of infamy', was simply intolerable. We often discussed such ideas and similar thoughts whenever we had the time.

The unnecessary chicanery of our instructors disgusted us both. Time and again, despite his best efforts, one of our number would not have stowed his locker in perfect compliance with regulations. Boatswain Hansen in particular, feared by everybody, would strike at every inspection by selecting a victim and emptying the contents of his locker on the floor. The delinquent would then have to pack everything into his sea-bag lightning fast, double to the upper deck with it, empty it out and then bring down, at the double, each item individually and put it in his locker according to regulations. Members of the ship's permanent company would stand observing at the 'tween decks, encouraging the delinquents with foul abuse. Some recruits collapsed exhausted during this punishment which was called a 'Flaggeluzzi'. There would never be an officer in attendance when it was being carried out. Lücker and I took the greatest pains to ensure that our lockers looked like an advertising photo for the Kriegsmarine and were fortunate enough therefore never to be victimised.

Every Friday our company had to proceed, singing at the tops of our voices, to a building ashore near the anchorage for our floating barracks. The evil reputation which had preceded this locality was confirmed on the first day. Its rough-hewn instructors had a seemingly inexhaustible vocabulary of insults for 'you Mummy's darlings', 'you spineless jellyfish' and so forth. I was not afraid of the water, but it cost me an effort to allow myself to be lowered ten metres down in the so-called *Tauchtopf* (dive pot). Beforehand we had to learn how to buckle the Dräger safety vest on correctly. This was a flat vest equipped with an integral mini-oxygen bottle, nose clip and mouthpiece. 'You won't be wanting to drown when your boat goes down! With the safety vest there's always a chance for you!'

The instructor shouted to a colleague: 'You are still up here in the dry, you coward! I still have you on the safety line! If you feel unwell down there with the sharks then just give it a tug. But woe to you if you try to spin me a yarn. I can pull you up at any time, but if you are only pretending to feel unwell I'll give you hell until you're glad to be healthy again! Right, now put on your lead belt to keep you down. Before that fix the nose clip of the Dräger on your hooked nose so that no water can enter that way into your luxurious body! Now put in the mouthpiece and in you go!'

To another I heard him shout: 'You slowpoke, do you require special treatment? You can have punishment exercises later until your arse boils!' This and similar encouragement could be heard everywhere, and when it was my turn I forced myself to go down quickly. Below was an imitation of the deck and conning tower of a U-boat. I had to circle the turret once and because the lead belt held me down, and despite the lift of the safety vest, I had to be hauled up on the rope. That evening Lücker and I concluded that if it came to it, the safety vest was more a psychological aid than a real safety feature. We both also received the bad news in letters from our mothers that our fathers had been called up, Heinz's father to the infantry, my father to the Gebirgsjäger.

Our training in the *Tauchtopf* continued on other Fridays. Next we were taught to escape from the control room of a U-boat at a reasonably shallow depth. For the purpose we had to go down three floors of the building to where a watertight and pressure-resistant steel hatch in a 'bulkhead' was opened and we found ourselves in a mock-up of a U-boat conning tower. Naturally we were well versed by an instructor beforehand in what awaited us. Three men at a time wearing their safety vests were to stand inside a *Luftsüll* (a steel tube between a hatch in the ceiling and the imitation control room).

'Strictest discipline! No jostling! Now we shall let the water flood in. That will compress the air in the control room. Because of the pressure the water will not rise into the *Luftsüll*. When the hatch at the top end of the *Luftsüll* opens you may enter the *Luftsüll* one by one and allow yourself to be swept up as the water rises. We want no panicking and keep your nerve at all costs. It's already been done a thousand times. Even you can learn how a man may escape from a sunken U-boat.' My heart beat like never before. When finally I was swept upwards I felt more than relieved. The following Friday we had to repeat the process but without the life-vest. It was emphasised that when rising we had to force the air out of our lungs several times to equalise the pressure and so avoid internal injury.

We called Saturdays 'grind days'. In that ice-cold January of 1942 we were chased through ice and snow clad in our thin drill dungarees carrying field pack and carbine. This was supposed to toughen us up to the standard expected of a U-boat man. On the third 'grind day' Boatswain Kruse ordered suddenly, 'Gas masks on!' Then we had to run ten kilometres.

At a moderate jog I passed several checkpoints on the seemingly endless route, fighting against nausea to reach the finishing line totally exhausted. Kruse was waiting for us there in his warm greatcoat. In a rage and without waiting for his order I ripped off the gas mask. Kruse said we had been amongst the first to finish. Lücker and I looked back in disbelief to our struggling colleagues. Some of them had collapsed and remained where they fell. Only by calling upon our last reserves of strength did we manage to make our way back to the *Wilhelm Gustloff*. At supper in the dining hall it was rumoured that Kruse had been ordered to report to Lt-Cdr Bornstein to account for this forced march. It changed nothing. In the weeks which followed, Kruse remained one of the most feared slave-drivers.

There was a change for me, however. Apparently a certain reputation had preceded me from Bergen op Zoom, for after one of our many periods of instruction, our platoon leader Sub-Lt Unverzagt detained me and asked courteously if I would like to be his valet here on the *Gustloff*. We all knew him as a calm, intelligent officer and therefore I agreed without much reflection. I was not without experience as a valet. I was surprised on the first evening when I reported to Unverzagt to be asked: 'Ordinary Seaman Staller, I have heard that you are a quite passable violinist and you played for a youth orchestra in Munich. is that correct?'

'Yes, sir!'

'For heaven's sake, Staller, why didn't you make it known? I had to find all this out from your shipmates! One of our violinists in the officers' mess has been suddenly transferred out to a boat. Suggestion: instead of cleaning duty with the others, would you play with us in the evenings in future.'

'Yes, sir!'

Sub-Lt Unverzagt asked if I had a violin, and when I told him it was at home he requested that I write immediately to my mother asking her to send it on at once. He would personally guarantee that the instrument would be returned to my home should I be drafted unexpectedly and could not send it myself. Lücker expressed his pleasure at my appointment and confessed that it was he who had recommended me as a musician to our platoon leader. Over the next three months I escaped much evening chicanery of our training instructors by my membership of the officers' mess quartet. It always amazed me that our officers seemed to tolerate these many punishment measures silently or in ignorance. It was repeatedly made clear to us, however, that as future U-boat men our training had to be especially harsh, but as I saw it this 'Flaggeluzzi' and similar nonsense had little to do with it. Once I heard Petty Officer Hansen say: 'Running upstairs before going to sleep makes you hard, you sissy. Later you will thank me for this on your U-boat!' Against that kind of arbitrary action we were totally helpless. The officers appreciated me as a musician, however, and so now and again I was treated to a glass of good wine or champagne in the wardroom.

At the end of our three-month stay on the former 'Strength through Joy' ship almost all of us were scattered. Lücker and I were lucky enough to be drafted together to Swinemünde on the gun-captain course. Before we left, Sub-Lt Unverzagt gave me a copy of the book *Wir hielten Narvik*. As dedication he had handwritten in his clear script:

'*Trotz allem Pech ein fröhlich Lied*
Nun Schicksal schlag nur zu.
Wir werden seh'n, wer früher müd',
ich oder du.
In Dankbarkeit, Ihr Leutnant Unverzagt.'
('Despite all the bad luck, a happy song
Now Fate will decide.
We shall see, who becomes weary first,
I or you.
In gratitude, your Lieutenant Unverzagt.')

That evening was the last time I ever saw this officer, whom I held in such great esteem. On 26 June 1944 he was lost aboard *U-719* west of Northern Ireland, depth-charged and sunk by the destroyer HMS *Bulldog*.

At Swinemünde we were lodged in four-man cabins aboard the steamer *General Osario*, anchored in port. Lücker and I were members of the same fifteen-man squad; he was in the neighbouring cabin. Over the next few days we were made familiar in theory with the individual components, range, handling and care of 10.5cm guns and also lighter weapons. Additionally all of us could dismantle and care for hand weapons such as MG's and machine-pistols with our eyes shut. This did not keep the slave-drivers off our backs in their efforts to 'make us hard'. For even minor infringements and before our first shooting training some of us got to know very well what it felt like to carry a 45kg shell. One evening it was my turn.

Boatswain Birkdorn did not feel that I had given him a smart enough salute[1] just before curfew when returning from town with Lücker and other classmates. As a punishment I had to play 'Bunny hop' which involved hopping around the entire upper deck in the squatting position and cuddling a 45-kg shell. Birkdorn followed me round slowly, showering me with foul-mouthed encouragement. When at the end of the circuit I could only stand erect with the last effort of will he called out, 'You could lift a woman weighing a hundredweight, but it's too much for you to give our enemy a small gift of our love! Would you like to slacken off now, Ordinary Seaman Staller? I advise you not to, otherwise I shall find time for you all night! Then we would find out which of us comes off worse!' I gritted my teeth in rage. Finally at the pre-determined finishing line I laid the heavy shell as gently as possible on the deck. Birkdorn watched me every second. Several of my colleagues before me had collapsed during this procedure. Although my knees trembled and I had to breathe deeply, in that moment I felt strong.

After we had gone over and over the operating drills, the dismantling and re-assembly of the gun and aiming the thing until we were sick of it, one day we sailed out for the first time into the calm Baltic on several small gunboats. There we were shown a tug towing astern at a respectable distance a yellowish-white net mounted on a wooden barge. Our boat was to fire the first round at the mock-up. Aiming through my optic I advised the range values. I was given the order 'Permission to fire!' and hit the firing knob. I noticed with

---

1. In the Kriegsmarine a *Matrose* was an Ordinary Seaman; a *Matrosen-Gefreiter* an Able Seaman and a *Matrosen-Obergefreiter* a Leading Seaman. There were three further grades of Leading Seaman; *Matrosen-Hauptgefreiter*, *Matrosen-Stabsgefreiter* and *Matrosen-Stabsobergefreiter*. The Petty Officer grades (without portepee) began at *Bootsmannsmaat* (bosun's mate), *Oberbootsmannmaat* (senior bosun's mate), *Steuermannsmaat* (coxswain's mate) and *Obersteuermannsmaat* (senior coxswain's mate). Chief Petty Officer grades carried the dagger (portepee) and wore the peaked cap, insignia of rank being worn on the shoulder straps. Aboard a U-boat the coxswain (IIIWO) *Obersteuermann*, two senior engine room hands, *Obermaschinisten*, and the senior radio officer, *Oberfunkmeister*, were of Chief Petty Officer grade. In the Wehrmacht, in specific circumstances NCOs as well as officers received the military salute from subordinate ranks.

surprise how the small boat cushioned the powerful recoil of the gun. Then I saw that simultaneous with the explosion of my shell a white fountain of water had reared up towards the grey heavens halfway between tug and target.

Our platoon leader Chief Petty Officer Kerner was standing behind me and began to rage at once: 'Can't you take decent aim, you sourpuss?' He was in his early thirties, a long-serving naval man of medium height and stocky who made an uncouth impression. 'Are you completely mad?' he roared. 'With your first round you almost sank that innocent tugboat, the pride of our Baltic Fleet!' Standing with arms akimbo he could hardly control his temper. 'That will have an unpleasant aftermath for you, you spineless jellyfish! Do it again! This time decently! I'm sick to the teeth of you sloppy gunners! Load! Permission to fire!' This time I hit the target, but this did nothing to mollify our platoon leader.

In the evening we were punished with the 'special treatment'. Then we members of the Kerner platoon sank exhausted in our cots. In a dream I saw the tug in flames and at six was frightened awake by the bosun's whistle of the duty petty officer making his way down the corridors. Petty Officer Müller looked rather satisfied this morning, but we were unable to understand why this otherwise so surly man should look so pleased with himself.

An hour later we found out what was on the schedule for us today. Until then nobody had paid any attention to the almost imperceptible gentle rocking of our depot ship moored fast in harbour. Now I and probably quite a few others were filled with dark forebodings as we went up on deck and saw the storm-tossed Baltic. Kerner drove us with more gusto than previously down the gangplank to the gunboat, and hardly was the last man of our platoon on board than we cast off and headed out to sea. My legs spread wide for balance, I stood at my station near the gun at the bow, glanced at the tense faces of the gun crew and held firm to the boat's rail. Scarcely had our nutshell left the calm waters of the harbour basin than its dance began. The bow dipped and rose, spraying us with great curtains of water. Threatening dark clouds raced across the skies. I was thrown back, lifted up more gently and then sank down in one or other direction. I held ever tighter to the rail, felt alternately hot or cold, sweat ran over my forehead. After a few minutes my stomach began to revolt. I thought; 'Sea sickness? What would they think of it on a U-boat?' I told myself at all costs not to vomit. But when Lücker did so a few seconds later, my breakfast came up. Lücker was wailing: 'I am going to die. My limbs feel heavy as lead. Comrades, I want to die!' Kerner stood near us with legs spread wide, resilient and flexible, toe-poked Lücker several times in the side and shouted angrily, 'Control yourself, man! Get up!'

The boat's commander, Petty Officer Kudowsky, a middle-aged man, hair greying at the temples, now left the bridge and looked around threateningly: 'Look at these sissies! And you people want to be German sailors?' An indescribably contemptuous glare fell on the still prostrate Lücker. 'You'll be able to die soon enough! But not here on my boat! A German seaman has to get used to rough seas. That goes for everyone. Get up! Man the gun! We're almost at the target!'

Kudowsky gave Kerner a challenging look and then returned to the wheelhouse with a rolling gait. Kerner raged: 'Now finally we've got the type of conditions you're going to find on a U-boat and you lazy swine want to slack. This will not do! We don't have an opportunity like this every day. Ahead to port I can see the target between the waves. Load! Permission to fire!'

I still haven't worked out how I managed to conquer my seasickness. When after many misses and only a few hits we made fast alongside our depot ship at dusk, I collapsed exhausted on deck. Some of our squad were laughing and joking, the heavy seas not having affected them. On the contrary. When the rest of us pushed away our supper, the unaffected pounced on it with evident relish and added it to their own lentil and sausage stew.

We were not subjected to the feared 'special treatment' that evening. Before I finally fell asleep I was beset by the worst doubts that I could ever accustom myself to such heavy seas. We soon recovered from it but remained depressed and looked forward to our future as sailors with anxiety. The storm did not abate overnight and I fought all day long in the gunboat against vomiting and actually succeeded.

Our gun-captain's course ended in the last week of July 1942. We all paraded on deck in our walking-out uniforms. I cannot remember a word of what our company commander said in his parting address. Every man on the course received his posting: next morning I took the train to Bremen.

I never saw any of my squad again. Towards the end of the war I discovered that Lücker was aboard *U-257* when the boat was lost in the Atlantic on 21 February 1944.

Chapter Two

Working-Up in the Baltic

With two other ordinary seamen I occupied a room in the building of the former police barracks at Bremen, not far from the Deschimag shipyard. Our simply furnished lodgings rather reminded us of home. Even if strict military regulations were in force here, the new surroundings had something of a family feel about them for us U-boat men because they were run by the so-called 'U-boat Mother'. I do not recall her name, but that first evening I heard that this middle-aged woman of very strong character had lost her husband in the First World War. He had been the commander of a U-boat. Probably for that reason she considered the U-boat men in the naval home as her boys. She knew that a new boat was waiting for us at Deschimag AG Weser.

In 1942 the air defences of the Reich were still so strong that an air raid alarm was a rarity. If the sirens howled in Bremen it never bothered us much. Nevertheless all occupants of the former police barracks had to take turns standing fire-watch in the surrounding coffee-roasting factories to raise the alarm immediately in the event of fire.

U-188 was a Type IXC/40, one of the big boats developed for long-range operations. She was the last of five built at Deschimag and had the builder's number 1028. Her keel had been laid on 18 August 1941 and she was launched on 31 March 1942. The boat was already afloat but completion work was continuing around the clock. Over the next few days we were crowded together at desks in a classroom near the shipyard where engineer instructors used diagrams to explain the compartmentalisation of *U-188*, its equipment, armament and numerous technical details. I also got to know other members of the crew. Besides myself there were other inexperienced newcomers who looked up to the veteran 'old hands' as I did, although only a few of them had previously sailed on a boat of this type. They summed us up with quick appraising glances. It was clear to everybody that before long our lives would depend on each individual's devotion to duty, his readiness to fight, his comradeship and cooperation and not least also his ability and knowledge.

From the first moment we newcomers felt accepted into the comradeship of the boat as a result of the respect for our superiors which had been drilled into us. I promised myself that I would always carry out the tasks assigned to me with the greatest responsibility. Lt Lüdden,[1] chief engineer Lt Kiessling (LI) and the two watchkeeping officers Sub-Lt Meenen and Sub-Lt Benetschik (I WO and II WO respectively) sat instructing us occasionally. I had the impression that this was partly a means of sizing up our attentiveness and ability to absorb information.

Four days later the other ranks were in the day room in high spirits, the NCOs grouping themselves around Chief Petty Officer Heinrich Korn (the coxswain, who would later act as III WO aboard) while we lower-grade ratings gravitated to our own circle. I believe that in no other branch of the Wehrmacht was so much store set by recognition of rank, discipline and unconditional obedience. Even now, in carefree mood, enjoying a few stiff grogs with our 'U-boat Mother', we sensed the differences in rank between us like an invisible screen. Engine-room Petty Officer Baumann sat with radio Chief Petty Officer Schulz recounting a few days he had spent at the Junkers works, Munich-Allach, in order to familiarise himself with the manufacture and operation of the Junkers air compressors which he called 'Jumbos'.

'On my last voyage with *Kaleu* Merten I was also on a Type IXC/40 boat, but there was no diesel-driven compressed air generator in the

---

1. In translation *Kapitänleutnant* ('*Kaleu*') is taken as 'Lt-Cdr' although it closer to senior lieutenant. *Oberleutnant* is taken as 'Lt', *Leutnant* as 'Sub-Lt' corresponding to Royal Navy ranks. Siegfried Lüdden commanded *U-188* initially in the rank of *Oberleutnant*, but was known aboard as '*Kaleu*' from the outset. He was promoted to *Kapitänleutnant* on 1 April 1943.

E-motor room. It is amazing what our engineers are able to come up with. They say that this Jumbo is capable of producing more compressed air for the tanks than the requirement.' We listened to this with great interest.

Chief Schulz replied: 'Let's not get carried away, Gottlieb. The Tommies aren't all asleep. I've heard they have developed equipment which can detect our boats at much greater distances. Let's hope that is only a rumour. It is all the more comforting to know though, that we shall always have enough compressed air over and above what we need for submergence and surfacing.' He looked around. 'And at least we shan't need to pump out the WCs by hand any more.' Laughter followed this remark. The 'U-boat Mother' entered the room with a smile and laid an accordion on the knees of Ordinary Seaman Heinze from Leipzig. 'Now show us what you can do, Helmut! And I want to hear you all singing to take your mind off things!'

After breakfast we marched with a song to the Deschimag yards where I went aboard our boat for the first time with other newcomers. Naturally I had a mental picture of the incredible narrowness of the boat's interior, but as I followed a works engineer inside I was overcome by a sensation of fear.

In the boat-familiarisation course of the past week, as a land rat from the foothills of the Bavarian Alps I had learned how the boat was divided into compartments. In the stern compartment were two nine-cylinder diesel engines, one each to port and starboard, each with an output of 2,000 shaft hp. These gave the boat a maximum surfaced speed of 18 knots. The E-motor room was located immediately forward of the diesel room and separated from it by a pressure-proof door. We were astonished at the confusion of pipes, levers and gauges fitted left, right and on the low ceiling. I was so impressed by it all that I was scarcely able to follow the talk by the Deschimag engineer. Pointing to the air compressor close to one of the E-motors he said: 'We hope that this equipment will live up to what Junkers promise.' The grey-haired man stood with a stoop immediately in front of me, and I saw a faint smile cross his narrow face with its funereal expression as he went on: 'Boys, if this box does what it is supposed to then you really do have one big worry less, for you will always have enough compressed air available for surfacing and everything else.'

With his free hand he gestured towards the two electric motors: 'These E-motors provide current and charge the batteries forward below the bow-room. On the surface they are linked up with the diesels by a coupling between the E-room and diesel room. When the boat is submerged they take current from the batteries. With this output of 500 shaft-hp the boat has a top speed submerged of 10 knots, but only for a maximum of two hours. At slower speeds and with lesser consumption of current they can keep going for considerably longer. You will all learn soon enough the tricks necessary to conserve the limited amount of air available for breathing.'

We gazed in wonder at the torpedo tubes and gave each other meaningful stares when we were shown the small, narrow cots, 'Klappen' or fold-down bunks, for use by the crew in the bow and stern compartments. We knew that on patrol when torpedoes would be stored around and under these drop-bunks the space to stretch out would be so restricted that one would have to manoeuvre into the narrow corridor just to turn in bed. So little space was available for us other ranks that we always had to share a bunk and you could only use yours if your opposite number was on duty and you yourself were off duty. At least we knew that in the working-up exercises in the Baltic we would be able to sleep in port, but at the front we would naturally not have such luxury.

After being shown over the boat we climbed the narrow steel ladder between the control room and conning tower hatches in silent and thoughtful mood. In naval jargon the boat was called a 'sea cow' on account of its size and range, and so none of us had imagined that its interior would be so narrow. Over the next couple of days, as future U-boot lookouts, we were instructed by shipyard engineers in the mechanism and handling of the hydroplanes, for when we made an emergency dive we would operate them.

The familiarisation period with the boat at Bremen passed quickly. On 5 August 1942, *U-188* was formally commissioned into the Kriegsmarine. Several senior naval officers were present and, together with Leading Seaman Willi Pollner, I was chosen to hoist the Reich war flag at the ensign mast on the so-called 'winter-garden', as we called the small platform aft of the conning tower.

Towards midday our 'U-boat Mother' organised a farewell meal at a restaurant near the shipyard. The wives of our commander *Kaleu* Lüdden and chief engineer Kiessling were also invited. They were not allowed to come aboard the boat, however, for it was considered that having women aboard a U-boat brought bad luck.

In the early afternoon we opened our 'U-boat packs' containing the functional shipboard wear, and dressed up. As lookout I received an issue of three grey-green overalls, a blue side cap, a long grey leather jacket, oilskins for bad weather, two blue pullovers, knitted blue underwear, rubber boots, fur-lined leather boots with non-slip soles, and thick leather gloves.

I paraded on the forecasing with other members of the off-duty watch as our boat left the shipyard. Later as we glided down the Weser we were allowed to remain on deck and enjoy the sunshine and fresh air. *Kaleu* Lüdden, I WO Meenen and his three lookouts stood on the bridge, and I noticed that they focussed their binoculars more on the land passing either side than the sky. In August 1942 we could still feel safe against enemy air attack in home waters.

Soon we passed Nordenham to port and Bremerhaven to starboard and then lost them both to sight. The diesels droned powerfully and harmoniously as we left the estuary of the Weser, ploughed through the North Sea and then cruised at slow speed through the calm waters of the Kiel Canal. Here some of us were given the job of peeling potatoes which at least kept us up on deck, sitting around our large kitchen pot and admiring the peaceful green scenery of Schleswig-Holstein. People waved to us from both banks of the Canal, and when we waved back we felt like the young heroes and saviours of the German people which Reich propaganda made us out to be.

In the evening we made fast in the naval basin at Kiel. From this 5 August 1942 onward we formed part of 4th U-Boat Flotilla at Stettin/Agru-Front (training group). We spent the night in a naval barracks, and sailed next morning for our first exercises in the Baltic. Two officers unknown to us had come aboard. We carried no practice torpedoes, therefore being off duty I could stretch out on my bunk with my arms folded under my head. In four hours' time I would stand my first watch with veteran Coxswain Korn, III WO of *U-188*, a boatswain NCO and another ordinary seaman. Karl Bauer forced his way along the gangway past my bunk and said with a grin, 'Man, Toni, without the torpedoes it's almost cosy here. You just need to get used to the air quality. I've got to go to the stern room to test out the head there, I only hope it doesn't have too many visitors.'

At that moment a loud voice came over the boat's inboard loudspeakers: 'This is *Kaleu* Lüdden.' His next sentences made such an impression on me that I can repeat them here almost verbatim: 'As you all know, the Baltic coasts are German, in German hands or belong to neutral Sweden or our ally Finland. Leningrad has been heavily mined by our naval colleagues and is additionally so well guarded that it is highly unlikely that we would ever meet a Russian warship in these waters. The Baltic is therefore our working-up area, even if the depths leave something to be desired for our purposes. We do not have unlimited time here. Every unnecessary day of practice is one day too many, for we are missing from the front. When we and this new boat have been moulded into an effective fighting unit, able to handle the demands of the most difficult emergencies, is not something for me alone to decide. Führer, Volk and Fatherland expect, however, that it is done in the shortest time possible, for only we U-boat men can prevent enormous quantities of war material being sent from the United States to Britain and its allies. Therefore the fullest personal commitment is demanded of each of us! We shall now dive our new boat for the first time!'

It became unusually quiet around us, the droning of the diesels at the stern fell away. Karl Bauer was forced to postpone his visits to the head and now stood equally tense as I in the longitudinal corridor. Despite the pale, greenish-blue emergency lighting used to economise on current while diving I sensed the amused looks of some of the veterans focussed on us from the empty torpedo room forward. I thought I heard the gurgling and splashing above me as the water flooded the vents, forcing out the air from which the boat derived its buoyancy when on the surface.

'Blow internal ballast tank! Close internal ballast valve!' Now I had the feeling that we were in a swiftly descending lift.

Surfacing about half an hour later I heard for the first time the hissing, whistling sound which the compressed air made as it was forced into the tanks again to expel the seawater ballast. The boat became lighter, I sensed it rising. This dive amused the 'veterans': 'The Old Man' – by this they meant *Kaleu* Lüdden – 'took the boat down vertically without power or hydroplanes,' they explained. Now one of them turned to address Karl Bauer, several of the other newcomers and myself: 'Don't look so pleased with yourselves! That was more gentle than in a lift. An emergency dive is something quite different! All bells are ringing and we go down steeply by the bows into the depths at full speed. If we are surprised and attacked on the surface, we have to disappear as quickly as we can.'

A few minutes later engine-room rating Hausmann came up from the diesel room and said, apparently in high spirits, 'Didn't you notice here that we had a leak in the diesel room? One of the visiting instructor officers must have loosened a pressure valve on the quiet. The exterior pressure when a depth charge explodes can cause that sort of thing. Our officer guest seemed very satisfied after seeing how quickly Engine-room Petty Officer Herbert Wolf got the thing under control. We just laugh at monkey-business like that.'

At that moment Karl Bauer returned from his inspection of the head. He had probably heard Hausmann's remarks and said with his usual self-confident grin: 'The other guest on board put some of the levers here and there in the wrong position to simulate situations which can happen in emergencies. The two visitors are now in discussion with our *Kaleu* and the chief engineer in the control room. They will be going ashore again at Stettin leaving us in the hands of our veterans.'

At Stettin next day we shipped practice torpedoes aboard. It was very heavy work, for a torpedo weighed thirty metric hundred-weight. The long, slim torpedoes were brought up to the quayside on railway trucks and heaved aboard by crane. From there the rest was done by muscle power. First we lowered four 'eels' at an angle through the pressure-proof forward hatch in the deck above the bow room to be stowed by the 'mixers' – the torpedo team – below the floor plating in the forward torpedo room by use of a block and tackle gear. The next four eels went into the bow torpedo tubes and two more were secured in the clamping fixtures below our bunks. Finally we loaded four more torpedoes through the torpedo hatch in the aftercasing. Two of these went directly into the stern tubes, the other two into the clamps below the bunks there. In addition to these fourteen torpedoes, our Type IXC/40 boat could take ten more on deck. There were five containers either side for this purpose, and when necessary they could be brought below deck while at sea. In the Baltic, these practice torpedoes would be picked up later by retrieval vessels. After their known running time they would finish upright in the water and so be easily spotted, but I never had the opportunity to witness this.

We practised and trained for the next two months without pause. When the sea was rough, several of my colleagues and I had to battle against seasickness. As soon as I got out into the fresh air I would recover rapidly and the symptoms would vanish. That was a great advance for me. As time went on, I already saw myself as an old seaman, able to look wind and sea in the face without a qualm.

As bridge lookouts we had to learn how to leave our positions on the conning tower when the alarm was given and slide down the outer struts of the steel ladder inside the tower into the control room without damaging our binoculars. The order in which this was done was fixed. I had to get in first carrying the bridge MG, and mighty quick so that the second man did not land on my shoulders. Nevertheless I picked up some bruises and abrasions by failing to duck away fast once I landed in the control room. In our oilskins and sou'westers – from time to time it was bitterly cold and wet up there – for a while we would be unable to sit at the hydroplane wheels as the boat dived. Even today I can still hear the captain scolding us as we two beginners failed to hold the boat at periscope depth (ten metres from the tower hatch to the surface). Gradually we got the hang of it and we were both not a little proud when the *Kaleu* praised us at last.

On the night of 6 October 1942 I was on the damp, cold bridge. Grey-black banks of mist limited visibility and enveloped the grey-painted conning tower of *U-188*, making it almost invisible. Our boat cleft through the sea at full speed. We were one of the grey wolves, a term of respect the U-boats had won for themselves for their ability to stalk enemy ships and sink a huge number of them. Today it was our task to pursue an eastbound German convoy and attack it with our practice torpedoes. *Kaleu* Lüdden was on the bridge with us. He wore his long, light grey leather jacket, his feet in fur-lined boots that were too large for him peeping out from under his leather trousers. The cap with its white crown, which only the commander was allowed to wear on board, distinguished him from the rest of us. On account of the poor visibility, he had decided to simulate an attack on the surface and also establish how close he could get to a convoy in such weather conditions without being discovered.

The commander now sat with his back to me on a small perch at the UZV[2] mounted on the tower coaming. As usual I was watching astern to starboard when III WO Korn called out, 'Dark shadow to starboard!' From now on I heard the calm voice of *Kaleu* Lüdden giving terse orders manoeuvring our boat into the most favourable firing position. I was strictly forbidden to concentrate my attention anywhere outside my allocated quadrant, but I risked it several times to look aside through my binoculars to gain an impression of the shapes of the reported ships. This breach of discipline passed unnoticed and I forgave myself on the grounds that it was important for me to know what ships looked like from the bridge at night and in fog. The Old Man passed his readings below from the UZV continuously to Boatswain Jupp Steimer, seated at the torpedo computing device into which he fed the target's speed. Our own speed parallel to the target was known of course. It was some time before we were at the right distance from the target, for Lüdden wanted to stalk him as close as possible. The course had to be recalculated once when the convoy changed its heading. I heard the commander observe quietly to the III WO: 'They don't seem to be beginners over there. Better therefore! We can take it that their lookouts are not asleep.'

Our practice torpedoes had no warhead and their running depths were set to pass below the target to avoid inflicting damage. Behind the eels in the torpedo tubes were pistons which were forced forward by compressed air to expel the torpedoes from the boat. Once ejected

---

2. UZV = *Zielgerät für Überwasserangriffe*: sight for surface torpedo attacks.

the two screws would counter-rotate creating a trail of bubbles on the surface only visible if the sea was calm and visibility good. Practice torpedoes had an occulting light astern enabling their path to be watched from the tower or if submerged through the periscope. As soon as the torpedo ran below the target ship a strip of lighting at the side of the hull would flash to confirm a hit. When our nocturnal surfaced attack terminated, *Kaleu* Lüdden announced through the shipboard loudspeakers: 'We would have sunk three ships from this convoy before the cruiser escort forced us away, but he would have been very dangerous for us if we were doing it for real. Our comrades on the bridges of the ships over there failed to spot our approach. We can therefore justly call ourselves grey wolves.'

Our officers and NCOs were not easily pleased. Often there would be much nervous tension aboard which gradually gave way to a certain composure in every individual. On one of our training voyages in the Baltic we were surprised suddenly by the onset of winter. The few parts of the boat above water were very swiftly coated with ice. We could only rid ourselves of it by repeated dives. To be on the bridge in this weather was unpleasant, to put it mildly.

After standing a four-hour watch we were frozen as stiff as our oilskins, almost useless for protection against the icy cold and biting wind. I stood beside Petty Officer Jupp Steimer in the E-room which also served us for drying and changing our clothing. I needed help to peel me out of my gear, as did the other three watch members. There was no heating on board, but here down below it seemed quite cosy. My limbs began to hurt as the blood flowed again, and in this narrow space I could only get warmed up by a vigorous rubbing down and a few knee bends.

Out of the corner of my eye I saw Jupp Steimer hang his frozen trousers by the braces from one of the steel rails. Then he said to Baumann, the motor-room petty officer: 'Gottlieb, our fur-lined shoes are soaked and frozen, and in this cold all the leather coats and oilskins aboard hardly prevented the four of us freezing to death up there.'

In his pleasant Hesse vernacular Gottlieb replied, 'But Jupp! Now it's calming down. In eight hours you will be as fit as a fiddle for another spell. Besides, the Baltic is nothing like so cold as the North

Atlantic. Although of course, even though it isn't now, I suppose it could get so.'

'Gottlieb, it's easy for you to talk down here in your cosy electric motor room. Talk of the devil and he will surely appear.'

'Of course, Jupp; but Petty Officer Braun in the engine room just passed the word that one of the diesels is starting to splutter: I heard if for myself a couple of times. That was why our LI Kiessling went to see the commander.' The two of them grinned, or at least Jupp Steimer did so once he had given his frozen cheeks a rub. I was also beginning to thaw out and Baumann added: 'Our diesel probably doesn't like the way the icy water keeps pouring down the ventilation shaft in this swell. In any case we can't rely on it for full power. That much is certain.'

Two hours later I was half warmed up in my cot when the news ran through the boat like wildfire: 'The starboard diesel has been shut down. We have been ordered to the yard at Königsberg for repairs.' For the rest of the day we headed for Königsberg on the one diesel and made fast in the yards there after dark.

Towards noon next day the always well-informed Karl Bauer told me in the naval barracks canteen: 'Toni, I've heard we're going to be here five to six weeks. Much longer than they expected. They are giving us a new starboard diesel because the old one has had it.' He grinned in his self-confident way and leaned towards me: 'And get this, Toni: all those not needed here are going to get leave. To replace the diesel engine, the casing has to be opened and then welded pressure-proof again. That can only be done by the technical people here.' I must have had a sceptical expression on my face for Karl went on: 'Man, don't give me that disbelieving look! As if I ever lied to you. You'll soon see, they'll send us on leave.'

Soon afterwards a Navy barge brought up our baggage to Königsberg from the 4th Flotilla warehouse at Stettin. The seabags contained our walking-out uniforms and everything else not needed on board. On 3 November the first of two groups were given fourteen days leave. On 27 November I left with the second group at four in the morning on the crew coach for Königsberg railway station. They split us up into smaller groups on the platform and a few minutes later we went aboard a train bringing back leave-takers from Russia.

When Leading Seaman Willi Roy and I got into one of the compartments, the grenadiers looked at us as though we were beings from another world. A young Army officer rubbed the sleep from his eyes in disbelief and asked us:

'What's this then? From which fashion house have you two escaped?'

Willy Roy retorted: 'Our uniforms only look so posh because we don't wear them in our U-boat. You should see the garb we have at the front. Compared to that, you're dressed quite comfortably.' After hearing that, almost at once the initial doubts about us turned into admiring stares in that crowded, smoke-filled compartment. Some of them bombarded us with questions. Roy had two successful front patrols behind him and described some of his experiences. His words made me shudder: 'Boys, we do what we can, but one thing is clear. The era of a Günter Prien, when a boat could sail undetected into an enemy harbour, is past. Our enemy's technology and armaments now make that a very difficult thing to do!'

The Eastern Front men told us of their privations, about the totally different dangers on the land front and the endless expanses of the territory. I listened in silence, thinking of my father, deployed somewhere in the mountains of Yugoslavia against the partisans. The remarks made by a couple of the soldiers were close to the mark of what was allowed: 'We haven't decided about war and peace, but about these batty politicians on both sides of the front. We poor swine must now face the music for this salad.'

We looked at each other in dismay. I sensed that the unspoken question now circulating between the clouds of cigarette smoke in our compartment concerned the encircled Sixth Army at Stalingrad: could we still save the Fatherland from Ivan, stronger every day, and the Tommies, the Americans and their allies: or were we going to lose this war? I was beset at that moment by the beginnings of doubt.

A middle-aged pioneer sergeant was seated on the wooden bench near the window, his uniform jacket half unbuttoned, and it seemed as though his Iron Cross and other decorations were as much a part of him as the buttons on his greatcoat. Now he stroked his stubbly beard reflectively and commented: 'Children, don't fill your heads with this rubbish. Of course we simple soldiers did not begin the chaos, but under no circumstances must we lose this enormous test of strength, for if we do Germany will go under. If the Red Army invades, then God help our parents, wives and children. The Ivans would murder them all. We must go all out to prevent that. And if our U-boat comrades can put the enemy's supplies on the sea bed, then we shall achieve it!' The train rolled on through snowy East Prussia, and the time to Berlin flew by.

In the late afternoon of 28 November I left the Munich-Salzburg train at Grafing, swung my seabag over my shoulder and was secretly irritated that even here I had constantly to deliver the correct military salute to every person wearing uniform who had a higher rank than I. How happy I was at last to find myself alone on the so familiar road from the station to Grafing Market and I hurried with long strides through the dusk to my parents' house on Gries-Strasse. Because I had not been certain at Königsberg until the last moment that I would be issued a leave pass, I had not informed ahead of my arrival. While now surprising everybody by suddenly appearing and being received gushingly by my mother and sisters I looked around. The small rooms on the first floor of the simple house seemed larger than I remembered them. I had grown so accustomed to the narrowness of our boat, where every careless move, or just by walking upright, could result in a collision with a lever, tube or some nook or other.

I was so pampered by my family and some friends during my short leave that to take my leave of them hit me hard. I had not felt quite right wearing my blue uniform when making calls, being in the streets or in some of the inns. Often I had had to learn, upon enquiring after this or that classmate or friend: 'Our Max fell in the Caucasus', or 'Franz has been reported missing at Stalingrad.' 'Our Schorsch was captured in Africa. They have told us he is in an English hospital seriously wounded.' 'We have been waiting a long time for a letter from Hermann. Let us hope he is still alive.'

When I met up again at last with my fellow sailors in the naval barracks at Königsberg, I felt a satisfaction and sense of belonging amongst them on this boat. For us all there was no question that we had to fulfil the expectations that had been made of us, and our duty. In this respect *Kaleu* Lüdden and LI Kiessling set the example, for neither had gone on leave, but during the period of repair had spent nearly the entire day with the boat in the shipyard. Their wives had travelled up to Königsberg, and I often saw them together in the town when we were allowed shore leave. Being the hand responsible for the stowage of the shells in their pressure-tight containers, and the small arms and their ammunition under the floor plating, I noticed that whenever I had to go through the procedure of oiling and polishing these armaments, and then replacing them as sparingly of space as possible, both officers were always present.

Towards noon on 10 December 1942 we were ready to sail. An icy easterly wind drifted thick swathes of mist across the waters as slowly we left the shipyard. Able Seaman Rötters stood beside me as rear lookout. In the calm channel of the Frischer Haff *Kaleu* Lüdden at my back ordered: 'Half speed ahead!' Scarcely had we reached the open sea than: 'Full ahead!' The reason for this was made clear by his quiet remark to Lt Benetschik: 'Now we shall see what this diesel is capable of. In an emergency we must be able to rely on it completely at maximum speed ahead. If it is going to give up the ghost, then better right here. If it happens later, boat and crew wouldn't have a prayer.'

On this voyage we practised everything imaginable. Amongst other things the commander simulated the case in which enemy anti-submarine forces kept us below for a long period and maintained the hunt for us. The air in the boat grew thick in the true sense of the word, all lighting was reduced to the barest minimum to economise on the batteries and only the instruments were weakly lit. Every man not required to work had to rest quietly. We all had to take as shallow breaths as possible, and the carbon dioxide-absorbent alkali cartridges got so hot after four hours that they had to be changed. In this exercise we gained a bitter foretaste of what might be waiting for us. When we finally resurfaced to air the boat I hoped earnestly never to have to remain under water so long again. The veterans made it clear, however, that a voyage submerged could last several days, and in a crisis we would have to wear our lifejackets. In order to make this exercise more realistic, the *Kaleu* had repeatedly altered course and depth at slow revolutions.

We celebrated Christmas 1942 in merry alcoholic mood in a naval barracks at Danzig. In mid-January 1943 Petty Officer Jupp Steimer and I received orders from Stettin to proceed to Esslingen near Stuttgart to fetch charts for the boat from a specialist printer. Jupp told me, 'Toni, this is an unmistakable sign that they are sending us soon to some far-flung place in the world's oceans. Therefore, tonight before we sail I don't want to find you here in the barracks under any circumstances. You should spend your precious time with your girlfriend. We'll meet up again punctually at the station tomorrow. Man, now off you go!' Naturally he didn't have to tell me twice, I got into my walking-out uniform and took the tram to Gisela.

After Jupp Steimer and I had delivered the well packed and by no means lightweight sea charts from Esslingen to *Kaleu* Lüdden we learned that *U-188* had been attached to 10th U-Boat Flotilla at Lorient with effect from 1 February 1943. Now everybody knew that the period of working-up was over and soon the word got round: 'We have just received a signal from the BdU [*Befehlshaber der Unterseeboote* – Commander-in-Chief, U-boats]: "Lüdden run into Kiel!"'

By now boat and crew had been welded into a single unit, for every man knew his job and the hand movements necessary for it. We lay for six days at the quayside of Kiel naval harbour. Our practice torpedoes were exchanged for twenty-four live torpedoes. Because of the narrowness of the area below the control room floor plates I had to store the shells, MG and machine-pistol gun ammunition in pressure-proof containers by myself. All the same, Lt Benetschik checked over my work very closely. Lastly, provisions were stowed in every available nook and cranny of the boat, and in many places hard sausage dangled below tubing and levers. Even the forward head was crammed to the last centimetre with tins. I heard one of the veterans observe: 'Boys, this is definitely going to be a long voyage. If fifty-four men have to share one toilet then that means reservation tickets. Let's hope that every one of us has the strength to pump out his shit against the resistance of the pressure tank.'

During the last night in our barracks beds I slept restlessly, and therefore I did not need the persuasive arts of Karl Bauer and others for garnish. Each man of us tried with every means at his disposal not to think of the dangers which lay ahead and had been explained to us by the veterans with such obvious relish. Nobody knew for certain, but all were convinced that our operational area could only be the North Atlantic.

Chapter Three

The Run from Kiel into the North Atlantic

At 0800 hrs on 4 March 1943 I paraded on the foredeck with all men of the off-duty watch not required below. Under a cloudless sky the waters of the bay shimmered a peaceful blue. We were all dressed in our U-boat packs. *Kaleu* Lüdden and the three watchkeeping officers stood on the bridge as our boat edged free of the quay. A Navy band started up, playing us off with a rousing march. At that the thought came to me how much I would like to exchange places with one of them and I got goose pimples. Later some of the others confessed the same. Just as we had been drilled, a group of senior base officers who had assembled on the quay to watch our departure received from us the regulation naval salute, right arm at the correct angle, hand touching the cap, faces expressionless.

Our boat increased speed quickly. A couple of female naval auxiliaries in dressy blue uniforms ran along the pier waving, trying to keep up. Within a few moments the voices of the men, the shouts of the women, the hum of the diesels and the music of the naval band turned into an indescribable noise. Soon our conning tower obscured my view of those we had left behind.

U-188 moved ever faster, the bow-wave began to rustle as the music astern became ever less audible and then finally died away. We had become very quiet. Only the hissing of the waves and the harsh screeching of the gulls accompanying the boat were still to be heard.

'Everyone below!' The voice of *Kaleu* Lüdden brought movement to our ranks and interrupted our thoughts. I was one of the last to swing myself through the tower hatch. I went from the control room to my bunk in the bow room and forced myself into the gap which the torpedo below it left me. Eyes open, I cast aside fresh anxieties: 'What will it really be like when . . .? Numerous questions overwhelmed me, and all remained unanswered.

In a way it came as a relief when after four hours I was summoned for mess duty to the NCOs' mess and could at last do something physically active. Some of the off-duty NCOs, amongst them engine-room Petty Officer Bischoff, were seated close together at a table set up on the floor plating of the so-called NCOs' mess. This area was criss-crossed by piping. Off-duty NCOs also had the folding-bunk system in which they shared a bunk with an on-duty comrade, their room also being a passageway. Every man coming from the control room or the bows and having to use this corridor pressed through the narrow passage even when the off-duty men were sat there eating.

When I took the freshly-stacked plates out of their locker and distributed them, I noticed that Bischoff turned his plate this way and that before placing it in front of himself. I had already been aware for some time that I was not the only one to whom he had taken a dislike. There was no chicanery on board, but nevertheless Bischoff had attempted several times to demonstrate his authority. That he was now thinking of blaming me for any spots or stains he found on the plates and cutlery he was given surprised me, and I was glad that I only ever had to come into contact with him when I had mess duty. I acted as though I had noticed nothing, went through the hatch and received from the cook in his tiny galley located between the NCOs' and Officers' mess the pot of steaming stew and a tray with freshly-cut bread. Fresh bread, fruit, vegetables and potatoes were only available during the early stages of a voyage. Later these glories would be replaced by tinned food, dehydrated potatoes and dried fruit.

The boat had a facility for distilling fresh water from seawater used for the batteries under the flooring in the torpedo- and other ranks' compartment in the bows. What distilled water was left over was filtered and then used for cooking. Only a limited amount of drinking water was available, and we had to use it sparingly. Therefore the mess duty men cleaned the plates and cutlery after use with seawater in a small metal bowl, P3 (Persil 3) being added as a softening agent.

My lookout duty on the bridge began at 1200 hrs. Relieving the No.2 lookouts under Lt. Benetschik went ahead very rapidly. Our watch under III WO Coxswain Korn had Boatswain Steimer as forward lookout, Rötters and I as usual had to watch the sea and sky astern. At the relief it did not escape my attention that Benetschik had advised Korn: 'Since 1145 we have been in convoy as per the sailing orders.' As he said this he pointed with an outstretched arm to two German motor minesweepers sailing together ahead of us and bristling with flak. We assumed that they would escort us through the Kattegat and Skagerrak as far as the North Sea to prevent our being mined. Our exact operational orders were known only to the officers.

We glided slowly past the coasts of the Danish islands. We still felt safe here, but knew that we had to be on the alert. We had heard that the enemy had so-called radar sets which could locate ships even in fog and darkness. On the surface we had to rely on our eyes and excellent binoculars, and when submerged on the hydrophones.

On 8 March when our escort released us in the northern North Sea I was again on the bridge. From now on we were on our own. More tense than ever before, I stood looking through my binoculars at my assigned quadrant astern. First I had to examine the waterline at the horizon where the sea and cloudy sky met. After that at the clouded skies through binoculars, then lower the glasses and search the sky with the naked eye. The operation described had to be without exception a constant and slow oval. Always I could hear the voice of my instructor: 'If you report an approaching aircraft too late, or recognise an enemy destroyer or corvette too late, this can mean the death of the whole crew, the end. Very much depends upon your concentration and endurance up to the last second of your four-hour watch. Danger for the boat can come from all directions, from any cloud or from the water. But take care: undue haste can also be prejudicial, such as when a seagull is identified as an attacking aircraft, or a ribbon of cloud on the horizon is reported as a trace of smoke. That kind of over-reaction is damaging because it causes unnecessary commotion. Therefore remain constantly on the alert, concentrated and always calm.'

A sudden drill tore me from my thoughts. *Kaleu* Lüdden ordered an emergency dive to 140 metres and then we proceeded submerged to check for leaks. While the men of the technical personnel led by our LI were fully occupied with this task, I had to lie still on my bunk, now a supernumerary. Scarcely had we surfaced again than Schulz in the radio room reported that we had been detected by enemy radar. We had a simple wooden cross on the bridge, made taut with wires, secured in a mounting fixture, the so-called 'Biscay Cross' or anti-radar device, which detected enemy radar transmissions through a cable to the radio room. Scarcely was the second watch under Lt Benetschik in the boat and the tower hatch closed than once more down we went 'into the cellar'. As usual they had brought down with them the MG and Biscay Cross. In my mind's eye I now saw Schulz seated at the apparatus in the small radio booth, listening studiously, but unable to detect any propeller noises. AB Koch, who had been on the bridge with Lt Benetschik's watch, told me later that they had had to renew the cable insulation of the anti-radar device at three exposed places. The false alarm had been caused by metal touching the site of the damage to the cable. Because the problem repeated itself several times over the next few days, causing much unnecessary upset and commotion and losing us time, the *Kaleu* was by no means distraught when soon afterwards the Biscay Cross broke up in very heavy seas and could no longer be used.

On 11 March we reached the Arctic Circle. The boat had to cope with heavy storms. As *U-188* pitched and tossed through the huge seas I began to feel seasick. I got to the WC at the stern just in time and my luck was in, for there was no queue waiting to use it. Hardly anybody noticed my distress. It was little consolation that I was not the only one. Later as soon as I went up to the bridge for my watch and into the fresh, raw sea air I recovered quickly despite the storm and the raging seas.

Before the beginning of my watch at 1200 hrs on 12 March I went to fetch my watch clothing from the E-room. The oilskins and leatherwear had not dried and Petty Officer Baumann gave me a sympathetic look. The boat was only rolling moderately and I hoped we wouldn't have to rope up for safety. When I climbed up to the bridge through the turret hatch, in comparison to the sea state on my previous watch I found that this was almost peaceful. The skies were hidden by a thick grey overcast. Because of alternate showers of snow and sleet, visibility was down to six or seven kilometres. About twenty minutes had passed when Coxswain Korn shouted: 'Hard to port! Drifting mine ahead!' A few seconds later I saw about 200 metres off on our starboard hand a dark sphere with horns bobbing up and down in the wave valleys. At the same moment I heard Lüdden hurry up to the bridge and say, 'Well done, Korn! That was a close thing!'

'Thank you, Herr *Kaleu*.' Korn's voice was as calm and unemotional as always. Not for a moment did he drop his binoculars from his eyes. Once again it was made clear to me how important our watchfulness was for the life of all on board.

On 13 March we were west of Iceland. We understood that there were German agents in American ports who reported the sailing of convoys and the route they would be taking to the BdU. Probably for that reason we had been ordered to the far north. Next day we sailed through the Iceland Passage with visibility always curtailed by blizzards. We knew that British air and surface forces were stationed in nearby Iceland. For this reason I was more than ever on my toes on watch. Bomber aircraft presented the greatest danger for us on account of their speed. We had to see them as early as humanly possible.

'Alarm!' I swung myself through the conning tower hatch and slipped into my seat at the wheel for the forward hydroplanes. Before the lighting for submerged travel was switched on, the light flashed on and off to warn every last man in the boat. Alarm bells shrilled loudly, nevertheless I heard Korn's report to *Kaleu* Lüdden very clearly: 'Destroyer on the starboard bow. He came out of a wall of snow dead ahead directly for us. Range about 5,000 metres!'

'His radar probably picked us up. We shall have to try and fool him.' A quick glance at the manometer showed me that we were at 100 metres, at the same instant for the first time I heard ahead of us the roar of exploding depth charges. Now I discovered how appallingly loud these sounded under water. Though fearful I concentrated on my hydroplane wondering if I would ever hear anything again in my life if the next pattern was only fifty metres or less from us. Our pressure valves would not have been able to withstand an explosion as close as that, and we would all die.

'Depth charges to scare us,' *Kaleu* Lüdden said. He was completely calm. 'Go to 150 metres! The deeper we are, the less effect these things have.' I wondered if this last observation was meant for me and Rötters at my side. In any case we were the only men in the control room hearing depth charges go off for the first time.

Now we heard the propeller noises of the destroyer directly overhead. I looked behind me and saw that *Kaleu* Lüdden had pushed his white-crowned cap back to his neck and was looking upwards like everybody else in the control room. Will he drop the next pattern now or from his stern? No doubt at this moment everybody was asking himself the same anxious question, and I caught myself praying, counting off the seconds and manipulating the hydroplane almost automatically. A pattern of eight depth charges fell behind us, and I had the impression that the booming explosions were farther off than the first group. The boat was shaken again by pressure waves. The pale lighting flickered. Shortly after he dropped about another twenty depth charges. LI Kiessling held our boat at precisely 150 metres with terse, softly spoken instructions. *Kaleu* Lüdden ordered the slowest revolutions possible while maintaining the depth and altered course. Then he muttered to Kiessling: 'We shall make this type uncertain with little zig-zags. Thank God he seems to be on his own. Against several of this sort we would have no chance.' Kiessling did not reply but while keeping my gaze riveted on the depth gauge I guessed that he nodded in agreement.

The destroyer was somewhere above us but we had not heard him for about fifteen minutes. He had turned off his machinery and was now listening down for us, occasionally his hydrophone equipment being audible. He was lurking up there like a hunter awaiting his prey. We knew that any of the next minutes could be our last. I glanced at Rötters beside me and saw the beads of sweat on his forehead, his sunken eyes staring at the manometer. Others may not have felt the same, but in this threatening situation I felt helplessly shut in, tied down at my position. Despite my fear I felt enraged that the Tommies overhead were trying to kill us, to steal our lives. I clearly remember thinking: 'It is a world gone mad in which men with a different field-post number try to send their opponents mercilessly into the other world, and are praised for it by their masters.'

In the boat no sound was to be heard apart from the soft hum of the electric motors. I experienced this game of cat-and-mouse, this lying in wait to kill people, for the first time that day. 'Will we be able to surface, or must we drown here like cats in a sack?' I asked myself this same question over and over while never letting the manometer above me out of my sight. After ten minutes the destroyer's propellers began to gurgle up and he started a search from not far off our port quarter. Twenty explosions broke the short deceptive pause for rest and rocked the boat violently as if held by a giant's fist. The weak lighting began to flicker again. Some areas of the boat reported damage. The screw noises now came up from the other side of the hull but they seemed to me not as close as before. As I wiped the sweat from my forehead I saw that *Kaleu* Lüdden's face had a tense expression but his eyes looked triumphant. He was standing at the periscope and I noticed Kiessling near him grinning in relief. This calmed me considerably and I thought: 'These two have taken this kind of punishment often enough before and now seen to think that we can dodge this bomb thrower.'

'Maintain minimum revolutions. Course south-west,' *Kaleu* Lüdden ordered in soft tones. Shortly afterwards the helmsman confirmed, 'Course laid in.' Although I had gained fresh hope, deadly fear was still crushing my chest with an iron fist. I was finding it difficult to breathe but I operated the hydroplane as calmly and surely as I had been drilled to do. The distance from our pursuer did not seem to have grown much greater. Depth charges kept coming down during the next anxious few hours, some threateningly near, then farther off. I had not been bothering to keep count of the explosions for some time, but they were still so loud that it took a great effort on my part not to show my fear. Although personally I had never been through a depth-charge attack before, I thought that the last pattern had been at our depth and not far off. In expectation of death, involuntarily I drew in my head between my shoulders. My assumption was immediately confirmed, for *Kaleu* said: 'Go to 130 metres.' Rötters and I concentrated all our attention on following this order.

The screw noises of the destroyer provided us with the acoustic evidence of his search pattern, sometimes distant, then threateningly closer. 'This fellow has enormous endurance,' I heard *Kaleu* Lüdden say in an undertone to Lt. Meenen standing near him.

'Let's hope he remains alone.' Meenen did not sound too sure about it, and I asked myself involuntarily, 'What will become of us if this Tommy has asked for support?'

While Rötters and I were constantly engaged keeping *U-188* exactly at the ordered depth, I was still plagued by fears that this accursed destroyer might extend his pattern and bomb too close for us to survive. We had already been under water for six hours. The air in the narrow steel tube was stifling. Now the passing minutes seemed longer than they had before.

Finally! Just after 1800 hrs the propeller noises began to diminish slowly but constantly. He dropped a few more depth charges for luck and then we heard no more of him. 'Let's hope his relief hasn't arrived,' I thought, and with this fear I began to doubt our good fortune. Chief Schulz opened the door of his small radio booth and reported: 'Destroyer is leaving fast on course north-east! No other screw noises!' The commander's voice sounded as calm and controlled as ever as he replied, 'Thank you, Schulz.'

At that moment, despite the low oxygen content of the air we were breathing and from pure joy I began to yodel. In all the pale bearded faces around me I saw exuberant relief. It was also not to be missed in *Kaleu* Lüdden's voice as he ordered, 'Come up to periscope depth.' Rötters and I had been given a job to do and never before had I been so pleased to comply.

Our *Kaleu* left nothing to chance. First he made a detailed 360° sweep through the main periscope, repaired after springing a leak during the recent storms. Next he searched the heavens with the sky periscope in case the destroyer had called up air support. Not until he was satisfied did he give the order to surface and air the boat. As Meenen and his lookouts climbed up swiftly to the bridge, Lüdden went to the chart table, ordered the new course and full speed ahead. The diesels roared, the used air was sucked out and fresh air streamed in through the induction shaft for distribution by the ventilation system to all parts of the boat. We breathed freely at last. While peeling off my oilskins in the E-room I established that as always after surfacing the first thing done was generate compressed air and recharge the batteries. As a matter of course we all behaved just as it had been drilled into us during our training: to act as if nothing unusual had occurred. Every man did his job. 'The boat and its crew is an inseparable unit which must always be functioning!' We had heard this particular sentence so often in training that it had become part of our flesh and blood.

On 21 March 1943 we reached our assigned operational area. The inhospitable cold desert of water, in which I often saw drift ice, told me personally very little about our exact position. As always, this was only known to the officers. It was a security measure: in the worst case scenario if we were picked up as the survivors of a sunken U-boat and made prisoner, we would not be able to answer the most adroit trick questions when interrogated. We simple mariners only knew that we were somewhere south of Greenland in order to meet up with other boats also ordered to this sea area. We also knew that we had to establish a picket line here in the far north: that is to say the distance from boat to boat in good visibility was between twenty and thirty nautical miles in order to sight a reported convoy. The first of us to find it was the so-called 'contact keeper'. This boat had to make regular signals to SKL (*Seekriegsleitung* – the Naval War Directorate) which would order other boats to make for the convoy, the pack of boats would then annihilate the heavily laden transporters and thus prevent these supplies getting through to our enemies.

U-188 had not come through the storms and the attack by the British destroyer undamaged. Feverish work was being done at various places on the boat. The storm had not only destroyed the Biscay Cross, but also loosened plating on the outer casing causing unpleasant noises audible throughout the boat. A large hole gaped in the deck near the 3.7cm flak and some of the upper deck valve flaps had been knocked away.

Whilst I focussed on the long rolling waves and skies astern, I noticed some unusual noises behind me on the bridge. Taking a quick glance back I saw ERA Hannes Arnold bringing up welding gear to the hole near the flak gun. So far as I could recall, there was also damage to the watertight forecastle which was open to the sea and allowing air to escape. Despite the dangerous proximity of the enemy, this problem had to be overcome swiftly. Willi Roy dragged a cable to Arnold and they began with the welding at once. They were below me and the spray of sparks interfered with my vision. Suddenly I saw a shadow on the horizon which I identified as a ship and was just about to give the alarm when I realised it was an ice floe.

The sounds of the repair work on deck drowned the almost pleasant rustling of the wind. While maintaining the search of my quadrant, I was seized by a sudden fear. 'If an aircraft or destroyer attacks us now, we won't be able to get under quickly enough. Waiting until this cable is down in the boat or cut away, and the men on deck have got below before us, we will lose much precious time. An aircraft is very fast and in this condition we would be offering him a target for his bombs which he could hardly miss. In addition, my comrades are welding not three metres below me using the current from one of our electric motors.' A minute later I asked myself, 'Is one electric motor sufficient to drive the screws when we are diving? Can they switch the other over fast enough so that we go down into the cellar with the power of both motors?' Walter Rötters had probably been thinking the same thing, for to my surprise he leaned towards me and against all the regulations put his head to my right ear and whispered, 'Let's hope this all turns out well.'

After about two hours I heard behind me the voice of our LI, Lt Kiessling. He was a mechanical engineer and at thirty-five years of age easily the oldest man on board: 'You've all done well, my boys! But now get all that crap below!' When we were alone once more on the bridge, Rötters whispered to me again, 'I bet the decision to make those repairs despite these gentle seas did not come easy to the gentlemen.' I pushed him away with my elbow, for at that moment the hand of our watchkeeping officer covered my binoculars. Without interrupting his own observation ahead, Korn wanted to check that I was alert. I confirmed this by knocking the glasses against his glove at which he took his hand away.

Towards 1600 hrs the mist grew denser reducing visibility to scarcely 800 metres. *Kaleu* Lüdden therefore came up to the bridge and I heard him say to Korn: 'According to Fiedler's radio report we ought to be in the path of the convoy. It seems that the navigational fixes of the other boats are as inaccurate as our own as a result of this fog. In the conditions it would seem more promising if we listened through the hydrophones submerged.' We dived. In the boat the tension in the total silence was almost tangible. Schulz's men operated the hydrophones, listening attentively. Lying on my drop-bed I tried to hear too and several times I thought I could make out propeller noises. Nothing happened. After a while I was roused from a restless slumber by the whistle of compressed air streaming into the dive tanks and I felt the boat rising.

Towards 2200 hrs the alarm bells shrilled and a blinking light gave warning of the dim economy lighting being turned on. At the same moment I heard the LI order: 'Everybody forward!' This would accelerate the dive. We had learnt to run in our socks so as to make no sound, and raced to the bow room. Seconds later we were all there crammed shoulder to shoulder smelling each other's body odour of dirty pullovers and shirts. The only shower on board was out of order. It was clear that we were heading downwards at a steep angle of about 45°. We reached out for handholds. Tins of food came rolling and rattling along the iron floor plating: acid came flowing from the accumulators in the battery room to ooze between the cracks in the plating.

'Everybody astern!' We climbed upwards towards the rear. With relief we felt how the boat came horizontal with the help of our body weight. We also felt, however, that the boat was sinking much faster than before and now with the stern stalled.

'Everybody forward!' Kiessling shouted. We sprinted off, tumbled almost silently one after another through the hatches and finished up crushed together as human ballast in the bow-room again. Depth charges thundered above us. Racing through the control room I had glimpsed the depth gauge above the hydroplanes not showing the increasing depth by single metres as usual but instead by ten metres and the needle was quivering close to the red danger field. Fear seized me as I saw in the faces of the old experienced hands horror, panic and a difficult to describe aura of helplessness. 'Is this my last hour?' I asked myself and then complied with the new order:

'Everybody astern!'

For an hour Kiessling chased us from one end of the boat to the other. We were running for our lives. Depth charges continued to explode above, but they seemed to be farther off than initially. Nobody spoke. We were maintaining a constant but tremendous depth. Somehow the LI had managed to trim the boat. Heads shrunk into shoulders, everybody seemed to be waiting for the enormous water pressure to crush the boat. I heard Karl Bauer standing near me say under his breath, 'Our big depth gauge stopped at 200 metres, but I saw the small gauge on the bilge pump showing 260 metres.' Despite my anxiety I began to calculate according to what they had taught us on the *Wilhelm Gustloff*: at a depth of 100 metres the pressure on our hull of Martin steel was 10 kgs/sq.cm: at 200 metres double that and now at 260 metres – 850 feet – according to Adam Riese 26kgs/sq.cm! Everybody could hear the sudden light crackle of the steel jacket and frames of the boat in the otherwise eerie silence. The only thing I saw in the faces of the veterans near me was naked fear. None of them had ever been in a boat this deep before.

The sudden hissing and whistling of the compressed air being fed into the dive tanks sounded louder than ever. Strained to breaking point we all waited for *U-188* to start coming up. The deafeningly loud struggle of the compressed air against the outer pressure at this enormous depth hurt my eardrums. Finally! In all faces I saw the burgeoning of hope and relief as the boat slowly rose, but there was a goblin in the works, for now we felt the boat rising very quickly like an air balloon in an up-current. A group of us at the bow heard Kiessling distributing orders in the control room. Then we felt distinctly that we were being rocked liked a ball on the waves at the surface. 'Are we a helpless and defenceless target for this destroyer's guns?' Everybody stood frozen with horror. We waited for the boat to be ripped apart by shells at any moment.

'Everybody forward!' The loud voice of the LI tore us from our anxiety. This time we went down into the cellar normally and at the usual speed, yet while each of us was returning to our assigned places in the boat we heard a pattern of depth charges exploding astern. With his usual nonchalant grin Karl Bauer remarked softly,

'God must have spread a curtain of mist around us when we were bobbing and weaving up there. They couldn't see us. Did Lüdden have a look round through the periscope?'

We were all still in such a state of shock that nobody had paid any attention to him. Later it was conjectured that at the first alarm dive a connecting valve had been left open so that instead of the bilge tank being pumped out it had flooded and made the boat that much heavier. The control room petty officer had worked out what the problem was and corrected it.

'Probably none of us will forget this 24 March 1943 if we ever get old,' I thought and saw in my mind's eye the terrified faces of the control room petty officer Hannes Arnold, Kiessling, Lüdden, Meenen, Benetschik and the other experienced hands. It had been deadly dangerous, otherwise it would not have taken its toll of these veterans as it did. Telegraphist Petty Officer Wilhelm Autenrieth interrupted my thinking: 'Destroyer course south-south-east has departed. No other screw noises.' One could almost feel the general relief. *Kaleu* Lüdden ordered: 'Go to periscope depth!'

Every man off-watch, and then the others in turns, celebrated the birthday of our boat. Since I had not been given mess duty, Karl Bauer, Wilhelm Rolfing, Willi Pollner, a couple of others and I sat on crates or on the flooring enjoying the tinned goulash and dried potatoes which the cook had prepared especially well today. The bottle of beer for each man released by the commander was much applauded. So youthful and light-hearted were we that the Junkers compressor being taken apart on the flooring only a few metres away could not spoil our festivities. The engine room petty officer, Baumann, and our LI were working at the repair with worried looks and obvious haste. Only Karl Bauer had noticed though: with a slight nod of the head towards the electric motor room hatch he remarked, 'Looks like we have too little compressed air'. Then he gave a boyish grin and went on, 'The next time we're down in the cellar and want to come up, we'll all have to blow or fart really hard.' Despite the seriousness of the situation everybody had to laugh at Bauer's happy face when he acknowledged: 'But until now they've always managed to solve everything.'

At night the diesels began to roar, the boat trembled and then the rumour spread: 'We are pursuing at maximum speed a convoy ahead of us.' At midnight I was due to be on the bridge and looked forward to see how this hunt on the surface would develop. At last we were ourselves the hunters. What would be my experience of the coming attack? Towards 2300 hrs Kiessling made his way fast from the diesel room to the control room passing my bunk. A few minutes later I heard that the starboard diesel was being disconnected. At 2345 hrs I stood in my oilskins with our III WO Korn and the others in the control room and put on dark goggles to accustom our eyes to the darkness. While still waiting to climb up I found out that the commander had decided on this immediate repair to the diesel in order to be fully operational next morning. We lost the convoy and the diesel repair was not finished until 29 March.

New problems cropped up. The newly-welded housing for the Junkers compressor broke apart during reconstruction. This could not be repaired with the tools on board. In future only the electric motor room compressor would be available to generate the compressed air so important for our survival. The question was, would it be enough for the job?

During the course of the next few days we were forced repeatedly to dive by anti-submarine escorts. It put a great strain on our nerves and I wondered how much longer the boat would be able to take it. Even though we simple mariners were not well informed, we considered it certain that we had been put on the track of a fresh convoy and had been ordered to another operational area.

Chapter Four

11 April 1943:
The Attack on Convoy ON 176

On the night of 9 April [11th in original is a misprint, the boat attacked the convoy in the early morning of the 11th. Tr], *Kaleu* Lüdden stood with us on the bridge. We had relieved Meenen's men shortly before one by one, so that there would be no gaps in the observation. Everybody in the boat was on edge. For several hours we had been the contact keeper on a convoy which kept changing course. The moon was bright and visibility good. *Kaleu* Lüdden was determined to keep a distance of between twelve and fifteen nautical miles between ourselves and the convoy so as not to lose the dark shadows from sight as soon as they made a turn. If they came nearer, Lüdden altered our course in order not to be seen by one of the smaller shadows, the escorts, and forced to dive. Once again, total concentration, good eyes and the outstanding binoculars were required.

On my next watch from midday to 1600 hrs on 10 April the sky was cloudy and the sea rough. From time to time a scarcely perceptible smudge of smoke would appear from the direction of the convoy. The engine room personnel of the freighters and tankers could not prevent this completely. The smoke would only appear above the ships for a short time and then disperse. It was our job to watch out for this telltale sign and not lose sight of the mastheads which were just visible on the horizon. It was the exciting overture for the coming night's planned attack. This contact keeping, which I was experiencing for the first time today, was known by the veterans as the 'Fight of the Long Knives'.

'Keep a lookout for aircraft!' The admonition of our watchkeeping officer was superfluous, for we were all as much on our toes as we could be.

I knew for certain that below us at the chart table in the control room every movement of the convoy and our boat was being plotted and transmitted by short-signal to SKL. While suppressing my excitement I asked myself: 'How many other boats of our group could we summon up by means of our short-signals to lie in wait or pursue the convoy?'

After four hours' lookout duty I climbed down into the interior. The smell of more than fifty sweaty men, of diesel oil, lubricating oil, rotting food and mouldy bread blended with the aroma from the kitchen and the tiny WC. All this together with the continuous rolling and pitching of the boat and the feeling of being imprisoned in this cold, damp tube made me giddy and numb. Shortly after 1600 hrs I checked over the shells and small-arms ammunition, and then was allocated messboy duty and therefore had only very little restless sleep before ascending punctually at midnight to the bridge.

It was 11 April 1943. *Kaleu* Lüdden sat between the two forward lookouts on the small seat before the UZV on the coaming. Seeing him there it became clear to me at once: he wanted to attack on the surface, more dangerous but faster and more effective, and using the smudgy-dark horizon at our back for cover. My heart was beating faster as I asked myself how this would turn out. Could we get through the chain of escorts consisting of fast and nimble destroyers on the surface unseen in order to get close enough to stalk the merchantmen? With deep breaths I calmed myself with the thought that Lüdden would certainly know what he was doing. A squall came between the convoy and *U-188*. With a determined and resolute voice the commander ordered a change of course to starboard in order not to lose sight of the enemy ships during their irregular changes of heading. For some time I could only see through my binoculars the dark heaving seas and the rain spraying down from the low cloud. Lüdden said to Benetschik: 'We have to stay on them at all costs.' A little later I heard the watchkeeping officer behind me shout: 'Shadow fine on the starboard bow.' Therefore the convoy had turned south in the darkness and was making directly for us. Now we stood on its starboard side. Immediately the commander signalled SKL: 'Grid square AJ 9364, course 240 degrees, speed eight knots'. Then he ordered: 'Full speed ahead!' His observation to Lt Benetschik told me that we would run ahead of the convoy on its present course and slip through the belt of escorts as soon as the weather permitted.

For quite some time we kept a measured distance ahead of the convoy. I could make out the large dark shadows clearly through my binoculars. The many ships were in columns on a broad front: we had stationed ourselves to lead the starboard column, as it were. The smaller, faster shadows of the escorts seemed much nearer than before their last turn. A very sharp watch was being kept by us all. Suddenly the most advanced destroyer detached and headed straight for us. Scarcely had I made my report and seen out of the corner of my eye that the commander had also noticed than the destroyer fired a series of starshells from his medium guns. The previously dark, heaving sea on either side of our conning tower was illuminated over a large distance and one of the shells poured brilliant light over our bridge for seconds. It was so bright that one could easily have read by it. I stood as if paralyzed and thought, 'Now it is up with us. We won't escape these destroyers.' Despite my fear I admired the commander, passing his orders with complete calm into the speech tube. Our speed increased to maximum ahead. The feared chase never took place. The Tommy lookouts had failed to see us.

There may have been several reasons to explain the behaviour of the escort. He might have got a radar fix (the equipment of the time had only limited range depending on the sea state) and then lost us again. He might have spotted our wake visually for a short time when for a few minutes moonlight shone through the cloud cover. He might also have heard our short-signal to SKL and thought that it came from a U-boat very close to the convoy. All this went through my head in seconds and I came to the conclusion that the opinions of the old hands were also valid: aircraft were more dangerous than destroyers. Thank God there are no bees in these skies.

Fighting men quickly forget what lies behind them, but the horrors of the recent pursuits by destroyers were still fresh in my memory. I had to get used to it and forced myself to be calm. Apparently it was not so easy to get a definite fix on us, and our commander was an old fox who had experienced many similar situations though never before as commander. As if in confirmation I heard him tell our watchkeeping officer, 'They probably feel very safe over there. Their radar seems to be defective or not to have the best of operators. Perhaps they have got one of the type on board which only provide them with a limited lateral field. Meanwhile we know their habits. Soon they will turn to port. The shadow of the rain clouds make us almost invisible. We shall make sure they don't spot our wake by proceeding at half ahead.'

Lüdden sounded as composed as ever as he ordered everybody to battle stations and all torpedo tubes flooded. Although I could hardly see our dark frothy wake my heart missed a beat as the commander steered U-188 astern of the destroyer. Now I could see the Tommy astern. Occasionally we were close enough for me to make out the structures on his afterdeck. I could not see what was happening ahead of our bow, only hear. They were not torpedo hits by other boats but the muffled growling explosions of depth charges which I knew only too well. 'Rahe or Uphoff are probably having their share over there, diverting attention from us.' The commander's remarks confirmed my own impression. Finally, finally, came the last questions and orders before firing: 'Firing angle?'

'Angle 70 . . . angle 75 . . .' Then the energetic order: 'Fire tube I, tube I fired! . . . fire tube II, tube II fired!' The torpedoes in tubes III and IV were released at other targets. What happened next is better described by the War Diary than I can do it.[1] The entry is for 11 April 1943 beginning at 0549 hrs:

After 94 seconds torpedo hit on tanker in rear third. Tall white column of smoke rose up at seat of detonation. Tanker buckled inwards astern and sank by the stern after 45 seconds. Second torpedo missed. 0552 hrs two torpedoes fired, hit on overlapping steamer to the right, running time 118 seconds, second hit heard after 131 seconds. Thick, dirty smoke from explosion and glare of

1. The strange circumstances surrounding the attack by U-188 on westbound convoy ON 176 on 11 April 1943 are not all evident from Staller's account. I have placed a Translator's Note at the end of the book in clarification. (Tr)

fire abaft forward mast. Steamer hidden shortly after explosion by turning hard to port so that its fate could not be observed. Glare of fire not seen again afterwards. Consider probable that sank quickly following hit. Medium sized freighter, estimate 5,000 BRT (gross registered tons).

The cloud cover was suddenly thinner. The wind drifted a few swathes of mist over us and away. The Northern Lights were not as bright as ordinary daylight, yet we could see farther and more clearly. I was slightly surprised by this reversal. As we turned away – the commander was probably searching for more victims for our stern torpedoes – I was only able to see briefly and partially in my quadrant the devastating effect of the torpedoes we had fired. The ghastly explosions resounding far across the sea's surface set my teeth on edge. I spared a thought for the poor sods dying out there.

Although I expected a destroyer to appear on our tail at any moment, and I would have to report it immediately so that as usual we could dive fast within seconds, I had to force myself to keep a sharp watch. Meanwhile the commander was standing close behind Rötters and me, his binoculars to his eyes. He was taking note of every detail of the work of destruction. Then he ordered softly, 'Watch out for escorts!'

'Steamer ahead to starboard!' Benetschik's shout seemed to electrify the commander, for he collided with my shoulder as he turned. This could only be a straggler which for some reason had lost contact with the convoy. What happened next went ahead swiftly: 'Rudder hard to port! Tubes V and VI fire!'

While Lüdden ordered a change of heading to get us out of the dangerously close sphere of action of the escorts, I told myself how lucky we had been so far not to have been spotted by the optics and equipment of the escorts and those in the wheelhouses of the merchant ships. Now I watched the lonely straggler passing us slowly 2,000 metres off. Scarcely did I have him in my glasses than torpedo V exploded in his forecastle and he sagged. I shall never forget the dreadful sound of that explosion resounding across the water. Shortly after the second torpedo hit astern. Aside from the magnifying effect of the yellow-red glow of the shipboard fire against the darkness of the night the ship looked gigantic. Seconds later came a dull rumble as his boilers exploded, enshrouding the freighter in white clouds of smoke and tearing the stern asunder. As the ship began to sink in the icy waters I had to force myself to resume the correct observation of my quadrant through binoculars, reproaching myself: 'Man, Toni, take care. You know how quickly we can be attacked! Don't be distracted!' I heard more torpedo hits astern where I believed other boats to be at work. Occasionally I also saw the light of fires.

Whilst outwardly composed and carrying out my duty as lookout, inwardly I was in turmoil. On the one hand, I instinctively felt pride in our triumph that the ships we had sunk with their supplies for the enemy's war effort diminished his fighting ability. On the other hand I felt deep sympathy for the merchant crews who had had to sacrifice their lives in the ordeal. 'Were the boys over there older than us? They would surely have preferred to have gone on living.' A thousand thoughts circulated in my head. 'Why is this war so ruthless and cruel? Because we soldiers belong to nations whose leaders prefer to fight instead of talking with each other reasonably. They over there were also continually indoctrinated into believing that every seaman had to do his duty for his people even if it meant risking his life for this better future . . . Thus they and us alike became torpedo and cannon fodder . . . The oath of allegiance is binding internationally, and I know for certain that in Germany every man who deserts the colours or refuses to obey orders is put up against a wall or hanged without mercy . . . Was it the same with our enemies? . . . Orders are international! And the duty of obedience too! . . . This forces each and every soldier to abandon his right to be a thinking individual . . . How will that be after this war? . . . Woe to us if we are completely defeated . . . How would my superiors in rank react if they could read these, my thoughts? . . . What would they think themselves if they could demand unconditional obedience of me and all their subordinates?' Such questions I could of course not answer myself.

Despite the feelings by which I was beset seeing ships and their crews go under from such close quarters, I kept up my unceasing and thorough examination of the horizon, sea and skies. We wanted to survive! Suddenly I remembered my father's words: 'After every war the law of the victor holds sway, only the defeated can ever have committed war crimes. The victors tell you precisely who the guilty parties are.'

'Watch out for escorts!' The voice of the commander tore me from my reverie. Then I heard him call down through the speaking tube: 'Reload all tubes! Rudder hard to port. Full ahead! Course . . .' We were going after the convoy again. Before I was relieved I heard *Kaleu* Lüdden say to Lt Benetschik: 'Rahe and the others are keeping the escorts so busy that they have no time to come looking for us, therefore we have to get back to the job in hand. The weather front brewing up there is made for us.'

Chapter Five

One Calamity After Another: We Head for Lorient

W hen changing in the E-room I saw Rötters take off his dry underwear and give it a beating to remove the layer of salt. I followed his example and also gave my burning skin a rub-down and felt better for it. Acrid smoke was coming from the diesel room. I had a quick look inside and saw Petty Officer Bischoff, LI Kiessling and other figures working with serious faces at the exhaust piping of the port diesel. A stinking, greyish-blue haze of smoke was drifting around the diesel room, and the men, coughing and spluttering, took it in turns to escape into the E-room to take deep breaths before returning to their work. Great demands had been made of the diesel for hours and as a result of the exhaust becoming overheated the port pipe had fractured and they were trying to plug it. I also noticed how Bischoff gave a resigned shrug of the shoulders as he pointed to the welding gear and acetylene bottle on the flooring. The fumes were already spreading through the entire stern section, and I hurried forward quickly. Here the air was a little better but getting worse. Despite this the mixers were loading the heavy torpedoes into the tubes. The torpedoes having been moved down, our bunks had been lowered and provided more space, but I was unable to enjoy the unaccustomed freedom of movement because of the stinking air. I had a handkerchief over my nose to filter it. My eyes were burning, but at least I could shut them, unlike the mixers at the torpedo tubes.

Breathing became more difficult. The contaminated air caused headaches, and some of the men began to throw up. Finally the loud roar of the diesels diminished, and the air gradually improved since at half ahead none of the exhaust gases escaped through the temporary repair into the boat. I read years later in the War Diary that despite the report of only restricted operational readiness made to SKL, we had been ordered to make a fresh attack on the convoy. This never came about, for a destroyer forced us down. He was probably unable to get a fix on us for he dropped his depth charges uselessly into the sea and departed much sooner than we expected. It was our guess that he had more important matters to attend to and was therefore prepared to let us off.

By now everyone in the boat knew that the Junkers compressor had given up the ghost and our E-room compressor was no longer reliable as a result of depth-charge damage and long-term overloading. This meant that we were not guaranteed our compressed air for breathing when submerged nor for blowing the tanks when desirous of surfacing. We were aware of this but nevertheless everybody seemed relaxed.

Towards the end of my watch, shortly before 1600 hrs on 24 April I heard Korn behind me report: 'Periscope ahead to port!' Almost immediately our commander appeared on the bridge and ordered: 'Full ahead!' *U-188* surged forward with a foaming wash. A little later I too saw the periscope jutting about a metre above the surface of that day's uncommonly calm sea. For about an hour our engines gave everything that was asked of them and I wondered if the patched-up exhaust pipe, though recently reinforced, would hold out. Naturally our enemies also operated submarines, and not until after the war did we discover that they tended to be technically more advanced than our own.

Once again I was soon crouching in the narrow magazine below the control room, caring for the shells and cleaning salt residue off the MGs when I felt the boat begin to roll violently as if in a heavy seaway. This interfered with the work in the diesel room to the extent that Lüdden dived the boat. Later I saw that our diesels resembled a field smithy. The cylinder head of the starboard engine had to be changed.

The commander's report to the BdU about the disquieting condition of *U-188* at last bore fruit, for on 25 April the word spread like wildfire to every corner of the boat: 'We are having to put into

Lorient.' At first I did not appreciate the purport of this order. Only after hearing an exchange between a couple of the old hands did I realise that in order to reach Lorient we had to sail through the Bay of Biscay, the great German U-boat cemetery. Over the last few weeks sprouting beards had changed everybody's facial appearance, but now in each face one could read the question distinctly: 'How are we going to get safely across this sea area off the French coast, monitored almost completely by the enemy, in this damaged boat?' Throughout the boat, repairs and checks were being made. I was spending much more time in the weapons hold below the control room than before. The entire steel tube was filled with determination to get through and survive. 'We have to do it: we want to go home again!'

On the evening of 30 April 1943, *U-188* reached the western Biscay. We had been forced to submerge by aircraft on three or four occasions by then. Their bombs had exploded so close to our wake that I thought they must tear the boat apart, or at least my eardrums. Horrified, we asked ourselves what more lay in store for us. Our reserve of compressed air and the charge in the batteries was diminishing due to the enforced dives. So briefly were we on the surface that neither could be recharged very much.

On 1 May we had been cruising on the surface for a short time when Korn reported a destroyer heading directly for us. Alarm dive. Rötters and I were seated at the hydroplane wheels when I heard Lüdden say to Sub-Lt Meenen: 'The bees sent him to hunt us down.' I would like to spare myself the detailed description of what happened next, but in a nutshell: Because of the diesel fumes circulating in the boat, the carbon dioxide content of the previously very thin air rose on this dive to between 2.8 and 3 per cent. We could scarcely tolerate the headaches and general vileness of it while Lüdden had to keep changing course and depth for hours. Moisture deposited on the naked walls and piping dripped ceaselessly and soaked us to the skin. Towards morning on 2 May the screw noises of our pursuers grew fainter, and the yearned-for report by Chief Schulz brought us relief.

Because I hardly dared to breathe and I could not see clearly the pointer of the depth gauge above me, the time Lüdden took before making his sweep of the surface with the periscope seemed to me unduly long. All I wanted to do was get up to the bridge, into fresh air. It couldn't be any worse up there. Those damn' Tommies couldn't be everywhere. With all my will I hung on to the wheel of the hydroplane until Lüdden's order galvanised me into action like an electric shock: 'Flak ammunition, MGs and machine pistols on deck! We have to air the boat and fight off the next attack by aircraft on the surface! Keep your nerve at all costs! Blow tanks!' Almost automatically I opened the hatch to the magazine, handed the cases of flak ammunition to Rupp the flak gunner and somebody else, passed up several machine-pistols with full magazines together with ammunition belts and followed them up to the conning tower with an MG as the last man. With a glance I saw that the portside MG was secure in its mount and Walter Rötters had the butt of the weapon pressed into his shoulder. While following his example, I breathed in the fresh sea air greedily. I felt slightly light-headed, but could see everything around me sharp and clear. Sub-Lt Meenen and his three lookouts were already observing. Each of them had a machine-pistol ready to fire hanging on the coaming in front of him. Lüdden stood astride at the centre of us, machine-pistol at his chest, binoculars to his eyes, turning slowly around his own axis. Two metres below me I saw Rupp on the metal seat of the flak gun, legs spread and stretched out moving the skywards-pointing barrel this way and that as if it were a toy. We all knew how it stood. Everybody knew how much depended on him and on his self-control in aiming and firing his weapon, and how fast the four-engined Whitley bomber flew for example, as well known to us from the classroom. If one of these aircraft patrolling in accordance with some set plan were to hit us with one of a stick of four bombs, that would be the end for all of us. It was again horribly clear to us how vulnerable and almost helpless we were in many situations.

Fear-filled and slowly the minutes passed. I was almost a nervous wreck, and I tried to stop thinking any longer about our plight. 'If Lüdden has decided on this desperate step, this must be our last chance. I will fight with all means at my disposal. I must aim coolly, shoot and get a hit at all costs as soon as a machine gets close enough to us. Them or us!'

'Aircraft astern, probably Whitley! Closing fast!' Wilhelm Rolfing's warning shout drew my eyes to a black point above the horizon along the line of our wake. The point quickly assumed form, sinking lower constantly, disappeared into cloud, and then came out making straight for us. While wondering in astonishment if he had X-ray eyes I became calm. I released the safety catch of my MG and thought, 'If he gets near enough I'll empty the whole belt into his knapsack.'

'Full speed ahead! Helm hard to port!' *Kaleu* Lüdders was bending over the bridge hatch. The attacker was flying for us ruler-straight and the commander wanted to check him with a fast evasive movement. In contrast to the helmsman the damaged boat responded ponderously, almost reluctantly. Now we could hear the aircraft engines clearly. I watched the enemy machine through the sight of my MG and when the range had closed to 800 metres I heard Lüdden cry: 'Fire at will!'

Everybody began shooting at the same moment and watching along the barrel of my hammering MG I saw the glass of the cockpit in the nose of the aircraft shatter. Probably Rupp had hit him with the flak gun. The Whitley was replying with all barrels. As it thundered overhead seconds later I turned and fired after the aircraft and was surprised that the flak gun remained silent. The bombs the aircraft had dropped fell in our wake.

'Alarm! Aircraft approaching to port!'

We dived rapidly. Sitting on my little bench before the hydroplane I was horrified to watch Meenen laying Rupp, bleeding from a wound in the chest, on the plating near the periscope. Had Meenen and Lüdden got the flak gunner down into the boat in time? But why was the commander taking so long? The boat was already cutting under! A torrent of water roared through the bridge hatch down into the bilges. The indicator of the depth gauge had my undivided attention but I could hear the commander's voice. It sounded unusually weary. 'Herr Meenen, I was not able to fully close the bridge hatch wheel with my right hand. The water pressure shut it.'

'Herr *Kaleu*, you have a bullet wound in your left shoulder!' At that moment everybody ducked as bombs exploded close by. *U-188* trembled and shook. We got over it quickly. Listening to Lüdden and Rupp being carried away behind me I thought: 'The worst thing about war is that one gets used to it. One gets used to all the shit.

Despite these endless attacks on our lives, every man of us functions just so as it was drilled into him.'

Meenen, at the periscope instead of the commander, and Benetschik were both in the control room. How long the deathly hush reigned in the boat I cannot say. The hum of the electric motors seemed softer than before. I found that strange, then realised that I was an idiot as the LI reported to *Kaleu*, 'We are running on only one motor. The batteries are almost empty. We have only enough compressed air to surface once more.'

Lüdden seemed to have made a quick recovery in his cot and despite the loss of blood was mentally wide awake. Only a brief moment passed and then we heard him say, quieter than usual, but in full control: 'Thank you, Herr Kiessling. Please bring me into the control room. We shall surface and ask for fighter cover. Until it arrives we shall have to survive on the surface as best we can.'

At midday on 2 May my watch on the bridge began. Before raising my binoculars to my eyes, I saw the unusually broad shoulders of Willi Beer at the flak. We now sailed for two hours on the surface without being detected. An hour previously FdU West (U-Boat Command West) had promised us four Ju 88s which should reach us by 1600 hrs. I stood at my position with a loaded machine-pistol as if on tenterhooks. Towards 1530 hrs I saw astern a dark point above the horizon through my binoculars and reported: 'Aircraft astern. Aircraft approaching quickly, probably a Sunderland!' The machine could soon be seen clearly. 'Sunderland approaching from astern!' I reported again . . . but what was that? Now I saw distinctly how the machine banked and turned away. 'Aircraft turning away!' My excited voice sounded strange even to myself.

Scarcely had my shout died down than Korn reported loudly: 'Four aircraft ahead to starboard!' Wild hope was kindled within me as he added: 'Four Ju 88s!' Unbounded loud jubilation broke out, and I too began to wave light-heartedly with all the others on the bridge and on deck. I could see them now with the naked eye flying in a search pattern. Korn grabbed the Very pistol from its mount on the coaming and fired a signal flare towards our aircraft. The Ju 88 flying to starboard lost altitude and a few moments later passed about 30 metres above us. The droning of its motors sounded like sweet music to our ears. I felt enormous satisfaction to see tears of joy drip from Korn's eyes into his beard. I drummed on the coaming with both fists, and my shouts were drowned in the general hubbub of joy: 'Ha! Not yet! Not this time! We live on!' Our long-lasting and enduring expectation of a quick death changed into an indescribable feeling of happiness.

Change of watch. As I ducked down under the air shaft into the control room I saw *Kaleu* Lüdden seated at the periscope. His face, or what could be seen of it through his brown beard, was pallid, and his sunken eyes glittered feverishly yet joyfully. He nodded to us without speaking as we went quickly to the E-room to peel off our oilskins. The diesel room looked much the same as it had four hours ago when I looked in through the wide-open hatch: Kiessling had been working there for hours with a couple of men, but the air quality was much improved and despite the chaos one could sense their hope.

Sitting on the deck in front of my bunk I drank a mug of hot tea and swallowed down a round slice of tinned bread spread with hard sausage. Minutes later I was crouching in the steel cell of our magazine, not even as tall as a man. Tired and raging inwardly, I began taking the MGs and machine-pistols apart, cleaning and re-assembling them. As I did so I asked myself angrily: 'Do we have to do this right now? We have fighter cover, will soon be in port and hardly need these things. But no. Petty Officer Bischoff requires me to report to him as soon as all these things are in a fit state for parade.' It is simply unbelievable how quickly salt water can coat even well-maintained metal parts with rust.

Because I had been assigned meanwhile to mess duty, my period off duty just flew by. I also spent the night watch beginning at midnight in the magazine because Lüdden and Meenen had decided to submerge for the night in order to allow work in the diesel room to proceed undisturbed and release our fighter protection in the darkness. Our batteries had been sufficiently recharged for us to proceed underwater at half ahead. Meanwhile I stripped, cleaned and polished with determination, so that Bischoff would find nothing of which to complain at his inspection. As I did so I asked myself what the bloated fellow had against me, and just then the hatch above my head was pulled up and Bischoff asked: 'How far have you got with it, Staller? How long are thinking of staying down there?'

'I shall be finished by 1000 hrs, petty officer. I shall report to you!'

'And about time too. When we arrive our weapons must sparkle like new!'

Shortly before ten on 3 May when I reported to Bischoff, 'As per your order, weapons and ammunition ready!' I was certain that he would find no fault with my work. My secret enemy descended into the steel chamber with an inscrutable expression and checked it over noisily and for a very long time. When he crawled back up to the control room he hissed: 'That probably was not all, Staller. I couldn't open all of the so-called pressure-proof containers for the shells. At least inside one of them it looks horrible. After your watch and mess duty you will have to go over them.'

When my bridge watch began I was tired but happy. It was a calming sight to see one of the German aircraft which had held off our persistent pursuers just above the horizon. We could sail on the surface using only the starboard diesel and even then on only seven of its cylinders, but this was enough for half ahead. I saw our Ju 88s turn away and heard Korn report down to the control room, where the commander was seated at the periscope with his chest thickly bandaged below a loose pullover: 'Escort being taken over by four minesweepers! Air cover leaving!'

Softly, calmly but with a firm voice *Kaleu* Lüdden answered from below: 'Thank you, Korn!' and after a few seconds he added, 'Now we're going home!'

'Jawohl, Herr *Kaleu*!'

At midnight on 4 May I began the last night watch of my first war patrol. Beforehand I had spent hours below the control room drying and polishing shells and now I sucked the mighty sea air into my lungs. Before taking up my lookout position I had a quick look over the bow through binoculars and saw ahead of us our *Sperrbrecher* – requisitioned heavily-armed merchant ships, packed with empty barrels and cork to make them unsinkable – which took station about 300 metres ahead of a U-boat to detonate any mines in its path. I believed I could see a dark strip of coast on the horizon, but then I remembered the admonitory words of our instructor: 'Never feel safe too soon. Even when you are running into port maintain your observation to the last second. Enemy aircraft do not advise you before attacking. You must therefore see them first!'

Although I was dead tired, I forced myself to keep my burning eyes open, searching the horizon, peering over seas whipped by the wind. It was a bright moonlit night. Shortly before 0300 hrs I saw concrete walls towering up to the right and left of us, then a narrow strip of the night sky glittering with stars above and finally a grey concrete roof appeared over my head. With a sigh of relief I let my binoculars drop to my chest. The noises of the diesel exhaust echoed strangely hollow against the concrete walls. We glided slowly into one of the U-boat pens built by the Organisation Todt at Bordeaux, Nantes, La Rochelle, Brest and here at Lorient for protection against enemy aircraft. Our I WO, Meenen, steered *U-188* to a mooring between two other boats already made fast alongside the pier. Our boat had suffered much from the weather. The protective layer of red lead was visible below the cracked grey livery. Rust had formed everywhere: on the bridge coaming, the flak barrels and on the deck gun. A thin layer of algae covered the wooden planks of the upper deck.

Meenen and Kiessling were helping our commander onto the bridge. Now that the tension of the past weeks had suddenly fallen away, I felt only a leaden tiredness. For a short while I was awake when I saw how Lüdden was holding himself very much under control, and how Meenen and Benetschik helped to bring the seriously wounded Rupp up to the bridge strapped to a stretcher. Safe at last. 'Now I can go down the gangplank and ashore, find somewhere to stretch out and switch off my mind,' I thought. First Rupp was carried off the boat on his stretcher to an ambulance waiting on the pier. Lüdden had his uniform jacket half unbuttoned over his dressing as he walked down the narrow gangplank upright but with unsteady steps. Meenen followed close behind him, arms outstretched ready to catch the commander should he falter. Then came the remainder of the crew, in strict order of rank. When Rötters gave me a poke in the ribs and said, 'Come on, Toni, now it's our turn,' I followed him like a robot and joined the ruler-straight ranks of the crew paraded on the quayside. It had all taken very little time. From my position in the rear rank of the three I had a partial view of

Kaleu Lüdden making his report to several high-ranking base officers before he went off in an ambulance. Not until later did I remember the characteristic contrast between the smart uniforms of these gentlemen and us 'front swine'.

We boarded waiting Kriegsmarine crew buses and drove first through a long concrete tunnel, then came out into the open to a dark, shining asphalt road crossing the fenced-in grounds of the base. As we passed the sentries at the gate I saw that the whole area around the bunkers lay in ruins. British bombers had tried unsuccessfully to bomb through the roofs of the U-boat pens. This had cost French civilians their lives. Driving through the ghostly, empty streets of the French port, I was so exhausted that I hardly noticed the excited and elated chatter of my shipmates. They drove us to a Kriegsmarine barracks compound on the outskirts of Lorient where we were to sleep six to a room. I sat on the second-best bed, kicked off my shoes and stretched out – just as I was – in my grey-green overalls on the yearned-for mattress. Subconsciously I noticed the others competing amongst themselves as to who would be first under the shower, heard them discussing the events of the past week in loud voices without getting the sense of what they were saying, reflected briefly on the fact that during the last two days I had had only two hours sleep and had spent most of the time crouching in the boat's moist, cool magazine. 'Let him sleep!' Those were the last words I heard distinctly.

Next day Rötters told me with a laugh that while asleep I had shouted out 'Alarm!' The only dream I recalled was one in which I was walking along a Baltic beach at Stettin with Gisela. I had held her in my arms and we kissed. When I awoke and recognised with some regret where I was, the evening sun was shining at a low angle through the barrack window, and I had a strong urge to pass water. My whole body was bathed in sweat.

Finding to my regret that I was alone in the room, I slipped off my overalls, my underwear and socks and felt disgusted with my filthy self as I threw everything to the floor. I stretched my limbs in the hot shower, washed my beard and hair with a perfumed French shampoo lying to hand, soaped myself over thoroughly, rinsing foam from my body repeatedly.

Dressed in my best walking-out uniform – our baggage had been brought to Lorient from Stettin – and freshly shaved, I met up in the canteen later with some of the crew who greeted me with well-filled jars of beer and glasses of wine and schnapps. At every table the men were laughing or singing along loudly to the melody from an accordion. The best informed of all as usual, Karl Bauer pushed a stool against the backs of my knees: 'Toni! You've got home leave with me on the second group. They've just started repairing our battered stovepipes tonight. If you ask me they can quietly take their time over it.'

My fourteen-day home leave came to an end too quickly, just like the first. I was very thoughtful as the leave train rolled westwards. At home I had been told that my friend Julius Scheurer and five of my former classmates had fallen in Russia. Waiting on the station in Paris I thought of our flak gunner Rupp, lying here in a military hospital. (Rupp died there of his wounds on 12 May 1943.) The morning of the following day, together with other men of the crew I was already busy helping fit out our overhauled boat in one of the Lorient U-boat pens for the next war patrol.

I had become one of the old hands and had a quiet look at the new faces. Some of the nucleus of our crew had been transferred to other boats, and two had gone on courses. It filled us with some satisfaction, however, that Lüdden and the other three officers would be sailing with us, that some of the new hands had had similar experiences as ourselves on other boats and the so-called hard core had been retained. An innovation made us scratch our heads: we would have a medical doctor aboard for this trip. What purpose would that serve?

For some time I had become used to expressing myself in the North German vernacular which was in predominant use aboard. I took at once to the slender and nimble new engine-room petty officer, Franz Heigl when, standing at the open hatch to the rear torpedo room, he called out in strong North German tones: 'Boys! In my old boat we always used to stow tins of meat longitudinally in the space between the hull wall and torpedoes. Hang on a bit before you secure the torpedoes. Staller and I will hand you down the tins.' With a crowbar he broke open one of the cases on the floor of the diesel room and passed me two tins which I forwarded to outstretched hands. Heigl smiled impishly: 'Naturally we shan't be able to tuck into these until you have fired off the torpedoes!'

I guessed that Heigl came from somewhere on the North German coast. That evening we sat at a table in the canteen at the naval compound and my respect for the petty officer grew when I saw the Iron Cross First Class on the breast of his walking-out uniform. As if casually he mentioned that he was an apprenticed copper-smith. He asked me, probably because I looked so young, how old I was and if I had a civilian trade. As soon as I told him that I had learned organ-making at Munich, with a laugh he slapped his thighs with both hands: 'Well, there we are then! We are almost neighbours! My parents had an inn and butcher's shop at Amperpettenbach near Dachau!'

Engine-room Petty Officer Baumann and Karl Bauer were seated facing us at the table, and Baumann remarked in his good-humoured way: 'Now we really do have two rascals aboard! Legendary what *U-188* expects of everybody!' We laughed, but later the conversation became more gloomy. Karl Bauer leaned forward and in low tones told us that during his leave at Kärnten he had met his uncle who was a major at the Bendler Strasse in Berlin. 'When he was talking with my old man in the smoking room I overheard their . Just imagine the statistics my uncle knows. Last year we lost eighty-five boats. This year it is already 200. And the sinkings of enemy shipping is falling off rapidly. At three million gross registered tons it is not even half what we sank last year. Since Portugal allowed the Allies to use the Azores as a base for their aircraft a few weeks ago, they can provide aerial protection to every Atlantic convoy. The blockade of Britain, the idea of which was to starve the island into submission, has therefore become meaningless. Furthermore, in this year alone 20,000 tons of explosives has been dropped on the Reich. How can that go on?'

As he spoke, Karl's voice had gradually got louder and we had not realised that it had grown quieter around us. Coxswain Korn surprised Bauer by appearing behind him, his inevitable pipe in hand, and laid the other hand gently on Bauer's shoulder. 'Bauer, I couldn't really make sense of the crap you were dishing out there.

You definitely misheard, or your honourable uncle has got his figures in a twist. All the same, I advise you to keep your wisdom to yourself in future.' Before Korn went, he gave an encouraging nod to Ordinary Seaman Heinze to start up a fresh melody on his accordion.

The following night several of us visited a house, surrounded by ruins, in which it was said that young French girls offered their services. The fee could be paid to the last pfennig in German currency. Everyone got what he wanted although the prophylactic measures were harsh.

The remaining days ashore were short on interest. There was enough booze without getting stinking drunk. What was coming next? Anything could be achieved with a little luck.

Next morning every man was aboard *U-188* hale and hearty. The carefree attitude and the usual busy activity shortly before a boat sailed seemed to me rather affected. Four nights previously two of our boats had left the bunker complex together and without escort. The commanders had probably thought they could sail out unnoticed through Biscay. Before a couple of hours had passed one of the boats had been seriously damaged and put back with many dead and wounded. A dreadful sight. The second boat had been sunk with all hands. Tonight we had been denied shore leave. Probably we – Lüdden's boat – would sail tomorrow night together with Piening's *U-155*.

Chapter Six

From Lorient to Penang

I had been promoted to Leading Seaman. In torrential rain on the night of 30 June 1943 we slipped out of Lorient behind our *Sperrbrechers*. Scarcely had the escort left us than our expectations were fulfilled by a Whitley bomber forcing us to dive. A brief time after cautiously resurfacing another enemy aircraft discovered us. Then a destroyer hunted us for hours in the old manner. He dropped his depth charges so close to the boat that inside it we were hurled to the deck or the ceiling. Water gauges smashed, piping hissed, water sprayed out under the force of the roaring detonations. Around me I saw pale faces looking upwards, their bloodshot eyes searching for the leak in the thin steel wall of our pressure hull which would mean our deaths. Nine endlessly long, fear-packed hours passed, and still the destroyer was dropping his canisters. A deathly hush reigned in the boat. The rating transmitting orders at the rearmost circular pressure door stated quietly: 'Shaft stuffing boxes leaking heavily.' Suddenly we heard the screws of a second destroyer, and the hiding place in the depths for us was narrower than before.

How the commander succeeded in shaking off these two pursuers was a mystery to us all, for we expected that every coming second would be our last. We made slow progress forwards, and even when we reached the open Atlantic our pursuers seemed to be everywhere, sticking to us. Several times in the distance we could hear Piening having the same problem.

When I came up on the bridge on the night of 7 July, I overheard from a brief muttered exchange between Lüdden and our watchkeeping officer that we had left the Azores north of us. On 22 July in a nerve-racking, hasty transfer in heavy seas we took on board 35 cubic metres of oil from Piening's boat. I was thankful that the skies wrapped us in dark grey, low-hanging cloud, and instead of observing the horizon I often caught myself looking at the supply boat wallowing in the long drawn-out seas. In the dark waters I was unable to see the hose binding us together like an umbilical cord, only the small boat which had brought the oil hose over to us. Naturally the commander was on the bridge. After completion of refuelling Piening wished us through his loudhailer, 'A good trip and fat rewards!'

A stiff wind which had whipped up suddenly swept the clouds before it. Minute by minute it grew brighter. Soon the pale yellow light of the moon spilled over the wide expanse of the ocean. We ploughed on southwards and alone. On this now peaceful looking sea I could see the shape of the globe by just looking at the horizon and the starry skies above us. Once again I reflected on the sense of this war while I and probably everybody else on board enjoyed the pleasant knowledge that on the last stretch we had been spotted much less often by our opponents.

Later, down inside the boat, the commander informed us through the loudspeaker unit that *U-188* had been attached to the so-called 'Monsoon Fleet'. 'Our destination is Penang in Malaysia. On the way we have to sink all rewarding targets which present themselves to our torpedo tubes. Four months are planned for this voyage with several detours.' As the loudspeakers crackled to announce the end of this unusually long address for Lüdden, it remained quiet for a couple of seconds. Then all began to talk across each other at once:

'Crossing the Line ceremony!'

'Cape of Good Hope!'

'Around the Horn of Africa!'

'So that's the reason why we've got khaki short trousers and short-sleeved shirts on board!'

'Malay women!'

'The Indian Ocean with its monsoon storms.'

'Malaysia is occupied by our Japanese allies!'

All these ideas swirled around madly. 'Four months! That's as long as four war patrols!'

Here in proximity to the Equator it seemed that the Allies did not suspect our presence. Nevertheless, in order to clear the bridge rapidly should an alarm be given, only one extra man was allowed up to take in the fresh sea air or have a smoke. But now staff surgeon Dr Esau sat up there taking the sun nearly all the time, claiming the sea for himself, without regard to the needs of others. For this reason he soon became the most unloved man aboard after a few days.

A few hours before we reached the Equator, great activity could be perceived in many parts of the boat. Because of the heat we wore only shorts and sleeveless string vests. For protection against the fierce rays of the sun the bridge watches wore sand-coloured broad-brimmed tropical pith helmets and cotton girdles to avoid kidney trouble. As I passed the galley coming from above and asked Gerhard Storz what stinking garbage he was brewing up for us today I was given the terse response: 'You'll find out soon enough, Toni. Then everyone will be able to ask stupid questions.' The control room petty officer standing near the cook grinned, grabbed my shoulder and gestured for me and others to go astern. I had gone a few metres when I saw our LI, Lt Kiessling, leaning back with folded arms against one of the numerous pipes. As I forced my way past him, he moved his head this way and that as if enjoying the mysterious unidentifiable odours wafting from the galley. Then he gave a quiet laugh and said to me, 'Don't think anything of it, Staller. Crossing the Line. Everybody has to go through it once.'

Some of the crew, that is to say all the officers, several petty officers and also a couple of ratings but not the doctor had already crossed the Equator several times. The majority of us would be doing so for the first time on that 5 August 1943. In order to avoid unpleasant surprises, Lüdden ordered submerged travel. No sooner was the boat under than some of those already baptised immediately put into effect their well-planned intentions. We awaiting baptism were all rather tense. Despite many dark hints as to the horror to come we thought it could not be as bad as all that, for there were thirty-two of us and the commander had only set aside an hour for the baptism ceremonial.

The hydroplanes were manned by two already-baptised petty officers, the E-room was staffed by more and now those for baptism and onlookers filled the fore and aft passageways both ending at the control room. I sat on the flooring squashed up against Bauer in the first row of onlookers, heard sniggering above me and watched in amazement as a kind of stage was erected in the narrow control room. Within a minute a rubber dinghy slopping seawater over the gunwales was in place before me. Coxswain Heinrich Korn sat on the periscope's folding seat, his makeshift throne. He was barefoot and clothed only in bathing trunks and a singlet. The fringes of a grey wig made of cotton waste framed his head and hung low over his eyes. The control room petty officer had a blonde plaited wig and a blue-white checked frock as Neptune's wife Thetis. She placed upon her husband's head a crown made of silver paper and handed him a wooden trident. Crown and trident identified Korn as the god of the sea, Neptune. His free hand was resting on a batch of handwritten certificates and notes.

Five of his attendants disguised beyond recognition held back the curious from adding to the crowd already in the control room, no respect being paid to rank or name. They even succeeded in making room for two large tureens, borne over all the heads from the galley. The guardians had to keep remonstrating: 'Keep back! We shall be calling each one of you forward soon enough! You will all see, what must happen here!' One of the two tureens was filled almost to the brim with a vile greenish-yellow and foul smelling liquid. When the guardians had carefully lowered it to the floor near Neptune and the inflatable dinghy, the god of the sea announced loudly and mischievously: 'Yes, we have it at last, our so lovingly prepared wine of the gods from which every baptismal candidate must take refreshment!' I did not like the look of this. Then Neptune said, 'Ah, and here we have our glorious ambrosia, food of the gods!' His guardians skilfully placed the second tureen near Neptune. It was filled with small greyish-brown pellets which we knew had been prepared by Gerhard Storz from flour, a lot of paprika, pepper, salt and vinegar. Many bearded faces around me were beaming in malicious expectation. The others were cautious and reserved, but each knew that we had to go through this ceremony and nobody must spoil the fun. Everywhere I heard excited giggling and then I saw Lüdden standing in front of the closed door to the radio room where the already baptised Schulz was listening out through his hydrophones.

The loud voice of Neptune spoke again: 'We have just crossed the Line separating the northern part of the earth from the southern.' Korn's announcement could be heard throughout the boat's loudspeaker system and for a moment there was absolute silence. 'I, Neptune, God of the water, Master of all oceans, seas and mires, condescend to advise those persons who have never before shipped across the Equator, that they must be cleansed of the filth of the northern hemisphere.' Here and there one heard giggles as Korn cleared his throat noisily before his powerful bass voice continued: 'In this cleansing of the filth of the North, obviously some people will not get off lightly. A few incidents in the northern part of the globe cry out loud for atonement. I must begin with *Stabsarzt* Esau, loved by everybody, for he considers himself indispensable on such a long voyage.' Neptune looked around before continuing: 'None of you hardened veterans and storm-proof heroes is ill! The Herr Stabsarzt is therefore unemployed aboard *U-188*. I have been told that he spends most of his time up on the winter garden and there deprives your crew of the space they need to breathe in desperately needed fresh air. Such an attitude is monstrous and must be punished forthwith. I consider that ten helpings of ambrosia and ten large quaffs of the wine of the gods is suitable to atone.'

While Neptune spoke, two of his attendants had, as if by chance, crept up on either side of the doctor as he was standing by the periscope, seized him as he resisted, dragged him before Neptune and held him fast. Another pair of Neptune's attendants forcibly opened the doctor's mouth while the fifth began to count out loudly: 'One!' Briskly he pushed the first pill into the delinquent's mouth and counted off the remainder hastily to ten. I saw Esau gag as he was forced to swallow the delicacy. 'Naturally it must be washed down so that everything is cleaned up inside.' I thought I detected satisfaction in Korn's voice as he nodded encouragingly to his helpers.

In order to see Lüdden's reaction to this disrespectful treatment of the doctor I had to bend forward. Would the commander intervene? He did nothing as the doctor's mouth was thoroughly cleansed with an oversize syringe made by skilful craftsman Petty Officer Heigl. Next he was baptised by having his head forced under water. The face of the physician showed no emotion as he received his certificate from Neptune. He had fallen quiet as he left and looked none of us in the face. In a surprisingly quiet voice I heard Lüdden say: 'Herr Stabsarzt. Come and see me as soon as you can. Carry on!'

Neptune was not flustered: 'From now on we shall move faster. Some of you are guilty of misdeeds, but none so bad as Number One.' One after the other he called us forward for baptism with a loud growl. Quietly I was calculating how many of these pills and drinks I would have to take when I heard: 'Bring forward Leading Seaman Staller!' I tried to put on a contrite face as I stood before Neptune. He spoke: "This indescribable young scamp, this rascal, comes from the Bavarian Oberland! On the first voyage with *U-188*, for disrespect to one of your petty officers he was thunderstruck to be awarded ten messboy duties as a punishment . . .' (here it was necessary for Neptune to consult his notes), '. . . and then he told shipmates, "He can stuff them up his arse!"' Korn interrupted the laughter with a movement of his trident. 'U-boat men! Time is short! It can suddenly become very dangerous for you! Stop interrupting me with your stupid giggling. We still have to get through five more baptisms! Anyhow, as I was saying, since Staller's manner of speaking and expressing himself have changed to his advantage and he appears otherwise to be conducting himself with decorum, I consider one pill of ambrosia and one drink of mead sufficient to atone!'

After what seemed less than an hour the entertaining ceremony ended and I received the written confirmation of my Undercrossing the Line.

'Clear the deck! Each man back to his station! Periscope depth!' Before I left the control room I heard Frau Thetis whisper to one of the assistants and Neptune: 'That with Esau might have done the trick.' I didn't see Korn's reaction and then routine took us all in hand.

On 26 August 1943 we rounded the southern tip of Africa at a respectful distance from the coast. Here we were received by such a hurricane as I had never experienced before. This change in the weather quickly dampened our high spirits. Once again on the bridge we wore leather and oilskins, our sou'westers as head protection and were buckled to the coaming to prevent being washed overboard.

Then so as to avoid the risk of damage to the boat, the commander decided to proceed submerged.

Over the next few days we headed north-east through the Indian Ocean on the surface with the coast of Africa to port, therefore west of us. Every time I climbed up to the bridge and had a look around before beginning my watch I would be deeply impressed by our great isolation on the so peaceful-looking surface of the sea. In daylight the mostly deep blue sky seemed reflected by the water. It lent it a greenish-blue colour of such intensity of which I would never have dared dream. In the reigning calm of the wind I loved it when we travelled through the great, gently undulating hills of water. The boat would glide quietly hundreds of metres downhill and then climb up again. However, I was warned 'Toni, the Indian Ocean is not always as peaceful as this.'

On my next daylight watch a sudden storm blew white spindrift across frayed wave caps. Above the howl of the wind, dull growling thunder could be heard, accompanied by incessant cobalt-blue bolts of lightning from the racing cloud low overhead. Once again we were strapped to the coaming. *U-188* was borne up on mountainous seas as high as a house, to be pitched from there into the raging abyss. After an hour the order came from below to come down. *Kaleu* Lüdden had decided to dive. Once again we tumbled dazed into the control room.

Lüdden seemed to be slightly nervous to me because we still had our full load of torpedoes. It appeared that we were alone. At 0300 hrs on 8 September in calm seas in the southern Indian Ocean we met up almost simultaneously with the boats of Henning, Schäfer and Junker. The rendezvous point lay in a chart grid square far removed from the merchant shipping lanes. The German supply ship *Brake* was also there waiting for us. We were to be replenished with provisions, lubricating oil and fuel. Lüdden wore only shorts, a dark blue pullover and his white-crowned cap and before addressing the neighbouring boats of Schäfer and Junker through his loudhailer he warned us to remain at maximum alert. Afterwards he quietly told Meenen, 'The Italian Cagni should have arrived here long ago with his boat. He probably knows that his new Government has changed sides and therefore decided to run into a safe port.'

Meenen replied, equally softly, 'I agree, Herr *Kaleu*. A fine brother-in-arms!'

Lüdden leaned over the conning tower hatch and shouted short, precise orders down into the boat. Junker and Schäfer were probably doing the same. We took station about 1,000 metres off the starboard side of *Brake*, Junker protected the port side and Schäfer the stern. When Henning's boat began to take on fuel, the absence of the Italian boat created a gap in the protection which we had to plug. After such a long and isolated voyage I rather took pride in seeing four German U-boats and the *Brake* afloat on the sea. At the same time I searched my quadrant conscientiously, but risked a glance aside at the *Brake* from time to time. In comparison to this ship our U-boats were very small. She was a tanker with an air of mystery about her: she was painted grey, flew no flag and had no name or port of registry at her stern. Her two masts were white: high on the forward mast, maybe 30 metres up, was a lookout in a small crow's-nest.

The replenishment went like clockwork. During my watch the following night, busy inflatable-boat traffic was conducted between *U-188* and *Brake*, towering high out of the water 100 metres away. We were the first boat to be reprovisioned. The foodstuffs had been taken by a German surface raider from American ships bound for Singapore or Penang. As I went down inside the boat, I immediately took my place in the chain of men hurriedly passing cases of tinned meat, bananas, bread and other delicacies from hand to hand. Towards eight o'clock we began shipping aboard lubricating oil and fuel. On 10 September – we were still undetected and all four boats had been resupplied – *U-188* headed north to loud cheers and good wishes. The lower deck suspected correctly that we were on course for the Gulf of Aden, hunting the fat traffic coming through the Suez Canal from the Mediterranean into the Red Sea, and which could not avoid passing in front of our torpedo tubes.

Uninvited guests had come aboard with the provisions. I was disturbed by loud shouts and commotion from down the passage-way. Later it was reported that the cook had seen a rat dash by. And we all felt the deepest disgust at the sight of cockroaches scurrying along the piping above our bunks. We began a ruthless hunt for the invaders. Afterwards, as was usual with everybody on board, dressed only in swimming trunks I lay prostrate on the wooden plank left sweaty by my predecessor. Scarcely was I asleep than I felt cockroaches crawling over my back and I got down to the floor plating in disgust. Rötters had the bed below me at the time and laughed: 'If the Amis have no more effective secret weapon than these things, then they will never beat us.'

'Please help me to get rid of them!'

'No, my boy. You will have to do that yourself. There seem to be fewer of them now. Besides, with you in the bed above mine, they won't drop from the piping directly on to me.'

'So, are you saying you won't exchange beds with me?'

Rötters' voice sounded as tired as I was: 'Toni, just let me sleep.'

At the beginning of my night watch on 12 September I was surprised by something completely unexpected. We were standing about 2,000 metres off from a blacked-out port. Behind it in the pale light I saw unlit white houses of what looked like an abandoned town with wooded mountains behind it. Only high up in the mountains was the odd blink of light to be seen. Apparently I must have looked as if I had seen a ghost for Korn explained: 'Staller! Here, right in front of your nose is Port Louis, the harbour of the island of Mauritius.'

Lüdden was at the forward edge of the coaming, binoculars to his eyes, and his disappointment was evident when he remarked, 'There are only small fry anchored here, none of them worth a torpedo. Has anybody contacted us? Cagni perhaps?'

The commander bent over the open conning tower hatch: 'Rudder hard to port! Half ahead!' Until then we had been almost invisible, the moon hidden behind the mountains of the island, but as we departed our wake did not go unnoticed, for at places along the shore and in the harbour searchlights glared suddenly and almost simultaneously, their fingers of light roved the sea for about three minutes. The beams never trapped us. We were already well clear when after about five minutes the searchlight activity resumed. Apart from that, nothing. Through binoculars I watched the slowly disappearing contours of the mountainous island astern and the enticing spots of light. I thought to myself: 'I've been 75 days on this boat. When it's quiet aboard, I can recognise each man of the crew

ton Staller. This photograph was taken after he had completed basic training.

Celebrating call-up at Grafing/Munich, autumn 1941.

Company commander of the training company, nicknamed 'The North Sea Terror'.

ll in civilian dress: instruction in collecting rations upon arrival at Bergen op Zoom.

e *Wilhelm Gustloff*, later the victim of one of the greatest tragedies in maritime history, served for hort time at the beginning of 1942 as a 'floating barracks' and was the domicile of Anton Staller d his colleagues during gunnery training.

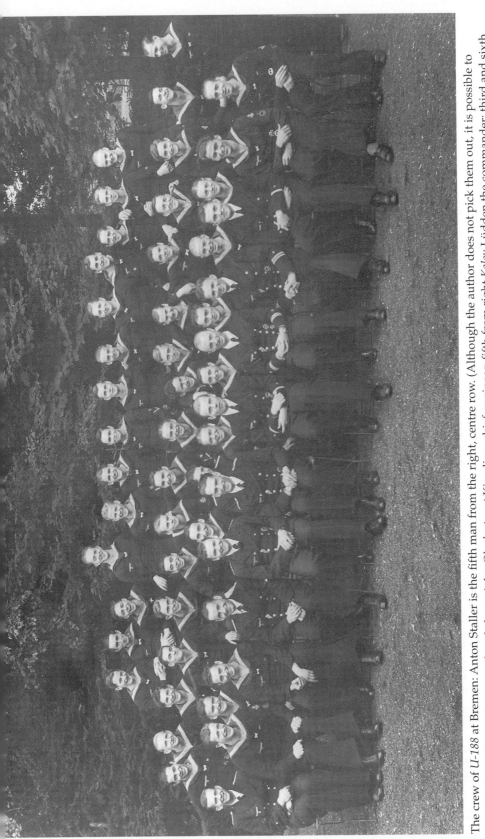

The crew of *U-188* at Bremen: Anton Staller is the fifth man from the right, centre row. (Although the author does not pick them out, it is possible to identify these officers: front row fourth from right, *Oberleutnant* Kiessling, chief engineer; fifth from right *Kaleu* Lüdden the commander; third and sixth from right respectively the two *Leutnants-zur-See*, Meenen and Benetschik.)

ewmembers and guests in the bow compartment of *U-188* during the commissioning: Anton
aller is at the centre, seated.

Lüdden in the commander's cabin of
U-188 as an *Oberleutnant zur See*: he was
promoted to *Kapitänleutnant* on
1 April 1943.

188 working up in the Baltic. Once winter set in ice would regularly coat the boat's upperworks.

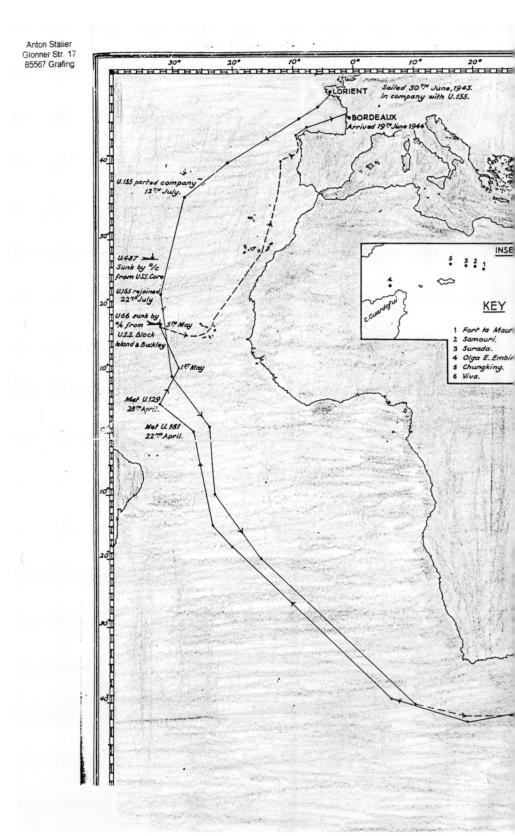

This chart showing the route sailed by *U-188* from Biscay to East Asia was prepared by the Royal

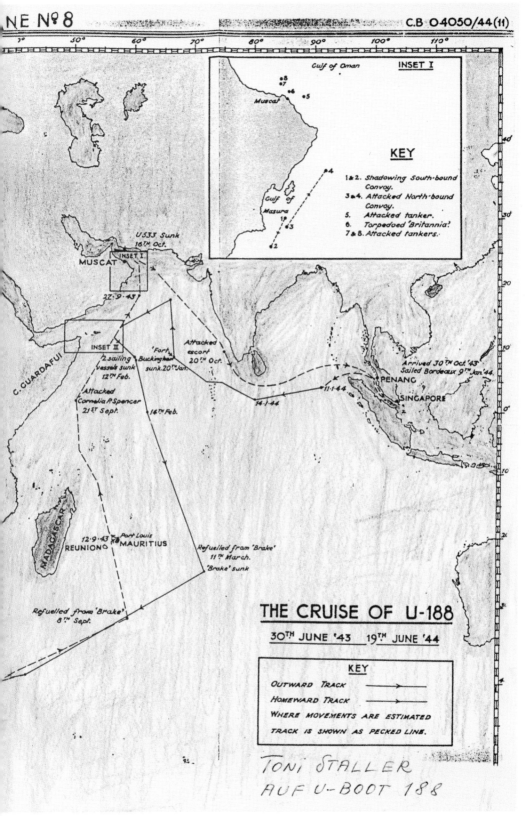

Crossing the Line certificate issued to Anton Staller aboard *U-188*, signed on behalf of Neptune and bearing the stamp of the 12th U-boat Flotilla but undated for security reasons.

...xcursion around Penang in Japanese Army lorries.

Anton Staller in walking-out uniform at Penang.

Christmas 1943 on a Singapore beach.

'Fifi', the boat's mascot.

188 in the Straits of Malacca, a dangerous region haunted by enemy submarines.

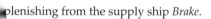
...plenishing from the supply ship *Brake*.

Tag Uhrzeit	Ort Wetter	Vorkommnisse
1941		Fangschuß Rohr IV.
		Z-Tiefe 6m.-Treffer Achterkante Brückenaufbau-ten.Schiff bricht durch.
1951	MQ 5869	Dampfer gesunken.-

Nach dem ersten Treffer hatte ich Zeit, mir den
Dampfer genauer anzusehen:-Klipperst. Klipperstéven-vorn 2 Schwergutmasten,
Kastenartiger Brückenaufbau hinter Schiffsmitte.Schornstein Ach-
terkante Aufbauten-achterer Mast-Deckshaus auf Achterdeck-Kreu-
serheck.-Ein Vergleich mit der Umdrehungstabelle erklärt die
achterliche Trefferlage.Es handelt sich um einen Amerikaner der
Cäsar 2 Klasse. Der bei 90 Umdr./Min. 15 sm. läuft. 7500 Brt.

1953		aufgetaucht-Im Trümmerfeld viele Kisten und Ka-nister.-Keine Überlebenden.
2000	MQ 5869	
2143	MQ 5976	Segler in Sicht - Kurs West -
2307	MQ 5971	Nach kurzem Feuerüberfall Segler durch Rammstoß

versenkt.-Muß nach schnellem Sinken schwere La-
dung gehabt haben. Größe wiederum wie ein mitt-
lerer Ostseeschoner.-

| 2336 | | Ausgang F.T.: 2006/9/520 |

Soeben versenkt Max Quatsch 5869 Amerikaner C-
sar 2 Klasse 7500 Brt.,280°,15 sm. 7.2. Max Quatsch 6747 4 Last-
segler, Westkurs mit 2 cm in Brand geschossen und nach Teget-
hoffverfahren versenkt.Ladung Baumwollballen.Rückmarsch über
Marqu. Lucie Wilhelm 45. 200 sm Etmale.   " Lüdden "

10.2.		
	Östl.Golf von Aden	
0000	MQ 5971	Beabsichtige noch einen Tag nach Osten auf Dam-pfertreck zu bleiben und dann nach Süden zur Ver-
0400	MQ 5985	sorgung abzulaufen.
0800	MQ 9112	
	NOz03,See2-3,1/4 bedeckt	
	gute Sicht	
1200	MQ 6755	Etmal: 192 sm, 4 sm.
	12°41'N,59°28'0	
1600	MQ 6787	Schatten in rw.108°,beim Näherkommen sehen wir,
1736	MQ 9124	daß es ein Tanker ist.
2000	MQ 6783	Ausgedampft 3°,11,8 sm.Laufe nach Stoppuhr
		2500 m querab.
2123		getaucht zum Unterwassernachtangriff.-Gestoppt
		94 Umdreh./Min. entspricht 11,8 sm. Fahrt.
2207	MQ 6753	Einzelschuß Rohr III.(letzter T3 aus Lorient)
	NO2-3,See2,1/2bed.	
	Vollmond,gute Sicht	

rw.   = 117,3°
σ   = 66,50
ß   = 21°
Vg.   = 11,8 sm
E   = 700 m.

Trotz peinlich genau ausgedampfter Unterlagen und
naher Schußentfernung ereignet sich nichts.-Nach
17 Minuten Laufzeit starke Detonationen,die im

| 2224 | | |

Boot heftige Erschütterungen hervorruft.Danach 4 leichtere Detonationen, dann Ruhe.Tanker läuft wild zackend weiter.
Annahme:Entstreckendetonierer,wie leider alle Lorienter Etos
der Unternehmung.Da Tanker mit gleichen Umdrehungen fährt wie
bisher, und unser letzter Aal verschossen ist-aufgetaucht-Rück-
marsch fortgesetzt.

Extract from the *U-188* War Diary for shortly before 10 February 1944 when east of the Gulf of Aden.

by his footsteps, his slight cough or when he clears his throat, even his manner of breathing. When will we finally get ashore in order to be people again?'

'Flying fish ahead to starboard. A whole flight.' Korn's voice sounded matter-of-fact, just as though advising somebody that his shoe-lace was undone.

'Not strange in these waters. But that really is a whole host of them.' Even *Kaleu* Lüdden seemed unimpressed, but I was curious and had a quick look in the reported direction. At the same moment to my left side below me I saw countless longish fish bodies, glittering rust-red in the moonlight, about a metre above the surface of the sea and for a short time close to the boat. About thirty to forty metres astern when they dived into a long rolling wave, the sprays of water they threw up sparkled and flashed in all colours of the rainbow. I was completely enchanted.

The commander made a half turn towards Rötters and myself. 'Keep observing!' Then he explained to us briefly, 'There are more than one hundred varieties of these fish. The ones here are as big as our trout at home. With their breast fins enlarged into wings they can fly up to 200 metres in 50 metre stages at an average altitude of one metre. Their asymmetric tail fins provide them with propulsion in the water and act as a rudder in the air. You will see them again and again here. You cannot eat these flying torpedoes. Moreover we are not here to go fishing.'

On 21 September, near the coast south of the Gulf of Aden, our WO reported towards the end of our watch at 1600 hrs: 'Mastheads 355 degrees ahead! Range twelve sea miles.' Lüdden was on the bridge within a couple of seconds exclaiming, 'Finally! It took us long enough. We shall approach him submerged.'

As I was not in the control room for the underwater attack after my change of watch, I quote what followed from the *U-188* War Diary:

Fired two, aiming point masts forward and aft. Running time 68 seconds, 63 seconds, range 1020 metres. Hit below wheelhouse, second hit under stern. Steamer settled about three metres deeper by the stern. When leaving conning tower broke surface briefly. Result was heavy fire from two medium cannon and several AA guns. Through attack periscope projecting above conning tower saw columns of water fountain up. No damage to boat. After trimming boat at 15 metres dived under steamer to other side. Waited ten minutes raised periscope again. Steamer still firing. Observed panic firing in all directions. As steamer still afloat after 45 minutes, coup de grâce torpedo aimed at wheelhouse (starboard side). Hit below mast aft. Inaccuracy inexplicable. The effect of this T3 weak. Steamer crew maintaining wild shooting. Crowded lifeboats hanging in davits. Coup de grâce aimed at forward mast, hit below funnel. Whole ship shrouded in steam. Bow rose quickly. Steamer sank. Modern USA-unit freighter, C-3 Class, 8000 BRT. Four lifeboats.[1]

Rötters told me after his watch that Lüdden had dieseled up to the occupants of the lifeboats to enquire as to the name of the ship: 'Toni, you should have seen how they all put their hands up and pleaded, "Don't shoot please!" Lüdden dived after that and so we remained undetected. They took us for Japanese. Apparently they murder all the shipwrecked as a matter of course. I'm glad we don't do things like that. Just imagine being ordered to shoot unarmed survivors!'

Later, when we four men of the bridge watch relief were getting our eyes accustomed to the darkness I heard Lüdden and Benetschik discussing the inaccurate performance of the torpedoes at such short range. Lüdden concluded: 'These faulty runners can't be blamed on us. It must have to do with the torpedoes themselves. That is what I shall report to the BdU. As for the reported aircraft, that can only be a flying boat from Aden heading for the survivors.'

On 23 September I awoke on my bunk bathed in sweat and saw Chief Schulz hurrying through the passageway with a slip of paper in his hand. With a sly smile he stopped in front of me, had a look

---

1. A T3 (LUT) torpedo had a pre-set gyro-angle and zig-zag course. It would run straight for a certain distance into a convoy and then make a zig-zag run in the hope of hitting something. The casualty here was the new US-flagged freighter *Cornelia P. Spencer*, 7,176 GRT, bound from Aden for Durban and sunk 300 miles off the coast of Somalia at 2°08'N 50°10'E. Her gunners fired seventy-five rounds of 3in calibre. Of the 68-man crew, two gunners were killed, the sixty-six survivors being picked up by Allied merchant and naval vessels later. (Tr)

round as though pretending to search, then surprised me with: 'Oh yes, here he is! Leading Seaman Staller, we telegraphists are always best informed about everything.' He bent towards me, extended his hand and said with a laugh, 'Don't look so dejected. I can't count you in the ranks of those who have come of age but nevertheless, my congratulations on your twentieth birthday! This . . .' – he thrust the paper into my hand – 'was added at the end of a radio signal. I copied it up for you. A privilege for us long-distance voyagers. Your parents don't know where you are serving, but they haven't forgotten your birthday.' I looked with surprise and pleasure at the slip of paper, and Schulz hurried back to his radio booth.

Six days after the unexplained defective torpedoes *U-188* pursued a convoy off the Arabian coast, got ahead of it at maximum speed and waited for it to come up for a night attack. As usual great tension reigned before an attack. I was fascinated by the bright phosphorescence of the wake, something I had never seen in other waters. It seemed to me as if greenish-yellow lights were coming up out of the ocean depths. There! As surprising as usual and initially minute, through my binoculars I saw appear above the mastheads of the convoy a tiny point in the sky. 'Alarm! Aircraft approaching from astern!' We dived at once.

In the control room from my place at the hydroplanes I heard Lüdden say to Meenen, 'The aircraft is now directly above the convoy. I am guessing they've got a fix on us. Three steamers, seven tankers and a modern destroyer can just sweep past us unharmed at seven sea miles distance. Please have a look for yourself.' I glanced behind me and saw Meenen seated at the periscope seat, Lüdden with a thoughtful look on his face standing near him.

Shortly before 1500 hrs we surfaced and set off after the convoy at full speed. I felt how the whole boat trembled under the effort being made by the diesels. Towards 1600 hrs at my back Kiessling said: 'Herr *Kaleu*, request permission to shut down the starboard diesel. The lubricating oil pressure has fallen so much that it is endangering the engine. I cannot say how long the repair might take!'

During my watch the following night we came across another convoy near the Arabian coast. Visibility was favourable, prompting Lüdden to consider a surface approach. Then he had to order us down to periscope depth. We all recognised the screw noises of a destroyer making directly for us extremely fast. 'Rudder hard to port. Go to 100 metres!' Rötters and I obeyed the order with fast movements of our hydroplane handwheels and heard the destroyer pass by us directly astern. There were no depth charges. We were all more than happy about this but it puzzled us for some time why we had got away with it so lightly.

Meanwhile the convoy went on its way, Lüdden watched it through the periscope and announced: 'Duty aircraft towards the convoy. Apparently keeping course with it. We shall attempt to put space between ourselves and the convoy and be ahead of it at sunrise.'

Later the fever of the hunt on board left me restless on my bunk, wet with sweat. At twelve midnight on the dot I was back on the bridge and heard the LI inform Lüdden that two exhaust valves on the starboard diesel were broken. I was unable to follow the discussion but we all heard the outcome of it: 'We shall therefore wait to see what happens and keep going for the convoy!' The rhythm of the motors implanted itself in me. The exhaust gases were forced out sometimes muffled, then rumbling loud again.

Towards the end of our watch the sea was like a mirror but dense mist over the water made the horizon so milky and turbid that it was hard to distinguish sea from sky. Back down in the boat I was messboy again. Before approaching the narrow table at which the NCOs were seated I had to dry my forehead and sweaty upper body with a towel. In the damp heat there was great tension which everybody did his best to hide. In order to concentrate my mind elsewhere I checked over the small arms in the magazine below the control room. Here it was two or three degrees Celsius cooler. Scarcely had I stretched out on my bunk than the expected jolt went through the boat. Three more followed at short intervals.

On the other side of the corridor Rötters turned on his bed to face me: 'Finally, Toni, we have got rid of our four bow torpedoes!'

'Well that's something new.'

We laughed and now we could imagine what was happening above. We felt *U-188* turning, then came two jolts at the rear as the two rear torpedoes left their tubes. We counted off the seconds to the explosions. After about two minutes we exchanged questioning looks. 'That can't be!' Somebody in the forward torpedo room swore. 'What's wrong with our torpedoes?'

'Silence in the boat!'

After nine or ten minutes we heard explosions in the far distance as each torpedo destroyed itself at the end of its run. We did not dare express what each of us was thinking: 'Had our torpedoes been tampered with at Lorient? Were they set to run wild?' This idea was unimaginable for us. When during two surface attacks on tankers over the next few nights the torpedoes ran astray and brought down upon us dangerous defensive fire, our suspicions seemed to be confirmed. Uncertainty now began to make itself noticeable aboard in addition to the already present tension and the carefully suppressed excitement.[2]

Kaleu Lüdden ordered all torpedoes to be checked over, but none was found to be defective. BdU sent a signal that when firing the remaining torpedoes in the Gulf of Oman and on the route to Penang, *U-188* should keep as closely as possible to the zones indicated for attack. This was only possible submerged by day and at night we would expose ourselves to enemy gunnery. If we were forced to submerge, the war material afloat for the enemy would get through.

Two days later we were on the trail of a weakly-defended convoy. Now our overstretched diesels went on strike and we had to dive. The chief engineer and the diesel hands worked without pause to repair the damage. After more than three months unbroken stay in average temperatures of 45°C and 95 per cent air humidity in a stifling tube not only I had to force myself to keep quiet.

Once the diesels were operational again, Lüdden wanted to make up for lost time and now despite the onerous presence of enemy aircraft in the Gulf of Oman he decided to remain on the surface even by day. Although this made great demands on our nerves and taxed our concentration, we did at least find the cooling wind of passage on the bridge more pleasant than the sultry and oppressive atmosphere in the pressure hull.

---

2. See map 'The Cruise of *U-188*' at Inset 1 for these attacks along the coast of Muscat. On 5 October 1943 at item 6 'attacked Britannia', the 9,977-GRT Norwegian-flagged steamer *Britannia* was torpedoed and damaged by *U-188*.

The heat in the diesel room was a continual 50°C and could even reach 72°C. This sucked the last reserves of energy from our bodies. Drinking water had to be rationed, distilled water being needed for the batteries. None of us could drink as much as he needed, and although we all wore only swimming trunks, our bodies glistened with sweat.

Meenen and Benetschik described albatrosses to me. Until then I had never seen one of these fabled seabirds with a wingspan exceeding three metres. One night on watch quite unexpectedly and at close range I saw one of these birds gliding just above the surface of the sea. After recovering from a moment's shock I reported quietly to III WO Korn: 'Albatross astern to starboard.'

'Thank you, Staller. Ever seen one before?'

'Know them only from descriptions, Coxswain.'

Korn turned round briefly, looked at the white bird circling the boat in the moonlight and remarked: 'Well recognised, Staller! Possibly this bird will follow us for some time waiting for kitchen waste to be thrown overboard. Sometimes albatrosses set down on the water waiting to spot fish. Don't let yourself be distracted.' During my next watch at noon the albatross was still there.

'Alarm!' Presumably the five attacking aircraft were flown off a British aircraft carrier. We had to dive very quickly, heard their bombs explode awfully near the stern and now we found submerged travel quite pleasant because the steel pressure hull was cooled by the colder water.

The Tommies in their aircraft were stubborn and seemed to be sticking to us. Their crews knew the speed of a German U-boat under water and could calculate when at the latest it had to surface. Before retiring they would probably summon reinforcements to take over.

'Screw noises from north-north-west. Coming directly for us!' said Schulz' voice through the shipboard loudspeaker system. Then everybody could hear the gurgling thrashing noises of the destroyer's propellers. We spent the next twenty-six nerve-racking hours at mostly 80 metres depth at minimum revolutions ahead, the longest period we had ever spent below. When Rötters and I were ordered to relieve at the hydroplanes, one could hardly have described the air as such. It was still oppressively warm in our steel tube. We had used up our reserves of oxygen and the increasing levels of carbon dioxide sapped our will to survive. Rötters and I dragged ourselves to our places in the control room. On the way we saw some of the men dozing half unconscious. Although all had their mouths wide open, they were trying to take the shallowest breaths possible. Without exception the eyes of all were red-rimmed, and probably nobody had a thought other than: Fresh air! But above us death lurked in the shape of depth charges and shells; we all knew that to surface meant death.

I had hardly taken my place on the tiny seat alongside Rötters than there came a ray of hope. The screw noises above seemed to diminish, even though the last depth-charge pattern had been very close. For whatever reason, did the people above us think we had been destroyed? We were not doing so well, but at least we were still alive. *Kaleu* Lüdden was tottering into the control room. The chief engineer watched him through deeply sunken eyes. The control room petty officer and the coxswain were staring at him, and another dozen pairs of eyes followed every drag of his feet. 'Whenever will he finally give the order?' I asked myself. The soft hum of the electric motors droned in my ears, beyond that there was no noise. The commander stood for long seconds in reflection at the chart table before he said at last: 'Prepare to rise.'

'Boat prepared to rise.'

'Rise,' Lüdden ordered wearily.

'Blow tanks!' Kiessling's voice was loud. Compressed air roared into the dive tanks, and its repulsive whistling sound was today like sweet music to my ears.

'Go to periscope depth!' *Kaleu* Lüdden sat at the seat before the periscope and leant on the extended handholds.

'Boat at periscope depth.'

'Up periscope!' After anxious and endlessly long minutes came the final decision. 'Surface!'

With a shock I was awoken to a new vitality as I climbed the ladder to the bridge with the other three men of the watch. Greedily breathing in the cooler night air, the longed-for excess of oxygen made me feel dizzy at first. I had to hold on to the bridge coaming for a few seconds until my head stopped swimming. Then I expanded my chest, another nightmare over! I don't think I ever saw such a starry sky before in my life. No aircraft was in sight so far as the eye could see: the ocean was peaceful, as if it could never be anything else. Quickly I regained my normal composure, swept away the memory of the fearful hours we had just gone through and heard Rötter's angry remark: 'The air here has got as unhealthy meanwhile as the North Atlantic or Biscay. It's going to take some getting used to.'

Quieter days followed. The Tommies' depth charges had left us with only one gramophone record, and sometimes telegraphists would let it play over and over. Imagine 'Lilly Marlene' endlessly through the shipboard loudspeakers. The telegraphists told us that the song had been translated into English and French and could be heard on many radio stations. It seemed to be internationally loved. Soon there was hardly a man aboard who could stand the dark contralto tones of Lale Anderson any longer.

We sailed along the west coast of India. By night we saw lighthouses lit up as in peacetime. It seemed to us like an exercise when in beaming sunshine on 15 October Lüdden approached the harbour entrance at Bombay submerged and set *U-188* on the ground at periscope depth. Almost every man took a short look at the city and the pulsing life of the harbour. The periscope was so sharply focussed that I felt I was actually there ashore.

On 29 October 1943 towards one o'clock in the morning I was on the conning tower when we reached the ordered chart grid square off Malaysia in which we were to meet up with three other boats of the 'Monsoon Fleet' and be led by the Japanese into Penang harbour. Our diesels were barely audible and we rolled lightly in the swell. The sea glittered in the bright moonlight. *Kaleu* Lüdden was with us. 'We are probably the first here,' he opined softly.

'So it seems, Herr *Kaleu*,' the coxswain replied.

For an hour we turned a slow waiting circle at the rendezvous. Lüdden said, 'We ought to be seeing soon what our Japanese allies will send out to us in the way of escorts and pilotage. As you know, three weeks ago Henning's boat was lost with all aboard. Junker and Schäfer should have been here long since.'

Suddenly Korn shouted: 'Aircraft ahead to starboard!' Before Lüdden had got the machine in his binoculars, Korn added: 'Aircraft turning away. Japanese national markings recognised.' Almost simultaneously within ten minutes a Japanese torpedo boat appeared accompanied by two German U-boats, and I thought I detected relief in Lüdden's voice when he said, 'Things are going like clockwork today. Those two have also made it.'

While still watching sea and sky, I felt an almost uncontrollable joyful expectation of what lay ahead. 'We've done it! We are almost there! We can finally go ashore!' Meanwhile the three U-boats lay within hailing distance of each other. I turned briefly and saw the Japanese warship heading for our rendezvous with foaming bow wave. Despite the bright moonlight I could hardly make out his international flag signal, but finally read it with difficulty: 'Escort you to Penang'. Then the torpedo boat turned away and we followed in his wake. The boat to our stern had to be Junker. With the unaccustomed luxury of an escort I felt safer than I had for many months, but soon I discovered that the appearance was deceptive, for the coastal waters of Malaysia and Java were, as they say, infested with enemy submarines. I allowed myself some moments to subject the men on the conning tower of the boat astern to a thorough inspection through my binoculars. I identified a young lieutenant from Landshut travelling as a war correspondent. I had spoken with him briefly at Lorient. When the bridge watch was relieved, I clattered down into the boat very reluctantly.

Towards evening came the order to dress up. I found the sight of my shipmates in their khaki shorts and short-sleeved shirts amusing. I was just in the act of buttoning up my shirt when Petty Officer Heigl put his head through the engine room hatch and laughed: 'You look like a freshly dressed scarecrow on one of our cherry trees at home!'

All around one saw laughing eyes in bearded faces. Heigl came to stand at my side and looked along the passageway. Everything that lay behind us in time was forgotten. We had been more than four months on board, *U-188* had covered 19,331 sea miles. Finally, towards six o'clock on 30 October 1943, Lüdden announced through the boat's loudspeaker system, 'Apart from indispensable personnel inside the boat, everybody parade on the foredeck. We will very shortly arrive in Penang!'

In happy expectation, and in strict order of rank of course, we climbed one after another up to the tower, down the side-coaming to the deck and formed initially three ranks in loose order before straightening up military fashion. None of the officers attempted to quieten down our conversation. The thickly wooded slopes of the mountainous island formed the backdrop to the mole behind which lay the bright houses of Penang town.

Some of the hands prepared to throw mooring lines. The boat edged in at half ahead. We were the second U-boat to tie up at the Swettenham pier. How we had longed for this moment for months. The Japanese naval band in white ducks drew my attention. I saw the slim, small and graceful conductor raise his baton precisely as Lüdden ordered us to attention: *'Stillgestanden!'* A mental jolt ran through our ranks, for unexpectedly loud, full-heartedly and without error the band struck up the Badenweiler Marsch. Karl Bauer at my right said, 'They probably know that this is the Führer's favourite.' No sooner had it been completed than the conductor raised his baton once more and without a break a fresh melody resounded from the walls of the halls and warehouses. 'That's Beethoven's *Eroica!*' Deeply moved I recognised it and had to fight back my tears. Japanese and German naval officers in their white tropical uniforms ashore saluted, hand to peak of cap. Lüdden called out an order and now we all saluted.

To my left I heard Rötter's joyful voice: 'Toni, it's just like your birthday. Look, a present for each one of us! Finally land and additionally this gorgeous reception. Even the host of sweetie-pies on the quay over there seem to be happy. And afterwards we can drink all we like.'

'Yoohoo!' Karl Bauer sounded happier than ever. 'Aren't you thinking of brown-skinned girls and the tropical paradise of this so peaceful and undisturbed island?'

Our shipmate Friedrich Beck from Hamburg had lost his family in a bombing raid on the city. He seemed slightly depressed when he said to us, 'Naturally you're right. It really is a paradise that's waiting for us over there. But home is where the heart is.' Finally the long awaited order came, and we were allowed ashore.

Chapter Seven

Ashore in a Tropical Paradise

It was an unbelievably blissful feeling to have firm ground under one's feet again. After being welcomed officially by the German and Japanese base commanders we marched to our quarters not far from the harbour. We other ranks were put up in the gymnasium of a former English school. Although we had to sleep in tiered bunks we felt like kings, monopolised the showers for two hours, shaved and were about to set to work removing our flowing locks when Karl Bauer appeared and stopped us. We looked with astonishment at how well groomed he looked: white knee-length shorts, white shirt, bright grey canvas low shoes and fresh socks, holding a white tropical pith helmet to his chest and bowing repeatedly in the manner of the Japanese naval officers we had seen at the harbour.

'No, children! Don't waste your chance! Regard me!' Bauer did a twirl, making sure we all noticed his immaculate haircut and smoothly shaved cheeks. 'You boring types have naturally nothing to do but waste your time washing your chops. Meanwhile I have got to know a very helpful Staff AB Seaman stationed here who took me to a fragrant hairdressing salon just around the corner. He even paid for me! With Japanese occupation money, with China dollars!'

He brushed aside our questions with a laugh: 'Just remain calm, comrades. This garden gnome' – he grinned conspiratorially – 'the Herr Staff AB Seaman is not exactly of Herculean build, also told me that our paymaster is on his way to us. As soon as you have your money I shall take you to the hairdressers! I guarantee that these pretty pussy cats will gave you first-class treatment. They lay you out on an upholstered hairdresser's chair. And all for pocket money! Now dress up in your tropical civvies.' The Japanese recognised

German other ranks by a black swastika badge on the chest, NCOs wore the insignia in silver.

Bauer made sure we put on the tropical attire, but it was not quickly enough for him: 'Come on, get on with it! NCOs and sergeants live in a hotel. We are all going to eat at the Élysée Palace. Sounds a real posh place. There we will be waited on! The officers have a villa requisitioned from the British. I know all this from my new friend, who works in the base commander's office. Oh yes; please do not say anything about our canoe to the hairdressing pussies or Tommy will know by the evening that we have moved in here. My new friend warns us emphatically: You must not confide in anyone here.'

On the short walk to the hairdressing salon I noticed a couple of old men with red lips chewing betel nut and heard the shouts of the vendors. Apparently the businesses were owned mainly by the Chinese and they sold wares of all kinds. Once a stream of red betel juice which a Malay shoeshine boy spewed out on the footpath landed just ahead of my feet. 'Did he do that intentionally?' I asked Karl Bauer.

'I used to think so at first,' he replied, 'but Horst told me that the betel chewers would never hit a passer-by. If they did so they would beg pardon a thousand times over and be overcome with guilt.' Then we entered the hairdressing establishment and I have to say that Karl had not exaggerated. Eight extremely pretty Malay girls attended to us brightly and skilfully, maintaining an almost unbroken soft chatter amongst themselves. When a delicate and very beautiful young woman finished giving me my haircut and then massaged my head with a perfumed lotion using tender circular movements of her fingers, she smiled at me with dark almond eyes, natural and free. She had the effect on me of an angelic being from another star. Probably I must have stared at her open-mouthed for suddenly she clapped her hands with a loud laugh and said something to her colleagues. At that they all burst into joyful female laughter which lasted for some minutes, pure joy of living which we had not known for so long.

After me Able Seaman Schwarzer stretched himself out on the long chair with a groan of relief while I sat at one of the small salon tables to enjoy a cup of green tea. I watched the nimble fingers of the young woman changing Schwarzer's appearance for the better minute by minute. Almost reluctantly Schwarzer rose after his grooming, stroked his head and the hair at the back of his neck and said, 'Toni! I should like to spend more time in such a pleasant establishment. I shall let them shave me here every day of our stay. I no longer think it is such a bad thing that the Japs have too few ships to keep the Allies far enough away from these happy shores!'

Petty Officer August Bischoff had joined our small group and now came up behind Schwarzer, laid a hand on his shoulder and said: 'Man alive! You old gossip! You never know if they can understand you. Naturally the Tommies have known for ages that we call in here to polish up our boats. But you don't need to broadcast our presence so loudly. Kindly keep your trap shut!'

It was already nearly 1400 hrs. We were served like princes seated at tables with white tablecloth in a pleasantly air-conditioned dining room. It was wonderful. I had eaten bananas and oranges before, of course, but papaya, fresh pineapple, kiwi fruit and the like were unknown to me. Fresh vegetables, wonderfully prepared rice, chicken pullet and best of all a very cold beer were just making me feel sleepy when *Kaleu* Lüdden, Kiessling our chief engineer, the watchkeeping officers and the medical officer Esau came in, gold insignia glittering on their snow-white shirts. We all sprang up from our chairs to stand at attention in salute, and they sat at a table reserved for themselves in the other half of the dining room. Rötters murmured: 'Well then, over there the inseparables are complete again.'

'At ease!' Lüdden ordered loudly, and then said at once: 'Now everybody listen up! Because every commanding officer is responsible for his crew even here, I am going to give you the rules of conduct which we have to keep to as guests of the Japanese in Penang.' Lüdden sat at his table, freshly shaved and with short haircut, smiling as he surveyed us all. 'I see that you have all just been well fed and outstandingly groomed. To the point: here on Penang off Malaysia and also in Singapore and the other two bases which the Japanese have placed at our disposal, namely Batavia and Surabaya on Java, espionage is as much a big thing as anything else in the tropics.' Lüdden looked from one to another of us. 'Therefore, no careless talk about ourselves, *U-188* or any of the other boats! Chinese business people, young men smooth as an eel, delicate geishas or pretty young girls all hawk this dubious espionage business for the British or Americans. Many of them also work for the Kempetai, the Japanese military police, which also has a secret service function. The Japanese are very courteous, but also very distrustful allies. At this point I would mention to you that the Japanese take offence if you decline a spoken invitation from them. Conduct yourselves accordingly. Now about espionage again: here many smiling faces work for money, others for sex and many others for both. For this reason everybody is strictly forbidden to dance in the Sakura park. You can have a look round this permanent funfair, but nothing else, for behind every smile is a trap. Ultimately we all want to get home. In ten minutes a photographer from one of the bases will arrive to take a picture of each one of us for our Japanese identity cards. You must always carry this ID with you without exception.'

Lüdden glanced at Kiessling before quickly adding: 'Oh yes, there is another thing. Something pleasant, before Herr Kiessling explains to you the nature of our stay. Naturally your entertainment is being provided for. The Shanghai Hotel has been hired out for all Germans. The employees of that sailors' home are kept under constant supervision. We do not attract so much attention there as we do in the town. I have been assured that everything is on offer to you during your free time.' Lüdden paused briefly and then nodded to our LI: 'Please, Herr Kiesling.'

Our chief engineer came from a small town in the northern Rhein-Pfalz, not far from Oberfranken. In his direct way he began at once: 'Men, despite it being so nice here, each of you will receive only ten days leave on Penang Hill. If you do not know where that is, you can soon find out.' He gave a smirk and then looked serious again: 'The German base commander has informed me that we have to repair all damage to our boat ourselves. The Japanese are already overloaded with repairs and maintenance work to their own boats. They are already short of yard workers and specialists, and the few they do have here are required by the Japanese Navy. The Japanese had assured us however that on request they will make available to us their repair halls, machinery, necessary materials and workers selected locally and vetted by the Kempetai. Our friends are also being put under increasingly heavy pressure by the Allies and have sustained serious losses. It will obviously not be easy for us but we have to sail back to Europe as soon as possible in a fully-repaired boat carrying raw materials which have become very scarce at home. Every effort will be required from every man for the repair work. Over the next few days each crew member will be assigned his job. We shall work every day but Sunday from 0730 hrs until the midday heat forces us to vacate the boat, therefore without a break until about 1300 hrs. The boat is to be guarded at all times. Each of you therefore will have to stand sentry duty at some time or another. We need to be absolutely certain that no unauthorised persons come aboard. I don't need to explain why. That's all for today.'

'Thank you, Herr Kiessling,' Lüdden said curtly and next turned to *Stabsarzt* Esau: 'Doctor, your turn please.' A scarcely-perceptible murmur preceded our physician's remarks. 'Naturally I am aware that you are all healthy. That is right and must remain so. Therefore I have been given the job to warn you against certain local dangers. Not only espionage but intentional infection lurks here for every man who dedicates himself to bodily love. Accordingly, hands off the elegant dolls in the street or in the so-called "Houses of a Thousand Pleasures" not controlled by us. The whole business is only allowed in the Shanghai Hotel where prescribed hygiene regulations are enforced! Everybody knows that venereal diseases inevitably result in the undermining of military ability and incur heavy punishment. Should one of you suspect that something is not quite right with himself then I ask that person to come to see me immediately. I can help you in the early stages. You may think that you won't catch anything. If you do, however, then please let's have no false shame about it. After our photo session everybody will be inoculated against malaria and other tropical diseases!' Esau glanced at Lüdden and finished off by saying, 'That was everything, Herr *Kaleu*'.

The tropical climate ashore was much pleasanter than the heat of our steel tube. That first evening ashore was spent by all of us stretched out on our beds even before curfew. That afternoon I wandered through Sakura Park with Karl Bauer, Rötters and AB Telegraphist Stahlberg. We watched the dancing pairs in admiration and resisted politely the beckoning hands and other unmistakable gestures of the predominantly dark-skinned beauties keen for us to do it with them. Watching the very limber and athletic dancing couples, however, it was not too difficult to decline. Although none of them said so, I suspected that dancing was not something they were good at. 'The Kriegsmarine taught us everything they could think of, but dancing was unimportant.'

Next day the officers did not release us until the heat in our steel tube was so great that you nearly burnt your fingers touching the bridge coaming. We worked hard right through the morning and after a refreshing shower took a siesta. Towards evening I went for the first time in company of shipmates to the Shanghai Hotel. 'Let us enter this House of a Thousand Pleasures' Karl Bauer said encouragingly and added in an undertone: 'According to my friend at the base, this enviable duty NCO in civilian clothes at the entrance is a salesperson for a ladies' fashion business in Frankfurt am Main.' As soon as we arrived at his desk he greeted us with: 'What will it be, gentlemen? In the rooms avoid paying for anything by buying vouchers of all kinds from me.'

'Are we the first?' Stahlberg asked.

'Exactly so, gentlemen. And now please choose: green tickets, one dance, twenty cents; cold beer, yellow, eighty cents; schnapps, blue, eighty cents. And to crown the evening: these soft pink tickets for Eva in Paradise. They cost only eighty paltry occupation dollars each. Dive in, gentlemen!'

Karl Bauer gave a hearty laugh. 'I have the gift of the gab myself,' he said, 'but I'd love to have your patter.'

'I am honoured by your praise, sir. And now according to regulations I have to make you aware of the house rules.' The duty NCO pointed to a list near the door. 'I do not like to receive complaints afterwards.'

None of us bothered with the rules, for Stahlberg insisted, 'Let's get on with it, boys. I have a tremendous thirst. Tonight I have two hours' dogwatch on the canoe. Beforehand I need to reinforce myself.'

Colourful Chinese lanterns spread a subdued light across the dance hall and in the small foyer on the first floor. Palms, almost dried up, supported to the height of the ceiling, stood between the tables grouped along three walls around the dance floor. At the bar and some of the tables forward were small groups of waiting girls. Delicate Chinese girls, brown-skinned Malays, dark girls originating from the Indian sub-continent and so-called 'cocktails', girls of mixed race, who looked at us with smiles. On a podium near the bar some musicians lounged in front of their gleaming instruments. A colourful plaque on the wall announced that these were 'The Hawaii Boys'.

Stahlberg led the way noisily to a table near the dance floor and at once the startled band grabbed their instruments. Seconds later we were dumbstruck and stood listening in shock as a melody well-known to us all drifted sweetly across the room in greeting:

'*Heimat, deine Sterne,*
die strahlen mir dort am fernen Ort.
Was sie sagen, deute ich ja so gerne,
als der Liebsten zärtliches Losungswort.
Schöne Abendstunde,
der Himmel glänzt wie ein Diamant.
Tausend Sterne stehen in weiter Runde,
von der Liebsten zärtlich mir zugesandt;
in der Ferne träum ich vom Heimatland.'
('Homeland, your stars,
sparkling to me here at this distant place:
What they are saying,
I interpret as the tenderest parting blessing from my beloved.
Glorious evening hour,
The heavens glittering like a diamond.
A thousand stars around the sky
sent to me by my beloved.
Here so far away I dream of the Homeland.')

Deeply moved, I looked into the faces of the others and fought back tears. No doubt each of us was thinking at that moment of those we loved back home. And for a couple of seconds I saw the face of Gisela and her blonde tresses from that day on the Baltic beach at Stettin. The melody brought back to me her parting words: '. . . when you come back, Toni.'

The eyes of my colleagues glistened. Rötters ran a hand over his forehead in embarrassment. Then he laughed at himself: 'Why all the sad looks, boys? The commander will get us back home as safely as he got us here. He knows the Tommies' tricks better than they do themselves. As soon he takes our boat out, Lüdden will run his little zig-zags and waste their depth-charges as before. Why would they get us? Heads up, men!'

Some of them seemed none too convinced. Probably for that reason Rötters made a certain gesture which made us all laugh. Now he seemed calmer. 'Behind us are the dolls for dancing with, all medically approved!' Shortly afterwards, Stahlberg went off for half an hour with one of the slender Indian girls. The dance hall filled slowly with the men from supply ships and other U-boats. Even Bauer's new friend and others from the base offices arrived.

A petty officer and two men from Junker's boat joined us at our table. One said, 'We had two of the new acoustic torpedoes on board which home in on screw noises. When a freighter crossed our snout, our Old Man tried an attack submerged.'

'Those things are called Zaunkönig,' the petty officer interjected.

'Yes. And everyone knows that. The Old Man sat at the periscope, the hydrophones operator called out: "Torpedo running . . . leaving fast . . . still going . . . noise wandering . . . noise holding still . . . noise holding still." Yes, and then all of us began to get jittery when we heard the trembling voice of the hydrophones man through the loudspeakers: "Noise getting louder . . . noise on course for the boat . . . noise increasing!" Because our E-motors were at half ahead we were able to control the boat. The fast dive was successful and the damned Zaunkönig swished by above us. We were all pretty cheesy, I can tell you.'

I had become bolder after two whiskys, so rose and went with an unbelievably gorgeous 'cocktail girl' with whom I had had a dance earlier. I showed her my pink ticket and felt myself blushing. She just laughed, took my ticket, popped it into her small handbag, grabbed my hand and pushed her forearm so firmly through mine that one would have thought we had been going out together for years. As I was going upstairs with her on the pile carpet, I glanced round rather uncertainly. Stahlberg gave me a satisfied wave.

Not only the clean and almost splendidly furnished room with the silent fan on the ceiling impressed me. Later, when the pretty girl breathed a kiss on my cheek in that first floor room of the Shanghai Hotel I asked myself who had owned the house before the Japanese requisitioned it. In order to obtain the regulation certificate of disinfection signed by a sick berth attendant I had to submit to a treatment which involved some discomfort and was so humiliating that during the procedure I swore never to go there again.

Shortly before 2200 hrs Heigl, Stahlberg, Karl Bauer, his new friend Horst and I went down the broad steps in front of the house to the waiting rickshaws. I stood still and looked out over the sea at lights on the horizon. Horst noticed and told me at once: 'Toni, those are not stars but the lights of the mainland. If you turn around you will see the lamps of Penang Hill. It is so beautiful up there it will make you feel as though you are in Paradise. Apparently each one of your crew can go up there for several days!'

Not until twenty days later, after back-breaking grind on our boat, did I go with Heigl, Bauer, Stahlberg and seven others on the mountain cable car to Penang Hill as the third group. Boatswain Jupp Steimer had spent ten days up there with the first group and returned with a small monkey which he had bought from some of the local boys. The monkey became the darling of the crew. He slept with Jupp in his bed, held on to one of his legs as we marched to work and swung around the boat skilfully, fast and light as a feather from lever to piping without disturbing anybody. The little monkey had instinctively found the bunk which his master shared with another petty officer during the incoming voyage. As soon as the little goblin got tired he would curl up like a cat at the foot of the cot and nobody could wake him until he was ready. *U-188* had got herself a mascot.

On Penang Hill Franz Heigl and I rented a room in one of the white-painted bungalows. A few minutes later we were in swimming trunks and occupying deck chairs by the side of the pool. Our predecessors had by no means exaggerated. Very courteous natives provided us with all our hearts could desire and explained in a mixture of broken English, German and picturesque gestures that we should never leave anything of value lying about on account of the ever-present monkeys. These ever-curious and fearless inhabitants of the primeval forest performed their gymnastics with a loud clamour in the tops of the surrounding trees and got up to all kinds of tricks.

Towards evening a cooling wind set in. Our hunger was pleasantly appeased, we had had our fill of freshly-squeezed juices and had not rejected alcohol out of hand. Chattering happily we wended our way along narrow asphalt paths between the houses of the former British officers' convalescent home, then through the surrounding jungle. We were just looking at two colourful parrots in the maze of branches above our heads when Gerhard Rieger asked in his thick Saxon accent: 'Have you also noticed how this boy in front of the main house drops his head between his shoulders and protects the back of his neck with his hands? I was just slapping a mosquito. The British used to beat them?'

'Don't you know that yet?' Heigl asked, and Stahlberg called out: 'The Malay who served us supper this evening told me twice that "German misters are much better than English sirs". According to Jupp Steimer these Malays told him that the British would hand out beatings for the slightest insubordination. It may not be true of course, maybe they just want to curry favour with us.'

The days on Penang Hill passed as quickly as a delightful dream. Soon we were back at our daily toil aboard U-188. The boat had lain over a month at the quayside in Penang. The technical personnel sweated and slaved in glowing heat and my weapons had sparkled like new for so long that I was ordered to help out in the diesel room. The Japanese were always obliging, but had difficulties getting urgently-needed spare parts. Our technical wonderchild Heigl and other mechanics were allowed to use all the lathes and equipment in the Japanese repair hall as soon as the Japanese no longer needed them. Our motors were restored almost lovingly piece by piece and all the other repairs touched up. Our LI Kiessling was always on hand with advice and to help out. It was clear to everybody that our lives depended on having the propulsion systems and other equipment in the boat in perfect running order. Junker's boat had already sailed: we had given them letters for the field-post service at home. Soon U-188 would be ready to put to sea.

For several minutes on one of my dogwatches I watched one of the large monkeys prancing around on the ridge of the roof of the repair hall directly opposite. In the moonlight his outline was black against the backdrop of the jungle mountains, bathed in yellow light. I was wondering how he had got up there when I heard footsteps approaching. The monkey vanished. Seconds later my watch relief Stahlberg appeared around the corner of the hall. As I handed him the machine-pistol and was about to go he said, 'Man, what do you reckon to eating in the Blue Bird tomorrow instead of the usual boring lunch? You know the one I mean, the high class place the Japanese frequent. We've hardly any of our pay left. Are you up for it?'

'Just us two? None of the others are coming?'

Stahlberg gave me an eloquent smile. 'No. Some have better ideas, others are simply too lazy or don't want to miss their siesta. Another is even too miserly. So, it's agreed?'

'Good, I'll come. But now I have to get my head down for a couple of hours or tomorrow I'll be too lazy.'

It was around 1430 hrs that we took our places at a small window table on the first floor of the Blue Bird. Behind us two Japanese naval officers came up the narrow spiral staircase and one asked us in clumsy German-English with Japanese sing-song tones: '*Dürfen we uns sit down?*' The smaller man in white uniform gestured with one hand to his larger, slimmer companion and with the other hand to the two free places at our table. Stahlberg and I hastened to conceal our surprise and agreed.

Naturally the Japanese knew at a glance who we were. Scarcely were they seated than the larger man pointed to our insignia: 'Submarine?' We nodded. He took a silver-coloured fountain pen and a small notebook from a breast pocket, drew a ship and his friend asked, after looking at us both and then pointing to the sketch: 'Sunk?' accompanying this with a gentle movement of the hand which left no room for doubt that he meant a sinking ship. Of course we had sunk ships, we assured him, nodding eagerly at the same time and the two officers were now much more forthcoming and friendly. The sketch artist raised his thumb and then forefinger and began to count in Japanese. When I did the same, Stahlberg said loudly, 'Golf Oman!' and added quickly for my benefit, 'It's really all the same, Toni. They've known about us all along.'

A Malay boy came to the table, spoke to the officers in Japanese and then we had no need to order for ourselves. The Japanese told us that we were their guests, and we remembered the warning we had been given that it gave offence to decline. So began for us a very pleasant and enjoyable afternoon. What we ate tasted excellent, although we could not be sure what it was, and our efforts with chopsticks caused amusement. No stranger to strong drink, Stahlberg put away a large quantity of rice wine as though it were water. This won him the admiring gaze of our hosts. It seemed to me as though the two Japanese felt honour-bound to follow, and they probably drank much more than had been their intention. Early evening culminated in an offer by the continually bowing Japanese to visit a Japanese tea house with them. When they saw how I glanced doubtfully at Stahlberg, and he merely shrugged his shoulders, the faces of the Japanese officers hardened. We therefore agreed quickly if half-heartedly.

We took four rickshaws. I heard the Japanese officer in the leading vehicle urging his driver in harsh tones to make haste. As we drove through the quiet streets of a villa neighbourhood, I heard Stahlberg in the fourth rickshaw behind me growl: "Toni, this is fun! Perhaps our officers even live in this neighbourhood! I believe this is Penang-Georgetown!'

We drew up before an establishment which we both took for a tea house. The bigger of our hosts paid all four rickshaw drivers. The other made a bow and pointed to the entrance, in front of which a Japanese naval rating was seated at his ease in a wicker chair but rose quickly and delivered a smart naval salute to the two officers. When one purchased some tickets there was a certain suspicion in my mind, and when we entered the hall lit softly by lanterns I had no doubts: 'This can only be a Japanese House of a Thousand Pleasures.' When I enquired of our hosts in German-English rich with gestures if 'disinfection' were practised here, one of them slapped me on the shoulders giggling and shaking his head. In amusement he led me into a room where well cared-for girls, some very young-looking, were waiting on a red upholstered settee. With ever-deepening bows we expressed our thanks to our hosts.

By signal *U-188* was ordered to a larger shipyard at Singapore on the southern tip of Malaysia. We left Penang on the night of 12 December 1943 and headed through the Straits of Malacca alone. Although enemy submarines were reported in the area, the Japanese were unable to provide us with an escort. To be on the safe side, Lüdden ordered every man not essential below up on deck wearing a lifejacket. We watched the sea, looking for the bubble trail of enemy torpedoes which we might be able to avoid if we saw them soon enough. To be exposed to the events of the war in this manner and not, as we veterans were accustomed, being amongst the attackers, bore down hard on our spirits. To be degraded to the hunted gnawed into our morale. The fact that every crew man had been told to write a second letter home for the next U-boat sailing told us that the first letter would not be arriving. That also depressed us, but nobody dared express what he thought. Instead, everybody tried to gloss over this unusual and threatening situation with coarse humour. 'Nothing can happen to us!' was the tenor.

After my watch from midnight to 0400 hrs I joined Jupp Steimer at the side of the winter-garden. Our little mascot, now named Fifi, was never far away when his lord and master was close to me. Towards 0700 hrs the cook announced 'Breakfast, gentlemen!' Without ceasing to watch the sea I asked: 'Albert, what are you offering us today?'

'Excellent coffee, fresh bread and freshly laid eggs. But the people here shouldn't get too excited about it though.' Wilhelm Authenrieth, Jupp, a few others and I were still watching the mirror-smooth waters of the Straits of Malacca some time after the cook had gone below. When eventually we turned round what we saw made us all laugh. Our monkey was sitting on a broad board amongst the eggs and had smeared himself from head to toe with the yolks. His fur was almost hidden under the thick yellow mass. Jupp grabbed the animal by the scruff of the neck, held him at arm's length and carried him astern. There, crouching down holding the rail, he gave the monkey a ducking. The squeals of the little fellow were soon louder than our laughter, the rustling of the wake and the noise of the diesel exhaust. When Jupp put him back on deck, the dripping wet monkey gave his master a hurt look like a child and shook himself briefly. After that he bounded off nimbly and skilfully to the bows, carefully avoiding the breakfast board on the winter garden which he had devastated.

During the voyage to Singapore, Lüdden succeeded in avoiding two torpedoes heading for us on the starboard side. After that we headed out of the danger zone at full speed. Luck continued to ride with us and on 14 December shortly after 0400 hrs we made fast at our destination.

The Japanese provided us with quarters on the outskirts of Singapore city, in villas almost on the beach, from where they drove us daily to work at the shipyard. *U-188* was drawn up out of the water at shed 52. The tiring grind was carried out in constant tropical heat. We cleansed the boat's hull of barnacles and other accretions, gave it a coat of quick-drying anti-rust paint and then fresh camouflage. Piece by piece we removed the heavy iron weights from the ballast keel. These weights were replaced by 310 tonnes of tin, 14.4 tonnes of tungsten and 1.5 tonnes of rubber, and 500 kilos of quinine and 200 kilos of opium were stowed securely. The Japanese were parting with some of the treasure of Malaysia, expecting in return that on our impending voyage to Europe we would reduce the number of our common enemy's ships.

U-188 had thus been converted into a kind of cargo ship. We were twelve tonnes overweight but would soon lose this through fuel consumption. To help reduce the excess I was given three Malay assistants and told to dismantle our deck gun, reassemble it in a warehouse for the Japanese and also bring the ammunition for it ashore. I had to work in the space created in the magazine by myself since there was only room for one person below, and very little of that. The heavy sacks were handed down to me to stack. I dripped with sweat. Everywhere one heard the sound of welding, hammering and riveting. The war cost all the nations involved fantastic expenditure. Repeatedly I asked myself what good things we could do with all the outlay in labour and first-class material instead of fighting each other with it.

We were all fed up to the back teeth with the work ashore. On the evening of 24 December 1943 we celebrated Christmas in tropical temperatures in the garden of one of the villas. We did not know exactly when, but we all felt that our stay in Malaysia would soon end. That evening, however, we simply wanted to enjoy hours under the starry sky, celebrating in happy and relaxed mood as if the impending voyage home was going to be no more dangerous than summer canoeing on some lake in distant Germany.

It was not only I who had anxieties. Others admitted later that they had asked themselves on that tropical night if it were actually possible to make the dangerous 19,000-nautical mile voyage and arrive home unscathed again. Now we all remembered our loved ones back home: 'Right now Mother and my sisters will probably be walking across the snowed-over market place at Grafing on their way to Christmas Mass. Will I ever have the chance to do that again?'

At 0700 hrs on 30 December we sailed for Penang. Because two enemy submarines had been reported in the Straits of Malacca we ran at maximum speed from One Fathom Bank and made fast in Penang the next day. In the evening Karl Bauer, Stahlberg and I took rickshaws to the Japanese tea house at Penang-Georgetown of such recent pleasant memory. As I feared, the naval rating at the door told us to clear off. So there was nothing for it but the Shanghai Hotel, our sailors' home, crammed full as one might expect on New Year's Eve. We were free until reveille, but knew that nobody would awaken us in the morning and so celebrated without heed as though this were the tropical night which heralded better times.

The customary final touches to fitting out for departure were applied on 2 January 1944. On the morning of the third day suddenly our mascot was missing. 'Jupp! Where is our little monkey?' Everybody asked Steimer the same thing. He became ever more surly and depressed. 'They can find better uses for the space for Fifi's bananas. The Old Man has been informed. Probably one of the blackguards from the base kidnapped him last night.' Once I heard Jupp reply in indignation: "Of course I've looked for him everywhere, you thickhead! It's like looking for a needle in a haystack. One thing is certain; we're sailing without him.'

The exact hour when we would sail was kept from us for security reasons. Fifi's fate remained a mystery during our last days at Penang. Had Jupp been ordered to leave him ashore? Had he really been kidnapped? On the whole perhaps it was better for both the monkey and ourselves. Who knew if he would be able to survive the long journey or, what was more likely, would find the endless voyaging submerged at the slowest possible rate of knots a torture and die. Nor was it out of the question that his loud chatter would imperil the boat when total silence was necessary.

Chapter Eight

The Calamitous Struggle
Back to Europe

A t 0100 hrs on 9 January 1944 I was a lookout on the bridge as *U-188* slipped out of Penang. My second watch coincided with the arrival of a Japanese cruiser and destroyer coming up from the opposite direction. Upon seeing us they showed us their narrowest silhouettes, and unlike all other Japanese vessels reacted to our recognition signal by turning away and leaving us.

We remained alone for days, always accompanied by dolphins. They seemed to enjoy sporting alongside us, showed no shyness and obviously considered *U-188* to be a playmate. Our watchkeeping officer had to remind us sharply on a number of occasions to remain alert.

For the first few days out our rations were enriched with fresh bread and vegetables, eggs and fruit but these soon gave way to tinned food. I hoped, while on the way to our operational area in the Gulf of Oman, that our voyage would continue as peacefully as it had begun.

On 17 January we were east of the Maldives. From now on we headed northwards. *Kaleu* Lüdden informed the crew through the loudspeaker system that since leaving Lorient at the outset of the round voyage we had covered 21,598 nautical miles, equivalent to a circumnavigation of the globe. The boat followed the western coast of India until on 20 January we came to the Arabian Sea. Here I experienced from the bridge the nerve-racking chase after a large and well-armed merchant ship sailing independently. The operation lasted 17 hours and brought us 170 sea miles to the south causing one of our diesels to overheat and not until 2200 hrs did we finish her off. This had been the UK registered 7122-grt *Fort Buckingham*, Bombay to Buenos Aires in ballast, eighty-nine crew, fifty-one survivors, sunk at 8°19′N 66°40′E. We sighted four lifeboats and a jollyboat with sails which gave me some feeling of comfort. From now on we had to expect to be hunted.

Enemy aircraft detected us in the northern part of the Indian Ocean and we suffered several attacks by British destroyers. Our monkey would never have survived the long periods of punishing strain and silence we all knew so well. The ghastly Asdic pings against the hull turned us into nervous wrecks. How Lüdden always managed to get us out of the danger area was a mystery. He seemed able to anticipate unerringly the worst designs of those of the surface above us and our faith in his ability grew hourly. When he asked a last effort of us, had us sit in darkness for hours to spare electrical current during enemy pursuits, made us breathe through potash cartridges to keep the levels of carbon dioxide down: we always knew that he made us do it because it was our only chance of surviving. The tension and anxieties of those days was written in our faces. Nevertheless, between 21 January and 10 February 1944, east of the Gulf of Aden, *U-188* succeeded in sinking the following merchant ships:

25 January; UK registered 7,130-grt *Fort La Maune*, Suez to Calcutta, general and military cargo, fifty-six crew all survived, sunk ENE Socotra Island.

26 January; 0225 hrs; UK registered 7,219-grt *Samouri*, Bombay to New York in ballast, forty-nine crew all survived, sunk ENE Socotra Island.

26 January; 1906 hrs; UK registered 5,427-grt *Surada*, Calcutta to Suez, general cargo, 103 crew all survived, sunk 40 miles ENE Socotra Island.

29 January; 4,677-grt Greek registered *Olga E Embiricos*, Durban to Eritrea with coal, crew forty-one, twenty-one survived, sunk 210 miles W Socotra Island.

3 February; 7,176-grt Chinese registered *Chung Cheng*, Calcutta to USA, 8350 tons ilmenite ore, ship sank at 13°N 54°20′E before boats could be got away, crew seventy-one, fifty-one survivors.

9 February; 3,798-grt Norwegian registered *Viva*, Bombay to UK, general cargo and tea, crew thirty-seven all survived, sank at 12°30'N 57°50'E.

As can be seen from the plate showing a page of *U-188*'s War Diary, at 2143 hrs that night of 9 February a sailing vessel was pursued and sunk by ramming at 2307 hrs, 'size again about that of a medium Baltic schooner'. Seven of these sailing freighters not worth a torpedo and carrying materials for the enemy's war effort were sunk in this manner. The record indicates that it was Lüdden's custom to approach boats carrying the survivors to offer provisions and water.

The War Diary page illustrated shows that on 10 February 1944 Lüdden 'intended to stay on the steamer track to the east for one more day and then head south to refuel'. At 1600 hrs a tanker was sighted and pursued, and a moonlit attack made in good visibility at 2207 hrs. The last T 3 LUT torpedo loaded at Lorient was fired at the tanker and 'despite the most meticulous calculations and close range' nothing happened. 'Loud explosion after 17 minutes' which 'shook the boat violently', then after four lesser explosions it fell quiet, the tanker 'zigzagging wildly' and escaping. Lüdden concluded that the torpedo had 'exploded at the end of its run, as did all such Lorient Etos of the voyage. Since the tanker is continuing with the same revolutions as before and we have fired our last torpedo-surfaced: continuing our return.'

U-188 received orders by radio confirming we were to proceed homewards and *Kaleu* Lüdden was notified that he had been awarded the Knight's Cross. Every man received a half-bottle of beer to celebrate. Drinking water was very scarce, which was a major privation in the great heat. Our provisions were also close to being used up. The tins which had been stored behind the torpedoes had split or cracked in the high temperatures and humidity. We had not been able to extract the rotted matter until we got rid of the torpedoes. At the first opportunity we fed it to the fish with great regrets. Although we all scrubbed and scrubbed, the vile smell lasted for days in the boat.

On 6 March AB Telegraphist Stahlberg confided to me that we had been sent to scout near a chart quadrant well away from all shipping routes prior to being replenished from the *Brake* with other boats.

Under overcast skies on the late afternoon of 11 March, the hoses of our old acquaintance began to fill our almost empty fuel tanks. Once our own refuelling had been completed we stood by with our flak gun manned to protect the other boats. Towards dawn on 12 March I was below when the word was passed that *Brake* had abandoned refuelling the other boats on account of the rough seas: the oiler and our half-flotilla was now heading southwards.

I was standing noon lookout. We were not far astern of the oiler. The weather had improved, visibility was good but I had a bad feeling I could not explain. After about fifteen minutes Rötters reported two aircraft above a trace of smoke on the port quarter. The *Brake* was 500 metres ahead, we could not make out yet what kind of ship was astern. Soon we received shellfire, the high plumes of water and spray advancing ever nearer. Lüdden ordered an emergency dive. Over the period of the next hour in the control room we counted 148 rounds hitting the oiler and fourteen heavy explosions. Later some depth charges were dropped and to our dismay we heard the familiar creaks and groans of a sinking ship. Immediately we were forced deep. Shortly after sunset we ran back to the site of the sinking to search for survivors. Apart from patches of oil the sea was deserted. The telegraphists received two signals within a short time of each other. Pich reported picking up all the *Brake* survivors and that he was heading for Singapore. The second message was for us, ordering our return to Europe at the most economical rate of fuel consumption possible.

On 31 March off Cape Town we had been almost three months at sea. Once in the South Atlantic we encountered a hurricane with breakers of such force that parts of the deck planking were torn away. Days later when relieved from the bridge punctually at 1600 hrs I had headache from the effort of observing and remained in the control room for a short while to rub my eyes dry. While I was there I heard Chief Schulz inform the commander that the high tension part of the radio transmitter transformer was broken: 'Herr *Kaleu*, we are working to repair the damage as soon as possible!'

'Thank you Schulz. Please report as soon as we are able to transmit again.'

Schulz hurried back to the radio cabin. All attempts to effect the repairs over the next few days failed. We had been living on hard bread and dry potatoes for the last two weeks. More alarming was the fact that our lubricating oil for the temperatures in these southern latitudes was too thin and our supply ship *Charlotte Schliemann* was reported missing. Our stock of supplies was melting like snow in the sun. Not only the faces of the men in the diesel room had hardened to masks. *U-188* could receive radio signals but not transmit in order to make other boats aware of our desperate situation.

Stahlberg told me confidentially: 'Toni, we're almost beginning to panic in the radio room. I think that even Lüdden is slowly getting worried. We are receiving request after request to report our position. It's enough to make you sick. It looks like we've got enough lubricating oil to get us to the Canaries. I heard Lüdden and Kiessling discussing it. There's a favourable spot on the coast of the island of La Palma they've settled for. Then all we have to do is swim ashore. Lüdden thinks we will have to scuttle the boat. Toni, if we don't get close enough to another boat to use our emergency transmitter, then I see it getting slowly blacker for us.'

Wearing only swimming trunks I flopped out on my bunk. After drying off, now I was sweating with the excitement. I scarcely noticed Heigl coming through the hatch from the overheated diesel room. Slowly, as if drunk, he made his way uncertainly past me towards the control room. Karl Bauer below me called out to him in a croak but as uninhibitedly loud as always, 'What's happening with us now? I mean, without any lubricating oil?'

'We've all got to piss on the shafts, you idiot!'

'Such a waste, man. You should use rancid butter instead. Tastes really vile lately.'

This stopped Heigl in his tracks. 'What did you just say? Butter?'

Minutes later we heard that the cook had received the order to break out all supplies of fats. Kiessling and the engine room personnel wanted to use them in an attempt to thicken the lubricating oil.

'I should have kept my mouth shut,' I heard Bauer say to himself. Then he called up, 'Toni, if all goes well, adding our provisions to the lubricating oil as well, they might even manage to get us past the Canaries. That would be good! This lousy grub! I bet that from now on we're going to get less to drink because the batteries use so much water. I'm parched! And all we've got left to eat is more hard bread and tasteless dried potatoes in teeny-weeny portions. Until now I never knew on how little a person could survive!'

Passing through the control room into the tower for my watch, I saw Lüdden with Kiessling, Meenen or Benetschik doing endless calculations at the chart table. It was a mystery to me how they thought we would sail past the Canaries at a couple of knots. Sometimes we combined one diesel and one E-motor. It was economical but only gave us five or six knots on the surface. The other attempts to see how much fuel consumption could be cut down by having the engines and motors in this or that arrangement made us increasingly more nervous. It seemed that the voyage was never likely to end. On watch in almost calm seas what we missed more than anything was the rustle of the bow wave and the refreshing wind of passage. Once Rötters whispered to me, 'This is like milking a mouse. We're hardly making any progress at all. If we don't get out of this soon we shall all die of hunger and thirst for the Fatherland. An amusing hero's death, don't you think?'

Before I could reply, our WO admonished us: 'Quiet! Keep observing! Don't talk stupid crap.'

Undetected we moved through the Atlantic northwards along the African coast. Forced to maintain radio silence we no longer existed for the Tommies since they were unable to get a fix on our radio transmissions. No aircraft came looking for us. U-boat Command also seemed to have written us off, for they no longer asked for our position or sent us orders.

From the southern tip of Portugal we sailed only by night and spent the days near the coast grounded, often at a depth of 100 metres. We could hardly keep ourselves under control: we were sustained only our will to survive and the obedience drilled into us. Again and again one man encouraged another: 'We must and will do it!' Following the Biscay coasts of Spain and then France finally we reached the Gironde Estuary and the miracle happened: on 19 June 1944 just after midnight Lüdden used our emergency transmitter to request an escort into Bordeaux.

After more than five months in our steel tube, 163 days, in which we often thought that we would not survive, we stumbled ashore exhausted but overjoyed. A handful of men wearing blue uniforms or grey leathers turned out on the pier to welcome us. It was rare to see a U-boat return from a patrol. For months past they had continued to put to sea, but very few ever came back. We did not fit the heroic image which our propaganda noised abroad, for without exception we all had matted hair and beards, hollow cheeks and eyes like golf balls. We looked more like malnourished jungle fighters than heroes of the nation which had lauded obedience. Still at the quayside we learned from ordinary naval ratings that the Allies had landed in Normandy. This was not encouraging news, but it was more important to us at the time to finally have *terra firma* beneath our feet.

Next day the news spread quickly that we were only the second of forty-three Monsoon boats to have returned. In horror I asked myself where all the rest were. Were we to be the last to come back? No, some with some with the Japanese, but surely all the others couldn't have been sunk?

We were told something about German miracle weapons which would soon decide the war in favour of the Reich. Our enemies were so worried about them that they were sending countless aircraft to bombard German towns without a break. The factories producing these weapons had not been located so far. Our duty as soldiers, and especially as U-boat men, was to hold out unconditionally to the last drop of blood, for these new, still unknown weapons would save us at a stroke. What should I make of all this? I remembered the oath of loyalty I took and also 'Render unto Caesar that which is Caesar's, and unto God that which is God's'. That is what I had been brought up to believe.

Once again Karl Bauer was better informed than the rest of us. Grinning as usual, he came into our room and reported: 'My friend Heinz Krause is a Leading Seaman, survivor of a sunken boat. Because he is fluent in French he is working at the local command office. I found out from him that the valuable part of our cargo is to be unloaded immediately. It is not certain that it will get to Germany because the French Resistance loiters everywhere. Well, you already know what they are; partisans. The important thing is that we have all been resurrected! They thought we were dead, and long since informed our families that we were missing, believed dead. Early this morning they sent telegrams to our homes retracting the earlier advice. Boys! Because we have stayed so very much alive, as soon as we've had our home leave, we can carry on the fight until victory. What do you say to that?'

I made a sign of disinterest and remarked sarcastically, 'Just Heil, Sieg and good hunting!' I was astonished at my own words. I can no longer recall the more cutting replies of some of my comrades to Bauer's piece of information. It was a good thing that nobody could read my thoughts, for these wavered between hope and deepest depression: Resistance? Until now one had always felt safe in France. For us it was almost like a second home. And now this? It could only be the beginning of the end. Before there had been clear fronts. Here was friend, there foe. Now between the front were partisans. Also amongst my comrades doubts had crept in about the leadership. Previously our convictions had been uniform convictions, now suddenly there was an invisible front through our hearts. For fear of being denounced none of us cared to confide in another.

Now at least we had before us the joy of furlough. Yet my anticipation was overshadowed by doubts and unanswered questions: When would this miracle weapon be ready, exactly when? How many innocent lives would it wipe out? These were the thoughts which preoccupied me before sleep came on that second night ashore.

Chapter Nine

Ten Months without a Boat

N ext morning Lüdden summoned me to his small office inside the U-boat bunker. I stood before his desk and gave him the regulation salute, staring at the new Knight's Cross at his neck. He seemed to notice this and an almost imperceptible smile darted across his face before he waved a telegram at me. 'Staller, your honoured father has made an application. He has leave and is presently at your home. He probably knows that you will taking leave with the second group. I am very happy to make an exception in this case. How long is it since you last saw your father?'

'Since being conscripted in September 1941, Herr *Kaleu*.'

'Well, almost three years then. Good. So you can start packing your seabag.' He smiled almost sympathetically when he added: 'There is a new regulation in force that leave-takers must not take more baggage with them than they can physically carry themselves. For every crewman of my boat I have organised tins of meat, green coffee beans in sealed cans, spices from Singapore and of course cigarettes before you go. Pack as sparingly of space as possible and try your bag out for weight before you go. You are leaving this evening with our first group. Have a nice leave, Staller!'

I saluted again and did an about-turn, inwardly rejoicing: 'Father at home? I'm going home this evening? Toni, you've fallen on your feet again!' In high spirits I set about packing at once and took little notice of the good advice with which my colleagues showered me. Franz Heigl and Karl Bauer would also be going with me in the first group and visited me several times in my barrack room. My seabag was extraordinarily heavy and it was very difficult to get it on my back without help.

In the afternoon Heigl brought me two large, well-rounded linen bags: 'Toni! These things weigh almost nothing. Why shouldn't we use our hands if Lüdden organised more than sufficient cigarettes for his men?' With a laugh he threw two others on Karl Bauer's bed. 'Karl! Your much-praised old man will definitely think more highly of you when he sees these spices and officers' cigars you're bringing him.'

'Many thanks, Franz. I still have so much to learn from you. Those will certainly put Papa into a happier frame of mind.'

Early that evening together with fifteen others from *U-188* I made my way to the waiting leave train at Bordeaux station. Nobody paid special attention to the flak guns and their Luftwaffe crews on some of the wagons. Only Big-mouth Bauer was unable to restrain himself: 'Hey there, grandpa! Are you going to shoot some holes in the air with that bullet sprayer?' An NCO of about forty tapped a finger against his forehead below the rim of the steel helmet and bent down to Bauer: 'You may soon be glad that we're coming along for the ride. There's no easy way to angle the Amis out of the sky! In contrast to you, however, they have respect for our quadruple flak!'

While I was still standing in the corridor of the coach I heard Gottlieb Baumann, normally tranquillity itself, say: 'Can't you shut your mouth for just once, Karl? These grandpas are not up there on the roof for fun!'

There were eight of us to each compartment. Our seabags were lined up in the corridor and our linen bags stowed in the luggage nets as the train jolted into motion and, blessed by the rays of mild evening sunshine, rolled out into the wine-growing plain behind the harbour town. At first I took part in the general conversation, then only heard the voices as if through cotton wool and was one of the first to fall asleep. Loud squealing of the brakes awoke me, and since I was sitting with my back to the engine I was pressed back in my seat. Darkness had fallen. Baumann opened the window, leaned out and shouted, 'Why have we stopped here in the middle of the woods? What's up?'

'Come down here, orphan-boy, and see this nice mess for yourself. The Resistance has blown up the bridge over the valley!' A voice I did not recognise ordered across the night: 'Everybody out. We are continuing on foot. There's a replacement train coming on the other side!'

We grabbed our precious linen bags, helped each of our colleagues shoulder his seabag and, cursing under our breath, stumbled in single file on a hardly recognisable meadow path near the railway embankment alongside the unlit train. Ahead we saw the locomotive standing close to the remains of the bridge. It had previously spanned a valley which cut deep into the countryside. Hindered by our very weighty packs we had to climb down a steep slope with much bushy vegetation: the smooth soles of our walking-out shoes were totally unsuitable for this purpose, and when as one of the last I arrived at the railway tracks on the other side I was streaming with sweat. A large, gaunt Army lieutenant came up and asked quietly, 'You were in the last coach? You all got over here? Despite your elegant footwear and those heavy-looking packs?'

'Jawohl, Herr Oberleutnant!' Gottlieb Baumann answered imperturbably, 'Our U-boat clothing would not have been much more use for the purpose.'

'U-boats? Do we still have any?' The lieutenant was silent for a moment and then explained quickly, 'A substitute train will fetch us away from here within the next half hour. You would be better off going forward, but it's up to you.'

Two hours later our substitute train halted at a bridge seriously damaged by air attack, but which could still be crossed on foot. Pioneer troops were repairing the damage, one could see the reddish-yellow sprays of sparks from the welding. Because we had followed the advice of the lieutenant and sat in the centre section of the second train, and impatient types had urged us to get a move on, we got to the other bank of the river quickly and found another train waiting.

After that it was stop-go without any obvious reason along open stretches. The months of tension still took their toll on us, for most of the time we slept. Thus I saw little of the delightful highlands which we passed by on the left side of the Rhine and did not awaken until we got to Karlsruhe. Karl Bauer standing at the open window saw me stretching and I had to make an effort to understand him because he had decided to speak in his thick Carinthian brogue: 'Back from the dead, late riser? The others send you many greetings. Three of the South Germans have already departed. Heigl accompanied Baumann off. Franz is getting something for us to drink from the Red Cross nurses.'

The station lay in total darkness below an overcast night sky. Silent figures passing by with rucksacks or field packs, most carrying a carbine, made a ghostly impression. A Luftwaffe NCO sat opposite me. I asked him for the time. He gave a quick glance at the phosphorescent face of his pilot's watch: 'Half past midnight, comrade. You can sleep peacefully. They are not coming tonight.'

In the pale light he must have seen my confused look for he added in quick explanation: 'Of course, you were asleep when I told the others. You were cut off from the world for so long on your boat. I mean the enemy bomber formations which fly over Reich territory almost every night.' He paused and then went on: 'I am travelling to Klagenfurt with your comrade Bauer. Our airfield is near there. There are far too few of us, ever more frequently we are having to attack those Flying Fortresses over the Munich area. Today it's so cloudy that South German airspace will probably be spared.' When I heard that I was suddenly wide awake as only ever before when the alarm was given aboard the boat. So it reached down there too. What would Grafing look like?

In the late afternoon the train, filled exclusively with military personnel, passed through Augsburg and across the Swabian-Bavarian plateau. The so-called 'Capital of the National Socialist Movement', Munich, was coming ever nearer. As the train rolled into the main terminus, a light drizzle sprayed through the glass dome, bomb-damaged at numerous spots spanning the baggage halls. Karl Bauer helped me shoulder my seabag and accompanied me to the door of the coach. On the opposite track was a black locomotive with the phrase 'Wheels must roll for victory' painted in white letters on its side.

As I jumped down to the platform, Karl asked me sadly, 'Toni? How much longer will they have to roll?' Instead of replying, I raised my lightweight linen bags and took my leave of him with 'Take care!'

'See you in four weeks, Toni! We've earned it!' After a few metres a lieutenant of the flak with greying hair at the temples and a very pretty flak auxiliary at his side approached me. Mentally almost at home, I forgot to salute, and I heard him shout behind me, 'Man, don't you salute any more?'

Quickly I dropped my two linen bags, walked back with correct military stride and passed him given a smart salute. 'You arse with ears,' I thought and grinned.

'Why are you grinning provocatively?'

'I am not grinning, Herr Oberleutnant, I am making a face to show my pleasure at serving!' The girl looked at me with amusement. 'I hope he didn't see that' I thought, but his eyes were riveted on my silver-coloured U-boat Front Clasp.[1]

'I will hope for that for you.' He see-sawed on the tips of his boots and seemed to consider what next before remarking: 'Beat it, man.'

Still grinning inwardly, I turned about, picked up my two linen bags and went with long strides to the platform where the train for Rosenheim seemed to be waiting just for me. At Haar, an eastern suburb of Munich, I waited impatiently stared out at the so familiar landscape, freshly washed by summer rain. At Grafing I was the first of all the passengers to alight. Suddenly my seabag seemed light as a feather, so happy and elated and full of good cheer was I. Before taking up my linen bags, I saluted a very young panzer lieutenant getting on the train, then almost at the double I crossed the station forecourt and along the street to Grafing market.

Twenty minutes later my father hugged me with a loud cry of joy even before my mother and sisters did so. He whispered in my ear: 'Toni, that Missing announcement was the same as a report of death. But now we both have eight gifted days before I have to return. You really have four weeks of U-boat leave?' I merely nodded, for now my mother and three sisters all wanted a hug.

Later my father laid his hands on my shoulders and gave an embarrassed smile as he looked at our respective rank insignia. 'Babe, one thing is certain: we are two small, insignificant idiots in these mad times of war but have it better than many others with greater responsibility. Although I tried, for as you know I was in so-called protective custody, from the very beginning I was never able to

---

1. The U-boat Front Clasp for valour was instituted on 15 May 1944. The decoration was awarded based on the recommendation of the U-boat commander and subject to the approval of the BdU. In November 1944 the award was restructured into three classes; bronze, silver and the rarely, if ever, awarded gold (Tr).

change anything about how things developed. Now at least we might be able to save our skins.'

In those first nights I awoke my father and mother by shouting 'Alarm!' in my sleep, but this soon passed. In some inexplicable way, however, home seemed strange to me. I felt that I had changed and I found myself suffering from a kind of homesickness for my comrades.

In order to avoid having to salute anybody of a higher rank than Leading Seaman, I dawdled across the market place one mild July evening in civilian clothes. Near the Sirtl Wine Bar I went down a narrow alley which led to the Kastenwirt inn. They were showing a film *Das Bad in der Tenne* ('The Bath in the Barn Floor') in a room above the inn. Because of the title it was X-rated, nobody under 18 allowed in, as so much was in those days. Just as I was following two giggly old men, happy with expectation, up the stairs to the room, I saw at the entrance one of our local gendarmes standing at a table behind which a girl unknown to me was selling cinema tickets at a till. Without bothering to notice the aged policeman in his green-grey uniform with the Reich eagle on the shako, I pulled my coin purse from the pocket of my leather shorts and asked for a ticket. The girl looked up to Gendarme Dauner with a frightened look, and he covered her ticket roll with his hand and asked me, 'Are you sure you're eighteen?' For a brief moment I was speechless, then I told him, 'Unfortunately since 1941 and in the Kriegsmarine. What they're going to show us in there I have seen long since in nature!'

One of the old men in front of me turned and quickly confirmed what I said: 'Herr Gendarme Dauner, this is the Staller kid from Gries-Strasse. He went on the U-boats. Don't you recognise him?'

'My apologies,' the gendarme murmured, gave me a surprised stare and laid a finger in salute on the shiny black peak of his shako. 'I believe I once saw you recently in your uniform. You defenders of the Fatherland get younger every day.'

'That's very nice of you, Herr Dauner,' I replied with a laugh, and entered the cinema. Scarcely was I seated inside facing the linen screen than the light was turned off and the excited murmur of voices dried up. The harmless merry romp cheered me up. Back indoors I asked my mother if I looked younger in civilian clothes. She answered with a smile, 'Babe, you have really recovered fast, you look much younger now and not so tense as you were during the first days of your leave.'

My father was already back in the mountains of Yugoslavia when I arose very early on my day of departure and took my leave of my mother and sisters as quickly as possible. In Munich I met Franz Heigl, and we travelled back together. At every station we looked unsuccessfully for familiar faces and asked ourselves where the others could be. After each fruitless search, we slumped back disappointed in our corner of the compartment. Towards evening the leave-takers' train had just left the French frontier behind us when the brakes squealed and we heard the loud order: 'Everybody out! Low-flying aircraft!'

We jumped down from the train with members of various branches of service, ran across a meadow and separated. At the edge of a small wood beneath some bushes, Heigl and I found a spot between two naval-uniformed figures lying prostrate, faces covered by resting on their arms. We had heard the roar of aircraft engines and the chatter of fighter MGs approaching fast even while we were still running. The flak on the rear wagon of the train engaged the attackers with such accurate fire that they quickly broke off and fled. As I raised my head I recognised the US white star on three of the machines and saw that one of them was trailing a light grey banner of smoke.

Then I looked straight into the grinning face of Karl Bauer, and at the same time heard the pleasant voice of Gottlieb Baumann behind me. 'Well just look here! These two rascals are travelling in the same train as ourselves and not bothering to say hello. What kind of slovenly manners do you call those?' We shook hands happily, brushed ourselves down and wandered back to the train with no great urgency even when the same voice as before ordered: 'Can you go any faster, may I ask? Everybody re-board. Report any casualties to me!'

When Heigl and I went to fetch our seabags from our compartment in order to transfer to that of Baumann and Bauer, we found it covered in shards of glass from the windows. There were several bullet holes in the upholstery of my former seat. 'Toni, you're a lucky dog!' Heigl exclaimed. Now he was speaking standard German again and had dropped his local Carinthian brogue: much the same occurred with me. We were back amongst ourselves. In the U-boat bunkers at Bordeaux they immediately assigned us into teams to repair *U-188*. Meanwhile the second group went on home leave.

There was a degree of tension in the air following the attempt on the life of Adolf Hitler on 20 July 1944. Though we talked about the event, any commentary was studiously avoided. Only Karl said anything: 'For me, this Stauffenberg was a bungler. Why didn't he stay behind in the hut with his bomb? Then I could respect him as a hero. Now he's dead just the same and the Gröfaz[2] will keep on making great speeches urging us to hold out.' None of us interposed except Chief Schulz who said quietly, 'Don't talk so much, Bauer.'

From now on all members of the Wehrmacht had to salute with the arm outstretched in the so-called 'Hitler salute'. Nevertheless it frequently happened that superiors in rank would be given the normal naval salute and no difficulties would ensue. We did feel however that the attitude of the French civilian population had changed towards us. The Allies' Normandy bridgehead had long since developed into an advancing front. The French scented the change and we became daily less secure.

One night in early August 1944 two of our boats sailed, and two days later it was rumoured that both had been lost in Biscay with all aboard. It was clear meanwhile that *U-188* and other boats would not be ready for operations as quickly as had been expected. All the same, the order of the BdU came as a surprise: 'No boats to the enemy.' Demolition squads did their duty and made a thorough job of it.

All U-boat crews had gone through a long and thorough training. Now the BdU ordered us back to Germany. We were told we would crew new boats there. Gottlieb Baumann got to the heart of it with a question he put in doubting tones: 'Have they really got new boats for us?' Those who heard him could only react with a shrug of the shoulders.

The same afternoon Karl Bauer proved once more that he was always the best informed of us all. An hour before the crews of the

---

2. *Grösster Feldherr aller Zeiten*, the 'Greatest Warlord Who Ever Lived', a term commonly applied to Hitler in the earlier days of the regime.(Tr)

boats demolished in the bunkers were required to parade to receive fresh orders, he told us in the barrack hut, 'Boys, the second leave group is waiting at home for us. They took our seabags to the Baltic some days ago. Tonight we leave. They just don't know how yet. Every vehicle is needed at the front at the moment.' A voice in the background, I think it was engine room mechanic Wolfgang Reutzsch, remarked sarcastically, 'Don't worry about it Karl. We'll borrow vehicles from the enemy and hand them back after Final Victory.' Nobody thought this was funny.

Officers of the base command office interviewed each of us. They were looking for drivers. In those days drivers were much less common than now. Then we were ordered to go into the town and search every garage for usable vehicles which we had then to requisition. Moreover we were told to 'organise'[3] bicycles and bring as many as possible to the base. 'And as quickly as possible!' This was the strangest of all orders I had been required to obey until then, and it spoke volumes. We swarmed out. *U-188* crewmen stayed together in the town. The very critical observations made by some of the men in response to this order would have resulted in court-martials if they had been overheard.

In the late afternoon, engine room hand Effing drove a rickety old minibus bearing Lüdden and other officers out of the bunker complex. This was the only vehicle our group had managed to seize in running order although each of us did now own a bicycle. About 150 U-boat men were given their marching orders and permission to ransack the naval depot. None of the French bicycles was fitted with a back-pedal brake, and since we did not trust the conventional callipers fitted we followed Franz Heigl's advice and each of us took a pair of shoes with built-in iron toecaps and heels for emergency braking. Other crews followed our example.

Heigl also suggested: 'Boys! Do we really want to take these heavy cans of food and bottles of schnapps with us? You can booze after Final Victory. That is imminent! Best to take cigarettes, as many as your comfortable mount will enable you, and use them to barter for food with any amenable Frenchman!'

---

3. This word in the military slang of the time meant 'rustle up, no questions asked'(Tr).

It was already early evening when we left the previously so busy U-boat base in long lines two abreast on our stolen bicycles and pedalled in silence through the apparently deserted streets of the port of Bordeaux. Now and again to left and right I saw curtains twitching at windows. We had been given the strictest orders to cycle more than 200 kilometres daily if at all possible. Leading us was a sporting looking lieutenant-commander who set a hellish pace from the outset. My bicycle was almost new and a sweet runner. Our trousers were not bell-bottoms but we bound our loosely-fitting uniform trouser legs with cord through the eyelets of our boots. Thus we pedalled away, silently, taking deep breaths and inwardly raging at the fast tempo. Gradually the line of cyclists grew ever longer. Bent low over the handlebars we pedalled ever onwards, gasping for breath. So as not to attract low-flying aircraft we could not show a light at night and had to be alert to avoid collision with the man in front or the neighbour. The mood got ever more irritable and I heard remarks like:

'This guy up ahead seems to be some kind of slave driver!'

'Can he get the Knight's Cross for pedalling a bike?'

'If they need us so desperately, why don't they send a lorry?'

Towards midnight came the shout from ahead: 'Short break!' We sank left and right in exhaustion in the threadbare grass of a vineyard and I stuffed a square of chocolate into my mouth. Heigl pointed out: 'I just saw a sign, Périgueux 10 kilometres. That means we have come at least 90 kilometres.'

'The slave driver up there wants to earn us all the Sport Badge!' remarked the always cheerful Karl Bauer. Nobody laughed. Soon we all pedalling furiously again, puffing and panting through the moonlit summer night. Once we quenched our thirst at a spring near a farmhouse. The ruler-straight road seemed endless in the slightly undulating countryside. Apart from the unknown lieutenant-commander at the head of the column I don't think anybody had a map. The *U-188* crew had kept together as a group at the centre of the long drawn-out column. Braking became common to avoid collisions. Although my mount was one of the better models, I had no faith in the handbrakes and used my boots for braking. Sometimes there were so many sparks flying from the column that it was possible to make out what the road was like ahead.

A few hundred metres beyond the village of Les Cars the silence of the night was suddenly rent by the chatter of machine-pistols. Just for a fraction of a second I saw muzzle flashes, and then, quicker than ever practised previously on some barracks square, we lay under cover either side of the road. I heard salvoes hitting the road surface and the ugly hiss of ricochets. Only a few of us were armed, but fire was returned from the head of our column. After a few minutes silence fell.

'Report casualties to me at once!' The voice of our slave-driver resounded almost blood-curdlingly loud in the night. Only two men required light dressings. 'Our infantry training was therefore not a waste,' remarked Baumann in his soft Hessian tones. Chief Schulz replied angrily: 'I had been expecting something like that for hours. You can't expect the Resistance not to notice a stupid great crowd of cyclists a mile long. That was probably not the last time the partisans will have a crack at us.'

None of our bicycles had been damaged and some fifteen minutes later we were pedalling again with very mixed feelings. Our destination was the town of Limoges.

At dawn it was getting light very quickly when we heard aircraft engines roaring closer. Again we abandoned our bicycles, dragged them off the road and then ran as far as we could from the highway before throwing ourselves into cover. All the *U-188* men escaped the three bursts of fire without harm. We could see the Tommies seated in the Perspex nose of their aircraft. Watching them turn away Karl Bauer was just describing the five RAF aircraft as friendly doves of peace when he suddenly shut up. About fifty metres from us we saw two men being dragged to the side of the road. The column leader ordered: 'Each of you knows the route we are taking, has his written orders and pay/identity book with him. Assemble into small groups of five or six men to make yourselves less noticeable! One man is stay behind with the seriously wounded. I shall ride ahead to Limoges and arrange for the wounded to be brought to a military hospital as soon as possible!'

Franz Heigl cleared his throat and remarked: 'If he had had this wonderful idea a bit sooner, those two at the side of the road would

131

still be alive. Let this *Kaleu* go off. We from our boat will now form groups.' Quickly I aligned myself with Heigl. Hans Ferdinand, Herbert Bernigau and Karl Bauer joined us. The other groups formed equally swiftly. 'We are the leading five,' Heigl determined. We were the first to mount up and go. 'We can meet up in the town HQ in Limoges. Maybe they will have breakfast for us. If not, then we'll meet up on the way no doubt. Do your best, boys!' Heigl shouted back.

Next day some of the groups and ourselves found the hotel in which the local headquarters was located. We rested and got the finest food. The officers showed themselves to be very generous for they were in end-of-term mood in view of the advancing enemy front. On several occasions they expressed their regrets at not being able to let us have any vehicles. It was already dark when as one of the last groups we set off for Bourges. The unaccustomed strain of the previous day had had its effect on all of us, and now we pedalled much slower, almost at a comfortable pace. Only Heigl had a pistol. He said that he did not intend to use it because he thought there would be no point up against the much better-armed Resistance. We all found this reasonable. We knew that on the road in front of us were several groups of cyclists, therefore we felt almost safe and decided that during the next stages we would proceed in daylight. We slept the remainder of the second night in an equipment shed near the road with a guard posted.

Towards midday we gave the town of Châteauroux a wide berth on a side-road. There was low cloud and it was drizzling. Although this weather shielded us against low-flying aircraft, it failed to raise our spirits much. On the road to Bourges we came across Jürgen Krause of the Bordeaux base HQ who had had to stop and repair a puncture. His group had not wanted to wait while he did this. They said that other groups were coming up and he should join one. We all agreed to take him. He told us: 'Up until now I was with *Kaleu* Dommes' group. He kept us going fast but I don't know why. He also doesn't seem to need much sleep.'

At dusk we cycled through Bourges and found the former district HQ. It had been abandoned but they had left behind all their quality provisions. We satisfied our hunger and thirst in the spacious kitchen of the mansion and laughed at the undue haste of the Wehrmacht officers in leaving all this food behind. 'Didn't we see German defensive positions in front of the town? The Americans can't advance that fast!'

Nobody felt really threatened, but neither did anybody object when Heigl arranged sentry duties for the night, and he did not exclude himself. Jürgen Krause had a road map which we examined briefly, all deciding that next day we would take minor roads to the bridge at La Charité on the Loire and from there head for Strasbourg. Almost satisfied we then turned in and slept in the unaccustomed spacious beds.

The following day did not go as planned. Three times we had to help out with punctures and thus made slow progress, also being unsettled by hearing the noise of fighting to our rear and apparently getting closer.

'That sounds like tank guns! Why isn't our artillery firing back?' Karl Baumann asked.

'Maybe you're a silly ass,' Jürgen Krause replied, 'How did they advance so quickly? Probably the Americans made a surprise breakthrough.'

It was beginning to get dark when we went as fast as we could through a small wood and approached the arterial road which had been blocked all day by German vehicles flowing to the rear. Now it looked very quiet. Crouching down in a ditch at the side of the road we were studying the map again in what daylight remained when a few kilometres ahead we heard the unmistakable sound of loud explosions.

'So what was that then? The armoured spearhead can't have overtaken us!' Jürgen Krause guessed, 'That sounded like demolition charges!'

We remounted hurriedly in something approaching panic and without needing any encouragement pedalled off violently. Ten minutes later we reached the west bank of the Loire and stared without speaking at the ruins of the bridge, parts of which were projecting out of the water, washed by gurgling muddy brown eddies. On the opposite bank I could just make out in the failing light an Army officer near his Kübelwagen watching us through binoculars. We had got there minutes too late and probably made on him an impression of dejected abandonment. He made a gesture of the arm which we did not understand, got into the car beside his driver and left. We stared after the small car speechless for some time. Then we all seem to say at the same time: 'He didn't need to have left in such a rush as that!'

'You idiot! They didn't know we were coming!'

'I'm not going to be taken prisoner.'

'Oh, you think we want to be? We U-boat men caused the Allies so much death and destruction that they will shoot us out of hand at once. Even though I don't believe all that our Propaganda Ministry tell us, I fear that they might not be exaggerating in that.'

'Their tanks won't advance so quickly at night,' Heigl said, adding nervously, 'Or can you hear a Sherman perhaps? Well then, even the Americans aren't such great heroes that they would keep on going through the night. As for ourselves, however, we shall have to cross the river somehow in the dark.' This remark made us consider. He proposed: 'We should pedal up-river. Our infantry can't have confiscated all the boats and barges, we're bound to find one at least. Jürgen, you speak French: even though the Frenchies don't exactly love us, you can surely talk them into letting us borrow a boat.'

We set off without lights and hurriedly left the road behind us. The path along the river bank was difficult to follow. The hum of our tyres and the soft gurgling of the river nearby were the only sounds in the night. Suddenly artillery fire from the east bank broke the silence, and almost at once the rounds exploded with a deafening road behind us and made the earth tremble.

'That's just nuisance fire,' Hans Ferdinand muttered. Karl Bauer agreed. 'Obviously, nothing else. They want to mark the limits for the Americans. Let's hope the latter don't reply straight away. They've got so much ammunition they could sweep the whole river bank. Anyway, as you'll see, they'll set up the front right here on the river.'

'Can we have some quiet?' Franz Heigl's voice sounded annoyed, and then he said quietly, 'Jürgen, I think that's a fisherman's cottage with a boat shed.' Now we saw the indistinct outline of a small house fronting the river bank. 'You stay with the bicycles,' Heigl whispered before making his way with Jürgen to the front door of the cottage. I heard the soft knocking they made. Nothing happened. Then both drummed violently against the door with their fists, and Jürgen let loose a loud outpouring of French. The door creaked open. A weak light could be seen within.

After a couple of minutes Franz Heigl came back, returning his pistol to the pocket of his uniform jacket. Apparently the fisherman and his wife had never seen German naval uniforms before and looked at the two of them as though they came from another planet. A deal had been struck for six cartons of cigarettes, one from each of us for rowing us across the river. The Frenchman was getting the boat ready while his wife was preparing omelettes for us. Two of us would be conveyed across on each trip with our personal bicycle, upon alighting each passenger would pay the promised inducement in cigarettes.

While Heigl guarded the bicycles we went into the cottage. A woollen blanket covered the kitchen window as a blackout curtain. The room was lit only by the flickering log-fire in the hearth. A frightened woman stood before it, stealing shy glances at us. After Jürgen spoke to her reassuringly in French a smile lit up her face.

Since Karl Bauer and I were to go first she served us our omelettes at once. After we had eaten, a very large Frenchman entered wearing a Basque beret. His face was inscrutable but he looked pleased to see the stack of cigarette cartons on the table. The boat was small and packed tight with two bicycles, two U-boat men and the fisherman rowing. It was so dark we could hardly see ten metres across the water. After a while the boat grounded in a small sandy cove between some bushes. We unloaded the bicycles, handed the Frenchman his agreed inducement and then pushed the boat afloat again.

It was amazing how he could row unerringly to the tiny cove half an hour later to deposit Ferdinand and Bernigau ashore at the same spot. Another half hour and with Heigl and Krause our party was reunited.

Karl Bauer gave a deep sigh of relief and said, 'No captivity. Now we can rejoin our Mummies in Bremen! And always in the open air!'

'Since when does your Mama live in Bremen? You're from the Carinthian mountains.' Heigl's voice sounded lighter. 'There's nothing like getting away from here. An artillery battle can start up at any moment. I don't like this quiet. Difficult to believe we're here all alone. All mount up! Let's go!'

We cycled almost as far as the demolished bridge before turning off down a small road, keeping up a fast pace for about two hours until it began to get light and we found the road to Clamecy. We had no idea where the German defensive line lay. Had it been set up to our rear? At an isolated farmhouse our cigarettes and the French-speaking Jürgen worked wonders again. The sky in the east had just begun to redden when the farmer's wife served us an excellent, rich breakfast with a little tea and much red wine. Her husband showed us a place in his barn where we could sleep and hide our bicycles. It seemed that this married couple had not had any bad experiences with Kriegsmarine men.

Although these French people were unexpectedly friendly to us, we still kept one man on watch. In the early afternoon, fresh and rested, we remounted. It was unbelievable how quiet and peaceful it seemed to be here. We agreed to travel in daylight in future. We were never once bothered by low-level aircraft and kept going for four days in bright sunshine. Every evening we found ourselves lodging with farmers, always reserved but willing to feed us well in exchange for cigarettes. As time went on we even began to enjoy our Tour de France. We could not be held responsible for the apparent perplexity and wrong decisions of our U-boat leadership, and neither did we know where the front line was. We thought that probably it lay far behind us and we were in German-occupied territory. We pedalled ten to twelve hours daily, but our stops lasted longer. I noticed that nobody was keeping count any longer of how many kilometres we were putting behind us. We were beginning to take it easy a little.

On the late afternoon of our sixth day of cycling we came up against the reality on the approaches to a bridge near Dijon. Field-gendarmes were checking marching orders. We looked on distrustfully as a large, very slim sergeant entered our names on a list together with the date and time. Finally he gave us all a searching look and could hardly hide his amazement: 'So, meine Herren. You are by no means the first to turn up here today. I have never before seen so many U-boat men important for the war effort on a single day. The Navy also needs its men. Go briskly through the town by this main road. At the stadium on the edge of town you will be collected up and taken on by bus! And now off with you, and get a move on!'

This time it was I who could not hold his tongue. 'Our leadership should have realised it much sooner!'

'Can you make that judgement? I don't like repeating myself, off with you!'

At the assembly point sixty to seventy U-boat men were seated in the grass. Petty Officer Baumann and some of the *U-188* crew greeted us joyfully: 'So you're here at last. Gradually we are really nearly all here.'

'Have you heard? Our *Kaleu* Lüdden and his companions were taken prisoner by the Resistance. Effing was wounded, they killed Roy.'

We five looked dismayed, but then Baumann interjected: 'No worries, somehow or another they all managed to escape, except poor Roy of course. But the Resistance kept the *U-188* War Diary.'

'Bravo!' exclaimed Karl Bauer loudly. 'But why was the commander carrying the book through that inhospitable region?'

'Idiot!' Baumann replied, 'Lüdden was on his way to the BdU. The gentlemen in Paris needed our War Diary for something to read at night.'

'And now the Tommies in their turn will probably be able to see where in the world we went to, and what we did there.' Hebert Bernigau seemed quite indignant. Chief Schulz was standing near me. He raised both hands in appeasement. 'Now don't get your pants in a twist, boys. The Tommies have known for some time how many of their proud ships we have sunk.'

'Maybe,' Bernigau replied quietly, 'but we are forbidden to keep diaries and only officers can take photos so that nothing can fall into the wrong hands. And now this?'

'It's all the same.' Gottlieb Baumann spoke as calmly and cautiously as ever. 'The important thing is that the leadership has not forgotten us. They've even sent us buses so that we can get back to the U-boat front as soon as possible. That is very nice of them; I mean, of the BdU. And now you can sling your five bicycles with the others into the ditch since we definitely shan't need them in our buses!'

Towards dusk three ramshackle Wehrmacht buses arrived in the meadow. A naval lieutenant unknown to us had us parade for roll call. It appeared that sixty-nine men had reached Dijon. Nobody knew where the others were. Murmurs and whispered names passed through the ranks. Baumann said to me, 'The important thing is that half the *U-188* crew is present . . .'

'Silence! Attention! Stand at ease!' the lieutenant ordered. 'The first six men on the left flank will go to the first bus. The others will accompany me to the other two buses.'

Was it coincidence? We six men of Heigl's group had remained together: Chief Schulz, Karl Bauer, Heigl, Ferdinand, Bernigau and I. Now we boarded the dirty camouflage-painted bus. As soon as we got to the doorway we had a shock. The driver's windscreen was clear, but all other windows were thick with grime. The only seat was for the driver: the entire interior was taken by barrels whose stink of benzene was unmistakable. 'What's all this then?' Heigl asked the driver in field-grey. 'Are you a lorry or passenger coach? Where have you hidden your tool box?'

'Behind the flap near the door. What do you want that for? Maybe we'll have some breakdowns later!'

'You'll see what for.' Heigl took a tyre lever from the box, threw me a far from clean blanket and told me, 'Toni, you can lay on that at the back. I'll knock out the rear window so that you can see clearly and observe.

'What do you mean? Are you going to deliberately destroy Wehrmacht property?' The driver rose threateningly from his seat.

'Shut your trap, you fool. You'll be grateful when our lookout gives timely warning of the approach of low-flying enemy fighters. Our do you prefer to die in this filthy rolling crematorium with your unwilling guests? Until now you've been lucky. You can't have many miles under your belt.'

Before I reached my spot I heard Baumann's mighty blows with the tyre iron and the tinkle of shattering glass. Karl Bauer crept up behind me. 'Toni, I'll stay here with you. If there's a serious problem we can both get out quicker this way.' Heigl had finished his work on the outside of the vehicle, threw us the tyre iron and shouted, 'Pull me up, I'll lie with you.' We had spread the blanket, and as soon as he was lying prostrate beside us the coach set off. The other three crouched at the front door ready to jump out. The driver turned to us. 'Boys, you've done a good job there! Really a comforting feeling!' he shouted in recognition.

We drove through the night, as usual one of us remaining awake. At daybreak we were somewhere near Mühlhausen in Alsace. Before being shaken fully awake from restless slumber, Franz Heigl implored me: 'Toni, somewhere or other the bees will be starting up now. We have the advantage that they will have the sun in their eyes. It is absolutely essential that you see them as early as possible. We are relying on you!'

Once again I was dead tired but wide awake at the same time. The driver drove calmly and maintained the same speed. After about ten minutes I saw three specks in the sky. 'Low-flying aircraft behind!' The brakes squealed and even before the coach had come to a stop I jumped out. I was the first to land, rolled to one side and sprinted away. At that moment I had only one thought: 'Toni, run! If only one tracer round hits those barrels of benzene, the bus will explode in a gigantic fireball!'

Soon the noise of the aircraft blotted out the huffing and puffing of those behind me trying to catch up. As soon as the aircraft cannons began to hammer, I threw myself into a freshly-ploughed furrow and pressed myself against the earth. In my sub-conscious it registered that somebody was doing the same behind me and then I felt clods of earth spray over my back from a burst of fire. Somewhere ahead of us a quadruple flak was firing and against all the rules of combat that had been drilled into me I raised my head. The three attacking aircraft had already swept over us and away, but the last was in trouble, trailing a black-grey ribbon of smoke.

They had decided not to bank and make a fresh attack. Two of the three machines made off, and I could see the white star national markings they bore. Standing up I watched the third aircraft dive into the ground as a red fireball. Our bus was in flames but everybody was cheering, not least from old custom, the shooting down of the aircraft. All around naval men were brushing the dust from their uniforms. My own uniform was by now far from presentable.

'Any losses to report?' Nobody replied to the naval lieutenant, and none of them reacted when he said, 'We were lucky that the flak up ahead near the road junction is so well camouflaged and could drive off those damn bees.' Our transport leader paused before ordering: 'Now it's a bit tighter. All aboard the remaining two vehicles and let's go!'

The drivers protested that they had to refuel. 'This place here close to the quadruple flak is ideal. The empty barrels can be laid one on the other to gain more space.' This was agreed to, and a couple of us helped lift the full barrels out of our bus, roll them up to the filling point and work the handpumps and soon as they were connected up. Baumann objected: 'If we have to ride in this mobile incendiary bomb then we need emergency exits at both sides!' Once again we heard the sound of glass shattering. Shortly before leaving Heigl put me in the rear lookout position and then I heard Jürgen Krause plead: 'Everybody to the windows: keep your eyes open at all costs. None of us wants to be roasted alive.'

Our bus was now crammed full with anxious sailors with no room to move. It had begun to rain but this was not much of a comfort for we knew that low-level attacking aircraft would often drop fast and unexpectedly on their victims like hawks. We followed the bus in front, also packed, avoided Mühlhausen and the west bank of the Rhine and drove instead unseen along the eastern edge of the Vosges mountains via Colmar to Strasbourg. It was late morning when we jumped down from the barrels to the parade ground of an infantry barracks on the outskirts of the city, and I felt the tension draining from me.

Karl Bauer said with a grin but rightly: 'Toni, if the low-level fighters had found us not many would have survived,' and added in a loud voice in his free and easy way: 'I think that U-boat Command stopped looking ahead some time ago. On the one hand they need us for new boats, and on the other play with us like chips at the roulette table.' Karl broke off for a while after Chief Schulz interrupted him: 'Careful, Bauer, no more popular outbursts, if I may ask. Learn to control your slanderous tongue.'

A few minutes later I stood alone before the wire-mesh fence around the barracks square. The sight of ammunition bunkers and some heavy flak guns surrounded by earth walls was reassuring. I watched squads of flak gunners on a large meadow to the rear of the barracks receiving infantry training in the way I had hated so much. About sixty metres from where I stood an NCO bawled his orders. I estimated the age of these flak men to be around fifteen. As the squad passed within metres of me with their carbines, I saw their little-boy faces. I said under my breath: 'For God's sake. Are these boys the Watch on the Rhine?'

Hans Ferdinand had crept up to my side and said, 'Looks like it, Toni. Only these kids, the dubious miracle weapon and naturally ourselves in our new U-boats can still halt the defeat of the Thousand-Year Reich.'

'All U-boat men parade to receive orders!' The voice of the lieutenant tore us from our thoughts. We turned away from the barracks yard and its very young recruits. Twelve men were to occupy a room, and we had to make our uniforms presentable. We spent the rest of the day in more or less deep exploratory conversations, and games of skat and chess. An alert sailor had organised a 'People's Radio Receiver' from somewhere and installed it in Baumann's room. We listened to the melodies of the Wunschkonzert and the news broadcasts. The era of the Special Announcements was long gone. Meanwhile many were not so shy at speaking their minds in view of the ever-advancing front line.

At night we slept like the dead. Not until the evening of the following day did we stand in ruler-straight ranks again for the naval lieutenant. 'The man longest in service, or the senior ranking man of a boat's crew, will lead his men in the early hours to his new service office. I am handing every group its marching orders.' Chief Schulz was called first, and since I was in a good position I heard the officer say: 'As per the schedule you are leaving at 0925 hrs tomorrow for Plön near Kiel!' The word 'as per the schedule' were emphasised by this man, the only naval officer at the barracks. He finished with: 'You may dismiss with your men.'

Next day we ambled aimlessly in small groups from the barracks into the town intending to go on to the railway station. Nobody had separated us from the remains of our cigarettes or reserve shoes, and neither did anybody ask where the rucksacks came from which a few of the men were carrying. We made a brief diversion to see the cathedral and as we arrived by chance I found myself leading our small group. We found the great Gothic structure awe-inspiring, and particularly its impressive 142-metre tall North Tower which dwarfed the houses of the Old Town. As a trained organ builder I was naturally very interested in the outfit inside the cathedral.

I heard Gottlieb Baumann say, 'Schulz! Do you believe they've got a new boat for us? I simply can't. At the moment it all seems to be conjured up.' I had stopped to hear Schulz' reply when a few metres away somebody began ranting: 'Don't you know the Hitler salute? Don't you want to know it? Members of all branches of service must salute with the arm outstretched! I shall immediately cure your monkey business and also teach your stupid heap how to give a proper salute!'

I pushed my way forward and found myself looking into the angry red face of a young-looking Army lieutenant. A couple of our men had given him a correct naval salute instead of the Hitler salute. Around me I saw surprised, bewildered faces. The lieutenant's uniform bore only the Iron Cross Second Class and the Nazi Party badge. Petty Officer Baumann had probably noticed this for he made the rather unwise observation, 'Well, he doesn't seem to be much of a hero.'

'What insolence! I will not have it!' the lieutenant barked and, taking a stance on the stone steps before the portals of the cathedral ordered us to lay our baggage in front of him. Apparently this was not done with sufficient alacrity and now he see-sawed on the tips of his highly polished boots. 'March in single file, two metres between each man, saluting me with the Hitler salute!'

I sprinted to the end of the file and noticed the rapidly growing crowd of civilian onlookers. Scarcely had I passed the officer at the tail of the march past than he ordered 'All about turn and repeat left to right!' Now I led the file. This second march past was done to his evident satisfaction: 'So, you can all do it excellently. Why not then as set out in Army regulations in the first place?' His voice took on a mocking tone. 'To get you to remember it firmly we shall now train some more. Form up in three ranks!' This was done in such a slack manner that he seemed on the verge of apoplexy at seeing it. We had to turn about, run at the double, take cover flat on the ground, march! march! Do it all again!' We boiled with rage.

This went on for a few more minutes and then while I was taking cover I noticed some outraged civilians approaching the officer in a threatening manner. At that moment Schulz said to us, 'Unfortunately we shall have to cancel the tour of the cathedral. Everybody pick up your pack. We shall march off to the station, I shall be at the rear.' While doing this and brushing the dirt from our uniforms Chief Schulz said to me quietly, 'If this buffoon follows us, then I'll show him our marching orders and make him personally responsible for preventing us taking the train.' By now the lieutenant was in serious difficulties surrounded by civilians and lost sight of us. During our now very rapid march to the station we had to give the Hitler salute as per Army regulations but to our surprise we arrived at the station in time to leave on our train punctually.

Near Darmstadt we all suffered for Baumann. Conversations died away as he jumped up from his seat and went to the window. 'For God's sake, is this what it looks like now? I hope nothing has happened to my wife! Can they just drop their bombs anywhere they please? The day before yesterday I sent another letter to my Gretchen . . . ' Schulz laid a hand on his shoulder: 'Gottlieb, Fatty Göring seems to be powerless. But take comfort. Bombs are like all the other jumping crackers. Not every one of them goes where it is supposed to. Your wife is safe.' We hoped that was so.

We had almost guessed it: at Plön there was no boat for us. During the first two nights enemy bomber formations flew over our naval barracks and a little later the earth trembled as bombs fell in and around Kiel. On the third day we received new orders: Danzig. We could hardly believe what our informant Karl Bauer whispered around before our departure: 'Lüdden, Benetschik, Kiessling and most of the others are expecting us at the Danzig yard. Not Meenen, he has been given his own boat.' Heigl poked him in the chest with a laugh: 'You old gossip! You should become a news reporter, then we would all know well in advance where we're off to.' Bauer ignored him and went on, 'You will all soon see! Our new boat is more modern than *U-188* but is still completing. Almost the same Type of boat, but improved. They really are waiting for us! We are a battle-proven crew!'

Over the next few days we discovered that the situation was out of control. At Rostock our locomotive and some of the coaches went up in flames and we never saw a single German aircraft in the skies. Miraculously our group emerged unscathed, but our morale was lower than I ever knew it before as we continued our journey on foot. We tried to cheer ourselves up with mutual pithy statements. Karl Bauer seemed the most irrepressible: 'Boys, we must not lose this war. We must repel the threatened calamity. Personally I do not have so much belief in our Führer but much more in this new miracle weapon! We only have to hold out a little longer. Everything else will fall into place.' We fell silent in the face of so much confidence and asked ourselves if Karl himself believed in what he was saying.

We covered the remainder of the journey on various lorries and the last fifty kilometres on a Kriegsmarine crew coach, a so-called MTW, which Lüdden had organised for us. 'At least we can rely on our commander!' We were unanimous in this opinion. We arrived in Danzig in the late afternoon and spent the night at the barracks which we knew of old. The meeting up with the men already in quarters here was like a family reunion. After the days of hunger at sea we were very happy with the large tasty portions we were served. It created some hope within us but we suspected that within a short while we would be aboard a boat living on hard bread and similar shipboard fare.

Next morning when we paraded *Kaleu* Lüdden informed us: 'Herr Meenen was promoted and has been given his own command!' Karl Bauer at my side gave me a nudge. 'It is not certain who his replacement will be,' Lüdden went on, 'We are now all going to the shipyard so that we can see over our new boat. Herr Kiessling and I shall be remaining here until it is finally complete' – here he made a short pause for effect – 'meanwhile you will all be going with Lt Benetschik to a convalescent home for U-boat men on the lake at Tegernsee.' I could almost have jumped for joy. Everybody murmured in excitement and for a brief moment I saw a grin cross the otherwise always serious face of the commander. I could hardly stand still for impatience and joy. None of us was dreaming of being in the new boat, no matter how well built and solid it might be.

Shortly after our arrival at Tegernsee Lt Benetschik assembled us all in the day room at our U-boat home, the Hotel Eden. He was more affable than any of us could ever remember. 'From today onwards you can do and leave undone whatever you want. Build up new strength for what we shall be facing perhaps very soon. Naturally I don't want to hear any complaints about us and consider it to be self-evident that everybody conducts himself in an exemplary manner and never goes out without his documents. The important thing is that we can wander wherever we like. If we have to hold ourselves in readiness I shall give you good warning. Now the lady hostel warden will show you to your rooms.'

Loud and exuberant like schoolboys we occupied our two-bed rooms. Heigl and I shared the same room, furnished simply but comfortably. No sooner had we hung up our uniforms and clothing in the unusually roomy wardrobe than Franzl said to me with a grin, 'Toni, I'm off to see my Elli at Pullach. She's already waiting for me with longing. What have you got planned?'

'Franzl, I shall go to Grafing and surprise my family, collect my bicycle and some civilian clothing. If we have carnival licence to enjoy ourselves here, then I shall copy you, and do it thoroughly.'

In happy expectation we set out for the railway station. Despite our lively chatter we made sure that no misadventure similar to that in Strasbourg befell us. Our paths did not separate until Munich, and Heigl took the tram there. Because of the forecast thunderstorm I decided to pass the time until my train left in the waiting room of a transit hostel for soldiers opposite the railway station building.

Upon entering the smoke-filled room I gave out a few militarily correct Hitler salutes and then my eyes fell on the grey-green unfathomable eyes of a blonde Luftwaffe auxiliary three metres away. She was about to leave and had thrown her rucksack on her shoulders. Overwhelmed by such grace and loveliness, I took two quick strides to her side. She noticed me and was flattered, for she was happy to allow me to straighten the rucksack. My voice sounded husky as I asked her, 'May I see you to your train?'

The eyes of the young woman in the trim uniform gave me an

impish look. I felt my pulses quicken. I was electrified as I heard her dark, clear alto tones tell me: 'If you wish, you can even accompany me to my Luftwaffe barracks at Murnau, but it seems out of the question that my troop leader would tolerate the presence of a man in the camp.'

'I would gladly accompany you to the end of the world,' I said as we went to the door. I tried to give the impression that I was fetching my girlfriend. Some soldiers made some sneering comments which I studiously ignored. Chattering happily we crossed the station courtyard and I even surprised myself when I actually got on the train to Murnau with Michaela. Grafing could wait one more day for me. I would definitely be able to find somewhere in Murnau to spend the night.

Dark rain clouds covered the summery evening sky over Munich as the passenger train rolled slowly south. The internal lighting was left switched off as an air-raid precaution. There were only a few fellow passengers in our compartment and so the zestful Luftwaffe auxiliary from the Rhineland and I quickly got to know each other. She told me voluntarily that she had just spent fourteen days home leave with her parents at Frechen near Cologne and was glad that she had not been required to serve at Essen – or in any of the other cities constantly under threat of bombing. 'Toni, my troop leader is a pain in the neck. Although she allows herself any number of liberties, she is very strict with us, but all the same I have had some good times at Murnau.' Still very much under the spell of her alto voice and Rhenish dialect, I just sat there listening to her and kissing. She seemed to have some scheme in mind, for an idea occurred to her: 'Could you pretend to be my brother?'

'What would be the point of that?'

'Just imagine it, Toni. If I can pass you off as my brother, you would be able to spend the night in the camp. There is a place there for bombed-out heroes.' We giggled like children and began to plan the conversation with Michaela's superior. I couldn't lose anything by it.

An hour later I stood in the Luftwaffe barracks before the desk of the Pain in the Neck who wore the shoulder-straps of a lieutenant. She was unexpectedly pleasant towards me, asked about my U-boat experiences and I was shocked when she did not ask to see my papers. This resulted from Michaela having told her at the outset in a very plausible manner how we had chanced to meet up in Munich, had not seen each other for ages, and I had only a few days at Tegernsee before sailing again. The only difficulty was explaining how I didn't speak the Rhenish dialect of Cologne (which is 60 per cent Dutch). With great presence of mind I answered: 'Ah, in the Kriegsmarine we have to speak High German, and I have grown accustomed to doing so. If I accept your kind offer and remain for several hours with my sister conversing in your guest room, then my Rhenish way of talking will come back to me.' Amazingly this nonsense melted the last doubts of the troop leader.

Later, in a barracks room actually intended for high-ranking visitors to the camp, we congratulated ourselves on our successful coup. Michaela laughed: 'Toni, that was a fine caper. One can't just wait for the right circumstances to come along, one must bring them about oneself!' We spent the next few hours together undisturbed. At dawn Michaela reported to her post at the telephone exchange. I went back to the railway station satisfied. I met her quite a few more times in bomb-ravaged Munich and once she even aroused the envy of my colleagues by visiting me at Tegernsee, but just as quickly as we had found each other we lost touch.

Time slipped by. At the end of November 1944 we had to be present at Hotel Eden punctually at ten each evening, and it seemed only a short reprieve until we would have to leave for Danzig. I had had a painful throat for several days which I tried to hide from everybody and occasionally I had a feverish spell. I felt very unwell. I got away with it for some time but finally Lt Benetschik noticed and he sent me off at once to see the doctor.

After a brief but thorough examination the old country doctor asked me reproachfully, 'Why haven't you come to see me before? You must have been in pain for some time. You are a walking germ carrier!' He gave me a sad look. 'I can't let you return to your people under any circumstances or they will accuse me of sabotage!' I must have looked depressed for he added, 'Of course I can understand that you want to rejoin your shipmates, but in your present state you represent an irresponsible danger of infection for everyone. I am sending you at once to the Hanselbauer Luftwaffe hospital at Bad

Wiessee for a tonsillectomy. You will have to let your comrades go.'

The same afternoon I was seated on a surgical chair patiently holding a steel basin under my chin. It would be going too far to say that the surgeon treated me with anything resembling care. He removed my tonsils with something which resembled a loop and shouted at me when I began to choke. After surviving this torture I was put into a small attic as a precaution against infecting anybody else and quickly recovered there. Then complications set in which the ward physician found inexplicable.

During my stay at the Hotel Hanselbauer as the only naval man amongst all the Luftwaffe wounded I was naturally a curiosity but the Red Cross nurses pampered me secretly from the first day until my release on 23 December 1944. To my surprise I was then given fourteen days' convalescent leave. My best Christmas present!

My father was away but for the first time since being called up I was able to celebrate Christmas within the bosom of my family in the usual Bavarian winter wonderland. During those days when my mother and sisters cared for me so lovingly, now and again I caught myself missing the comradeship and iron unity I was used to on the boat. I wondered what kind of fool I was. Was this normal? Why did I feel in this peculiar way like a man stranded on a peaceful island instead of simply enjoying myself at home?

Finally I received orders to report to a naval transit camp at Zeven near Bremen. As I was shown into one of the rooms there on 7 January 1945, I met at the door engine-room rating Effing from U-188 who had just shouldered his seabag and was about to leave. He had been the driver of one of the buses in which Lüdden and other officers had left Bordeaux, being captured shortly afterwards by the French Resistance but had then been released. We greeted each other like long-lost brothers. I noticed his Black Wound Badge and asked him at once if he were fully recovered.

'Of course Toni, the doctors have given me the all clear. I was on convalescent leave until recently, now I'm returning to Kiel for another boat. Pity that Rolfing didn't make it when the Resistance attacked our bus.'

Heinz Effing asked about our bicycle tour and then he told me: 'On another matter. The day before yesterday I learned that Lüdden is dead. He was aboard a burning accommodation ship at Kiel and died of smoke inhalation. The crew has a new commander.' He saw how sad I was at our loss and before leaving the room slapped my shoulder: 'There are now enemy aircraft over the Baltic. Some of them Russian. Your replacement on lookout was killed during an air attack. Take care of yourself, Toni. I wish you well in this ice-cold transit camp.' Thoughtfully I watched him leave and scarcely noticed the curious looks of the others sitting in their greatcoats on the beds of the unheated room who had been following our conversation with interest.

The few barrack huts of the transit camp were overflowing with shorebound sailors. In the barely-heated office nobody could tell me where and when I would be drafted aboard another U-boat. Instead I was asked if by chance I knew someone who could do joinery.

'Why?' I replied as innocuously as possible.

'I asked *you* and not the other way around!' The office jackass was a greying Chief Boatswain who wanted to make it clear who was in charge.

'As an organ builder I am myself a trained joiner, Chief Boatswain.'

'Well why didn't you say so straight away? We are in desperate need of a new trained specialist in our workshops after they relieved us of our last captured hero. But we are still expected to keep up our daily requirement in wooden parts. Report at once to the foreman and make yourself useful!'

Leaving the office I was glad to be occupied and not have to sit in the room doing nothing. In the workshop it was comfortably warm. I put on one of the brown overalls and began work at a carpenter's bench following the instructions I was given. During my first few hours in the barrack hut converted into a workroom I was given doubting looks by some of the other sailors and the foreman carpenter.

This foreman was a very haggard civilian of about sixty. On the second day in friendly tones he gave me small special tasks. He also allowed me to bring my seabag to work and fill it every day with wood shavings and other wooden waste as fuel to heat our room. The same evening our room was warmer though not overheated. Colleagues came to visit us from colder rooms to warm up. This led to conversations about the recent war situation. I discovered that Aachen had been occupied on 21 October 1944. Along the Pfalz frontier it might not be possible to hold the West Wall. The Red Army had been on German soil in East Prussia for some time and they were threatening Silesia. Under Soviet pressure, Romania had declared war on Germany, Bulgaria had concluded an armistice in Moscow and before all that Italy had already changed sides. We were under siege from all directions, and it was a mystery to many in this transit camp how the fronts could be held just by desperate defensive fighting.

I hesitated to become embroiled in these discussions. The others seemed to know each other better, and I was not present during the day. Everybody was aware how quickly an incautious word could be considered as seditious if brought to the attention of one of our unforbearing naval judges. Perhaps others thought as I did: 'If the Allies cross the Rhine in the West, they do not love us but are the lesser evil. That might bring an end to the incessant air raids which cause such suffering to our civilian population. But what of the East? What will happen when the front there finally collapses? Only a miracle can save us then! Do we really have this miracle weapon?'

For myself personally I was convinced that as a small, insignificant U-boat man, the fortunes of war would make little difference to me and at that time I often recalled my father's words, 'Now at least we might be able to save our skins.'

Initially I was happy to have work in the carpentry shop and kept quiet. The transit camp lived up to its name, for many got their marching orders. As time went on I began to hope that there would be no boat for me. About mid-March we had a young rating from Hannover, not yet nineteen, in our room. He was very uncommunicative, taciturn, and after receiving his orders to report aboard an S-boat (MTB) in the Baltic he disappeared suddenly one morning. It was soon being rumoured that he had gone to his mother's house and they were looking for him. A couple of days later the military police brought him back. I felt unbounded relief that I was not assigned to the firing squad which would execute him in the courtyard of the transit camp before the assembled company and a naval judge. Because my work in the carpentry shop was deemed so important for the war effort I was even excused attending.

At the end of March spring came to the naval transit camp and we sensed the end of the war approaching. Despite all exhortations to hold out I no longer had any doubt that our miracle weapon would not be used. In my room I had now only one companion, wounded as a mechanic on an S-boat in the Baltic. He had been discharged into the camp from a military hospital at Kiel as recovered, and expected at any moment to receive a fresh posting. Others were long gone to ships or to the infantry. I kept my fingers crossed that U-boat Command would be unable to find a use for me or might even have mislaid my personnel file.

On 8 April I was with the foreman carpenter at the planing machine finishing some wooden parts, the purpose of which I was never able to discover. Early that morning we had heard bombs falling on nearby Bremen, but kept working. Towards midday I looked out through the windows, covered with a fine layer of wood dust. It had begun to rain, low dark clouds were being driven fast across the skies. For the remainder of the day, perhaps even longer, the city, often put to the test, and its surrounding region, would be spared the attentions of the bomber formations and low-level fighters. While thinking this a very old AB seaman with a glass eye called me into the office.

'Here, sign!' The Chief Boatswain pushed a movement order across the table to me and said with an inscrutable expression: 'Your seabag is being taken from here to the appropriate storage facility. Take only your U-boat pack and your necessities. In an hour you can take a lorry to Bremen. If you want to write a letter home beforehand, you can leave it with me before you go.' He handed me a postcard and pencil and added, 'How you get to your boat in Bremen is your business. But avoid any detours.' To my surprise the previously so unapproachable man rose to offer me his hand. 'Staller, take care of yourself!'

Chapter Ten

The Black Boat

I got off the lorry in Bremen near the Vegesack shipyard at the start of the quest to find my new boat somewhere in the yards, or what was left of them. The city was unrecognisable. All around, debris upon debris, bizarrely-shaped bombed-out ruins, burnt-out window frames behind smoking hills of ashes and mountains of rubble through which ghost-like forms rummaged for remnants of their possessions. Everywhere only old men, haggard women and hollow-cheeked, pallid children, empty expressionless faces and stooped backs. I was deeply moved by the sight of a five-year-old girl, head bandaged, standing before a heap of rubble watching her mother searching through it for something. It struck me that these children would never receive the Wound Badge. On broken walls the defiant proclamation: 'Our walls break, our hearts never!'

Hadn't my U-boat Hostel been hereabouts? I was unable to find it. Didn't our 'U-boat Mother' live here once? For long minutes I stood in shock at the corner of the tavern we had frequented before our first trial voyage in *U-188*. The building was one of the few which remained undamaged. On the street in front of the entrance pieces of furniture, household effects covered in dust, wash baskets full of twisted cutlery, scorched beds, mattresses and perambulators. Behind this heap of junk and misery a red notice was affixed to the wall of a house: 'Looters will be shot'. The miserable existence of an afflicted people still under the heel of the Brown rulers.

Inwardly in revolt I was about to walk on when I heard behind me, 'Your papers, please!' Three field-gendarmes with machine-pistols ready to fire had probably been watching me for some time. I gave the Hitler salute as per Army regulations, now as before a good start, and the sergeant studied my documents very thoroughly before handing them back: 'U-boat? Do we still have any?'

'I would like to think so, Sergeant!' I replied with as much zeal as possible.

'Well, make sure you get on board quickly!'

An hour later I found myself standing in dismay before a really old boat from before the war intended for thirty-six men. Presumably it had been only used for training purposes and then mothballed. In bitter disappointment I asked myself where we could now exercise in this thing undisturbed. Boat and crew one unit? It seemed to me to be farcical. I feared that thirty-five men and I were going to be sent to slaughter in this obsolete steel tube shortly before the end of the war for no good reason whatsoever. To be honest, at this moment I was seriously thinking of going underground somewhere. Then I thought of the execution in the transit camp, of the ever-present field-gendarmes and also the journey in the lorry to get here. We had driven through a street in which three men in field-grey were hanging by the neck from trees. As we passed by, the grey-haired lorry driver pointed to this sight through the front windscreen. Each man had a cardboard placard at his chest reading 'I am a coward'. The driver said to me quietly, 'My boy, my boy, deserting never pays.'

Holding my documents I stood despairing at the quayside comparing the boat's number in my papers with that painted on the small conning tower. I heard repair work going on inside. The questioning looks I was receiving from the sentry pacing the deck escaped me completely. 'Are you perhaps Leading Seaman Stoller?' I turned round in surprise, gave the officer the correct naval salute to the peak of the cap and shouted loudly 'Jawohl!'

He was aged about thirty, wearing blue trousers and a dark blue roll-neck sweater, the blue officers' cap on his blond head leading me to believe that he was the chief engineer, and when he gave me a casual salute in reply I saw dark traces of oil on his hands. The man reminded me agreeably of Kiessling aboard *U-188* as he confirmed my assumption: 'Staller, I am Lieutenant Seidl and the chief engineer here.' He nodded towards the boat and continued: 'We were waiting for you. Now we are numerically up to strength but we still have a great deal of work to do. Come with me: we have received orders to move downriver to Bremen-Vegesack as soon as we have got the diesels going again. They are going to fit us with a schnorkel and for the moment we cannot dive.' He pointed to a circular hole directly abaft the conning tower and directly above the diesel room which had been cut through the boat's pressure hull. I had noticed this opening before without being able to see a reason for it. My new LI led me aboard over a thick wooden plank and asked over his shoulder, 'You know what a schnorkel is?'

'Jawohl! When submerged the boat can suck in fresh air, discharge exhaust gases and so run the diesels!'

'Right! They should have delivered the apparatus to us here, but it got diverted and is now at Bremen-Vegesack.'

The LI was pleasant to me from the very beginning. I climbed down behind him through a narrow conning tower hatch into a control room of very cramped dimensions in comparison to *U-188*. A *Kaleu* and a sub-lieutenant were bent over a chart. The interior smelled of oil fumes. Deafening hammering and the hissing of welding torches from the stern room situated very close by awoke in me unpleasant memories. The whole boat was filled with the sound of work being done. The LI reported: 'Staller has arrived!'

The two officers stood up at once, standing very close to me as I reported myself. The *Kaleu* looked very young. He gave me a piercing stare with his steely blue eyes and said brashly, 'Well finally! Welcome on board, Staller. It's been a long time for us to even get a full complement! You were with Lüdden on *U-188*?'

'Jawohl, Herr *Kaleu*!'

'Excellent. At least another experienced U-boat man aboard.' He avoided mentioning his own name and pointed to the sub-lieutenant. 'Lt Marker is our I WO. You are with his watch. You will get to know the others. Make yourself familiar with the boat as quickly as you can. After that give our weapons a check over. Particularly our flak and the MGs!'

The LI had left us through the hatch to the diesel room and I wondered if this arrogant, snotty-nosed kid could really be my commander. Lt Marker glanced at my baggage and said, 'You will find your bunk in the bow compartment, Staller.'

The first thing I did was go through the boat and make myself known to the other members of the crew. I established that with the exception of the diesel hands only a few men aboard had previously sailed on a U-boat, and this gave me a feeling of grave discomfort. While I shook hands and looked the veterans in the eye it was clear to me that amongst these predominantly inexperienced men, some of whom gave the impression of being horribly eager for action, there was little chance of survival. Trembling inwardly I asked myself, 'Am I to die at the end of the war in this obsolete steel gherkin?' Then I had a comforting thought: 'For the time being we are unable to dive. It might so happen that I will be on the bridge when enemy fighters sink the boat here on the Weser, or corvettes or destroyers give her the coup de grâce on the open sea. From up there perhaps I could leap into the water. At the moment, however, this dingy weather is at least protecting us against air attack.'

The magazine below the control room was narrower than a coffin, but the extremely good condition of the MGs, the small arms and ammunition surprised me. On the other hand the small-calibre flak would only be of any use to us of deck in the hands of a first-class gunner. As time went on I felt hungry. How and from where the cook conjured up the excellent evening meal on his tiny cooking range nobody cared to ask.

Our III WO, Chief Boatswain Stahl, was ordered to proceed with me the following morning to a naval depot upstream. We were to collect the provisions, for which we had a list, using a small launch which belonged to the shipyard. During the short trip up the Weser, Stahl sat at the tiller, never taking his smoking, short-stemmed pipe from his mouth. He advised me: 'It's overcast, but keep a good lookout anyway! You can't trust those damn' bees! For safety's sake I'm keeping close to the riverbank.'

Half an hour later we entered a warehouse only a few metres from the river. The depot was undamaged and I stared in amazement at the supplies stacked almost as high as the roof. Inwardly I was furious at the thought that out there mothers and their children were going hungry while here was a storehouse with everything one could desire. While thinking this, it became clear to me how our cook could feed us so well. Stahl came here regularly. He seemed to be on close terms with the smartly-uniformed but miserly Staff Paymaster for I heard him say almost confidentially: 'Herr Staff Paymaster! We have plenty of room on our launch. Would you want to have these tins of Hungarian goulash, these tasty potatoes and the other delicacies bombed into waste? Have a heart! As soon as we are ready to sail we shall have to live on hard tack again at sea. The youngsters could do with putting on a bit of fat beforehand.' Stahl seemed to have convinced the depot administrator, for we loaded much more in the launch than we had on our list. On the return Stuhl smoked a perfumed cigarette and threw me a carton with a grin. The cook was expecting us as we tied up alongside below the conning tower.

Two days later at dusk I stood on the bridge with Lt Marker, Boatswain Schreiber and the still inexperienced Able Seaman Scholz as we went downstream. The diesels had been given only temporary repairs. They were to be given a thorough overhaul at Bremen-Vegesack with shipboard tools before the schnorkel could be installed. Where we would be going once that was done remained a mystery.

No schnorkel had been delivered to Vegesack for us. Our commander was furious. The calming influence in the boat seemed to be LI Seidl who suggested to our *Kaleu* that he should anchor as close as he could get to the U-boat bunker under construction. 'The works have a railway branch line. We should receive our schnorkel here. I must give the starboard diesel a very thorough examination with my men, and I cannot yet guarantee the port diesel. Neither are seaworthy yet, Herr *Kaleu!*'

'Tommy's tanks are coming ever nearer. They must not surprise us here under any circumstances.' I couldn't hear any more since I had to go up to the bridge with Senior Boatswain Stahl and the other two.

Over the last few days, a fairly friendly relationship had developed between Stahl and myself. He was the veteran of several U-boat patrols and was aware of my fears. Neither of us was keen to die for this crazy regime. We had just been given a list of provisions to fetch from the naval depot and jumped down from the conning tower to the deck. 'Has anyone come aboard this canoe meanwhile?' Stahl asked the young sailor doing sentry duty on deck.

'No, Herr Chief Boatswain!' The man had come rigidly to attention and Stahl remarked, 'We don't do things on a U-boat as though it were a parade ground.'

As we boarded another kind of launch Stahl told me, 'Yes, Staller, this fully-tanked beauty belongs to the guards for the forced labourers who over there' – here he pointed to the building site on the river bank – 'are building those monster U-boat bunkers. Our *Kaleu* seems to have good contacts, for I borrowed it from them.'

During the run along the bank of the Weser there were some gaps in the cloud above us and for safety I brought binoculars along to be able to identify low-level aircraft rapidly. Stahl seemed to rely on me completely, though he made the occasional searching stare towards the river bank. We had already left Bremen astern and were about one sea mile from the depot when the sirens began to wail. Stahl took the boat to full speed. The bow rose out of the water, and a few minutes later we made fast at the depot quay. From the city, farther downstream near our boat and the bunker building sites we heard flak chattering. Combined with the numerous bomb explosions and the growl of heavy aircraft engines it grew into a ghastly inferno.

'I'll just have a look to see who's home!' Stahl pushed against a large sliding door and we found ourselves standing in the warehouse before the cleanly-stacked treasures. There was nobody about. Stahl grasped the drawbar of a small cart with rubber tyres and told me, 'Don't have any false modesty about it, Staller. The gentlemen will only stay down in the cellar until the air raid is over. Therefore we do not have too much time to help ourselves here. Just look for the best items!'

We sprinted several times with our fully-laden cart between the warehouse and our mooring point. After about twenty minutes we closed the door again and ran to the launch, now low in the water due to the great weight of cargo. Nobody had disturbed us. We had been very selective in picking and even threw off the cart cartons already loaded to be replaced by produce of better quality. We put-putted slowly downstream with our ill-gotten gains. I stood with legs spread at the bow, leaning my back against the stacked sacks of potatoes and flour, big cartons of tinned meat and fish, and hard sausage. Ahead of us it had all fallen quiet at Bremen, and at its shipyard was working again. The not-very-effective flak defence had ceased fire and the droning of the homeward-bound bombers was growing ever fainter.

I turned once again to search the skies astern of us. In doing so I looked briefly into Stahl's serious face. He was standing to steer so as to see ahead above our cargo. He said quietly, 'Keep observing Staller, bees can buzz anywhere. Something else though. Yesterday when I went through the control room I heard an interesting conversation. The commander is more than upset that our little schnorkel hasn't come. He is worried that the British will get to our boat before the schnorkel does. He gave our LI the order to get the diesel repaired at once and to put a steel plate over the hole for the schnorkel mast behind the conning tower. Seidl objected that it might not be strong enough to keep out heavy seas. The *Kaleu* dismissed that as an exaggeration.'

Stahl pondered for a short while before going on: 'At the moment, nobody knows where the U-boat operational centre is located. It has ordered us to creep up to Norway without the schnorkel so that we can be involved in *Endsieg* from there. Staller, as an old hand aboard you ought to know this but naturally you must keep quiet about it. Today this will probably be our last barge trip on the Weser.'

'It all sounds fun,' I replied and continued to watch the skies. When next I glanced at Stahl he was calm, relaxed and smiling which suggested that he knew more than he had confided to me. It was clear however that there was no point in asking him any questions.

At the boat we were greeted joyfully at the sight of our rich booty. The cook led the unloading party, involved every available man in the job and within less than ten minutes the launch was empty and could be returned to its owners.

It was beginning to get dark when I went on the conning tower as its lone sentry. The sounds of loud workings in the diesel room could be heard. Shortly before I had seen an old Junkers air compressor dismantled on the floor plating of the E-room. In the bombing raid that afternoon the incomplete U-boat bunker near where the boat was anchored had been hit. A stately farm not far from the river bank had been reduced by the British bombers to rubble and ashes. A couple of Frisian cows lay dead on the meadow with outstretched legs. The parts of the bunker behind it seemed undamaged. When a bomb exploded ashore not fifty metres from the boat I ducked down instinctively. Since there was no aircraft to be heard nor seen it could only have been a delayed-action device.

Hardly had the reverberations of the explosion died down than I could not believe my eyes: I saw dark shadows moving at the edge of the giant bunker works. I adjusted my binoculars to short range and watched a guard in a grey uniform leading a small group of men, another guard bringing up the rear. They were forced labourers dressed in black and white striped jacket and trousers and similar cap. Each of them carried two buckets. I realised at once that these must be concentration-camp inmates.

The two guards stood to one side smoking while the prisoners set about cutting up the animal's bloated corpse. The sight repelled and outraged me, and made me ashamed. At Lorient and Bordeaux the bunkers had been built by a German workers' organisation. And now this. The scales fell from my eyes. How had they managed to keep all this hidden from us? If we were captured, we would have to pay for all these crimes! I no longer knew what to think or believe. I felt empty. Preoccupied by my observations and outrage, it did not at first register with me how quiet the boat had become. Marker the I WO came up with the other two men of our watch to join me on the conning tower, the diesels sprang to life and exhaust gases escaped noisily from the two rear tubes.

'What's up?' I whispered to my neighbouring lookout. Lt Marker heard me and explained softly, 'We are just going up to Bremerhaven to close over the schnorkel opening and check the diesels. Then we're off.'

As we moved away slowly from the river bank, the contours of our small boat combined with the grey-black waters of the Weser to make us into an indistinct shadow in the diffuse light of evening. Marker now noticed through his binoculars the bustle occurring around several of the cattle cadavers. He asked, 'Whatever's going on over there, Staller?' I gave him a brief account. Before he could react the commander appeared on the conning tower and said, 'Seidl and his men have finally managed to get our diesels in halfway running order. In my opinion this has lasted long enough. It does not speak well for the front experience of our LI.'

We lay three days at Bremerhaven. The commander became really nervous when he was informed that British armoured units were continuing their advance towards us. The LI reported that the diesels were still not operational. Seidl also could not and would not guarantee that the steel patch over the schnorkel opening was sea-proof. On the evening of the second day everybody heard the commander berating the LI in the control room: 'We are sitting here like a mouse in a trap! Will you now kindly show us what you are capable of! I have orders to sail within 24 hours. If you have not completed this long overdue repair by then, I shall have you and your men court-martialled!'

'24 hours. Jawohl, Herr *Kaleu*!'

The repairs to the diesel were actually accomplished, for the next evening we sailed. Our antique boat slipped out of the harbour like a thief in the night. Lt Marker, his three men of the watch and the commander stood on the bridge. We were heading for the Heligoland Bight and I heard the commander order full ahead. Then, as quick as a weasel, he disappeared below. Seconds later we heard him addressing the crew through the loudspeaker system: 'Men! We are duty bound to carry out our assignment. We have to bring this boat to Norway in order to continue the struggle from there. I know from a reliable source that our miracle weapon will be deployed in the next few days. The world believes we are already defeated. It will look on in amazement when it sees instead that we are capable of hitting our enemies in so devastating a manner as no enemy has ever been put down before. I have been assured that from German soil we can practically wipe from the face of the Earth not only British and Russian but even American and other enemy cities!' He drew breath and went on: 'As you all know, the victims of the Allied air terrorists were mostly women and children, the aged and those unable to fight. My own family for example was burnt to death at Dresden. I would prefer not to speak of that.'

At this point the commander paused for effect. 'Some of you seem to lack hope. But there is no cause for that! Soon all of you will see the miracle weapon which German inventive spirit has created.' I thought, 'He probably does not believe that himself.'

His address was interrupted abruptly. There was a jolt felt throughout the whole boat followed by strange noises coming from the exhaust at the stern and the bow-wave died down. This left us in no doubt that the diesels had had enough. We tossed and rolled powerless on the waves and I could see in my mind's eye enemy aircraft using us for target practice when daylight came.

I heard a loud exchange of words in the control room. Minutes later behind my back I heard the commander say to Marker with resignation: 'This boat is done for. Even on this short stretch the other diesel went on strike. The LI is of the opinion that using tricks of the trade we might be able to get to Wilhelmshaven and repair there.' Because I had to watch astern I did not see the commander bend forward over the speech tube but I heard him order the change of course. After that he asked Marker, 'What is your opinion about this development?'

'It is not surprising, Herr *Kaleu*.' The commandant was silent. I could not see his face but heard him return below. By day one cannot look inside another and read his thoughts, and less so in the darkness when his expression cannot be read. Nobody on the bridge spoke a word. Each of us stared through his binoculars. Yet I was almost certain that the others were as pleased as I that now we might not have to die in this floating coffin. I began to hope that with luck we would be spared that. Why didn't the Tommies come a bit quicker from Holland to East Frisia? Probably almost everybody aboard was hoping secretly that the diesels could not be made operational again in time. In any case I found myself often thinking that captivity was better than death even if we feared that our enemies would seek revenge for the losses which we U-boat men had inflicted on them. Full of hope and somehow light-hearted I thought defiantly: 'Come what may, I shall also survive it!'

When we disembarked at Wilhelmshaven towards midnight I was not unhappy. The LI and the engine room hands and even the commander remained on the boat while the other crew members went with Lt Marker and a rating from the base to the nearby naval barracks. On the way I tried to see something of the city, which lay some distance from the river bank. As an air-raid precaution there was a general blackout in effect and not the faintest glimmer of light was visible.

Not until morning upon leaving our rooms did we find that there were a couple of other U-boat men in the barracks who had finished up here for the most diverse reasons. Towards midday we learned that our boat had had a surprise visit from a technical investigation commission. Not only I was unsettled by this. Nobody put it into words but everybody wondered if our engines had really been as defective as the diesel hands and the LI reported that they were.

Shortly afterwards Seidl and his men arrived at the barracks. We had not been together long enough to know each other well but I thought I detected relief in their tired faces. Minutes later a rating came into our room shouting. 'No boat to the enemy! Go to the window, perhaps you will be able to see from there your old beauty being blown up. The demolition team is already on hand waiting to do its duty!' As I hurried to the window and bestowed a quick glance on the faces of the others, I saw serious but by no means sad expressions.

We stayed there for two days in nervous uncertainty, playing endless rounds of skat, surprised that sea and sky were so peaceful and that we hardly saw our officers and NCOs. Because everybody knew that the war would end in a few days we celebrated with a couple of bottles of schnapps which a clever comrade had organised from somewhere. 'Raise your cups!' We could hardly credit our good fortune: we had come through it! The great kitchen of the barracks was also inspired by the motto 'Nothing to the enemy' for we ate more richly and well as hardly ever before. We were not allowed to leave the barracks.

Chapter Eleven

Prisoner of the British

Around 0900 hrs on 3 May 1945, duty NCOs thundered through all floors of the barracks and ordered us out for roll-call in the courtyard. I took my place in the long ranks. A large number of naval officers had also fallen in near the barracks main gate. Everybody looked with deadly serious expressions towards the gate as we heard the rattle of tracks and engine noises.

'Those are tanks!'

'We will be made prisoner!'

'Will they separate out us U-boat men?'

'It doesn't matter! The main thing is that the war is at last over for us!' The courtyard buzzed with conversation. For some time previously I had become accustomed not to allow myself to be unsettled by the assumptions of my colleagues and therefore watched in silence as a British tank drew up to the barracks gate and aimed its main gun at us.

'What now? Will they make mincemeat of us as Goebbels prophesied?' Stahl was standing near me and I heard him say this. A small open car drove past the tank slowly and stopped about twenty metres in front of the group of naval officers. The driver remained seated in the jeep while a British officer alighted from the vehicle in what seemed to me a very relaxed fashion. He walked up to the group with a military bearing but not stiffly: an officer whose rank I could not see stepped forward from the ranks.

The German saluted by touching his hand to the peak of his cap. Then he offered his officer's dagger to the British officer. The latter gave him the British Army salute, holding the palm of his hand not down but facing outwards. He took the dagger, looked at it for a few moments, weighed it in his hand and then with a short courteous bow returned it to its owner. Was this the British chivalry in which until now none of us had been able to believe?

More British officers drove into the barracks yard and negotiated for some time with the senior German officer at the base. We watched in silence as lists were handed over to the British. A middle-aged petty officer from Seidl's diesel team remarked sarcastically: 'Now that's what I call German thoroughness. Probably the Tommies are now getting the list of our names.'

The tank at the gate drove in, and the British officers got in beside their drivers in the jeeps one after the other. The German district commandant now approached our ranks to speak. 'The British officers have just confirmed to us that an armistice is in existence for the North German region and we have to keep to it on our word of honour! From this moment on we are prisoners of war, but have to be our own guards!'

Because this gave rise to whispering in the ranks he ordered: 'Silence! More discipline please! We will retain all our uniforms with the insignia of rank, all orders and decorations. Every man is required to observe unconditional obedience. Under the agreed armistice the British have been assured that every German will obey their orders or those of Canadians if they happen to be here. With immediate effect the available provisions are to be rationed since the Allies are not able to feed the greater part of their prisoners for the time being.' At this point Stahl and I exchanged glances and we were both probably thinking of the fine provisions depot at Bremen.

The officer continued: 'Disobedience will continue to be punished under German martial law. Therefore conduct yourselves as you did before this armistice! You will now bring out all firearms in the barracks and lay them out here in the courtyard. From now on the possession of a firearm is punishable by death. That is all for now. Dismiss!'

Together with two colleagues I was given the job of collecting up all the weapons and ammunition in the barracks and stacking them in orderly fashion in the courtyard. Scarcely had we cleared out the arsenals than British lorries drove up and we worked intensively for an hour loading up all these carbines, machine-pistols, MGs and the like. As they drove off, all eyes watched them. What would my comrades be thinking, I wondered. Personally I was far from sad at not having to be surrounded by weapons all the time.

In the queue for food that day, a pair of angry ratings told us that they had watched the kitchen staff pouring water into the cauldrons for the men after the officers had eaten in the dining room. Despite that we were astonished that the disher-up filled our mess tins with a thin, watery soup with a strange taste, and seemed to be cautious about giving anybody too much. He rejected our protests calmly: 'Boys! Quite definitely we shan't be getting any more supplies. From today on we must budget what we have strictly. Nobody knows how long we have to make it last. Apart from that the Tommies are sending new prisoners in almost hourly, including stragglers from the Luftwaffe and Army!'

In the afternoon we U-boat men had a surprise. A British Army lorry arrived at the courtyard with our seabags. When my name was called I grabbed mine happily, for I had long believed it to be lost. Now we all had a change of clothing. The rumour was going round that from tomorrow we would be put to work, and our U-boat packs were better for this purpose.

Next morning Canadian lorries arrived and took us to abandoned German gun emplacements on the coast. Under the watchful eyes of the Canadians, all day long we brought up artillery and flak ammunition from the earth bunkers to the waiting lorries. We were pleasantly surprised at the friendly treatment we received. Some of them even passed us cigarettes secretly when they thought their NCOs were not watching. We were prisoners and as such happy to have survived the war. The victors seemed to share this sentiment. They had a somewhat different way of putting it but nevertheless the joy was felt in common that all this killing was finally over. All the same I always felt fear as soon as I heard aircraft engines. We all felt this sudden peace to be a bit eerie, and in any case difficult to get used to.

It took two weeks of hard work to empty out all the ammunition bunkers. The rations grew daily less. On the evening of the second day we heard the shouting of outraged sailormen. We leaned out of the windows of our room, banging our cutlery against our mess tins. Our complaint was that we were worse fed than the officers.

Everybody was chanting: 'Thick and strong was the soup, sailors drank it!'

A veteran petty officer advised us to keep quiet: 'But boys, where would the Tommies get provisions so quickly for so many unexpected prisoners?' He was interrupted: 'Pah! Then the gentlemen should be starving just as we are.'

The petty officer would not let himself be put off and said quietly, 'Over the last few days very many soldiers and civilians have fled the Russians and crossed the Elbe to us. The Americans in the southern part of the Elbe are apparently just handing the refugees from the Eastern Front straight back to the Russians! Just be happy that you can be here!'

'We are! But just give me one good reason why the officers should eat better than us!'

During our clearing-up work on 8 May the news reached us of the death of Adolf Hitler and the unconditional surrender of the German Reich. Without exception we accepted this quietly and with resignation. There were few who cared to make a comment: 'Probably the other side have got the miracle weapon.' Or: 'This Thousand-Year Reich seemed to me very long, and in the end it lasted only twelve years.' Or: 'They say we might have to fight alongside the Western Powers against the Soviets.'

'It's all the same to me. The main thing is, I keep on living.' I agreed with this, but I also thought about my uncertain future. I hoped I would be soon back home. I knew at least where that was, others had worse luck, for their home towns lay in the eastern part of Germany and had long been overrun by the Soviets. Many still did not know if their families had managed to get away before the Soviet advance.

By mid-May the Tommies themselves probably no longer knew how they were going to keep us fed. Canadians drove us out of the barracks in lorries, mainly naval ratings stood in the back with their seabags. Where we were bound was anybody's guess. The most hopeful thought we might be released. Instead the Canadians divided us up between a couple of villages in East Frisia, and I dismounted at Pilsum.

A German naval lieutenant stood by a jeep with a British officer and told us: 'You have liberty of movement north of the Ems-Jade Canal.' He indicated with outstretched arm to a brickworks at the edge of the village and added, 'Over there is a cook with a field kitchen who will provide for you and everybody else in the close vicinity as far as possible.' Then he warned us, 'One thing is strictly forbidden. Nobody may cross the Canal. We have to keep ourselves available here near the coast. The Canal is the demarcation line and is closely guarded!'

Together with six others I was billeted in the cowshed at a large farm. We made ourselves as comfortable as we could in an empty loose box, the usual occupants being in the meadow. First we scouted the neighbourhood and offered ourselves as labourers to a couple of aged farmers, but unsuccessfully since others had already been there before us. Next we played skat and went for rambles along the narrow field paths through the cow pastures. On the third day at the field kitchen all we got again was cooked broad beans and the cook was not moved by our displeasure. When somebody towards the rear of the long queue shouted forward: 'Hey, Hannes, can't you cook us something reasonable?' he snapped back, 'I feel sorry for you, boys! But this is all I have received. Try to feed yourselves. Earlier you were so full of good ideas!'

My own stomach was rumbling and when I heard that I thought to myself, 'The cook is not wrong. What did I learn a trade for? I can make myself useful with wood and plane.' That same afternoon I began to look for work in the village. After a long conversation an old master cartwright let me have the small room above his workshop and said, 'We have to stand together, my boy. My wife and I are waiting with longing for the return home of our son. Go over to our village smithy. Hein will be glad to make for you the tools you need for piano and organ tuning.'

A few days later I used my somewhat clumsy but serviceable equipment to tune the piano in the village tavern. During my apprenticeship as an organ builder in Munich my tutor had always been full of praise for my ear for music and now I confirmed with satisfaction that I had not lost the talent over the following years. The old but solidly built instrument in the guests' parlour was totally out of tune but by midday it sounded like new. It filled me with the deepest satisfaction when the old grandmother sat herself at the keys and began playing with beaming face. Her daughter was the proprietress at the time and stood with her own two small daughters behind her listening. The old lady did not want to stop playing but finally rose, gave me a hug and said spontaneously, 'Young man, you deserve not only lunch but also supper with us. Come into the kitchen.'

Very quickly we were on familiar terms, and I began to drool at the sight of the aromatic baked potatoes, fried eggs and fresh spinach. It needed a great effort not to serve myself with too much. The lady of the house encouraged me several times to tuck in. Her small daughter, four-year-old Marlene, told me while happily chewing and very trustingly: 'Did you know Toni, our papa is still in Russia. He didn't write us a field post letter until half a year ago. Grandma says that he will soon be home!'

Her mother probably saw my face fall and therefore changed the subject: 'Because all our healthy men were called up, we have to look after ourselves, Toni. We here in the marshlands can make ends meet to some extent. The tavern doesn't pay much at the moment but at least we still have our farm. I often ask myself how old people or women with children in the cellar ruins of Hamburg or other bombed-out cities survive. No doubt you have seen for yourself how some of these poorest of the poor drag themselves every day through the village street in order to barter the last of their belongings for food. They call it hoarding but they simply have to beg in order to survive. Naturally we give them what we can. But we simply don't have enough for so many.'

At that moment there was a knock at the door. An old, fairly self-assured farmer stood there. 'Please don't let me disturb you. I just heard how good your piano sounds again!' He turned at once to me and went on, 'I have a piano in my living room which is out of sorts. Come at once if you can!'

I reflected on this offer swiftly and weighed it up against the promised supper in the tavern before answering; 'Of course willingly! But I noticed while tuning the piano here that I need to work on my tools a little. I can be there by tomorrow at the latest!' He gave me exact instructions on how to find his farm and departed

From the landlady I learned that one of his sons had been killed serving with the Luftwaffe over England and another was missing at Stalingrad. Uncle Gustav, as he was known in the village, was hoping that at least his youngest son would return healthy from the United States to where the Americans had shipped him out. Uncle Gustav and his wife had only their 19-year-old daughter Trude left with them.

Early next morning I stood in the well cared-for living room of the farmhouse, which had an impressive reed-thatched roof. The gentleman of the house insisted that I call him Uncle Gustav and explained: 'My youngest son, Heinrich, plays really well on the piano. When he gets back from America, I want it to sound as good as the one in the tavern. But nowadays this old, out-of-tune thing plays its own tunes all by itself.' He glanced at me and saw my doubting look, then went on, 'Don't look so disbelieving, young sailor! It really is so! We don't know what it can be. Perhaps you can find the cause while tuning it. I have now to go and see a couple of soldiers working in my fields. Ask my wife or Trude if you need anything.'

Despite her buxom form the daughter came hurrying light-footed from the kitchen and was forthwith never away from my side. Her long blonde tresses reached to her hips and I confessed to myself that her bewitching, flashing dark eyes and enticing cherry lips unsettled me greatly.

When I took off the dark-brown wooden screen covering the piano chords I found in the lower sound box behind them a nest with newborn mice in it. This was therefore the reason for the piano mysteriously playing itself! When I showed my discovery to Trude we both broke down in laughter. Her mother's voice came through the wide-open kitchen door: 'It is very nice to hear laughing again in this house, but I should like to know the cause of this amusement.'

'Oh, mother, the young U-boat man from Bavaria just told me that once he found a mouse-nest in the piano at a farmhouse!' She laid a finger to her lips, winked and then said, 'With this piano it is nothing like so simple. It will take a bit of time before our old tinkle box stops making its weird noises. He can't begin tuning it until he's finished that.'

We nodded conspiratorially. Trude held out her apron, quickly I put the nest into it and she swept out of the room. All day I simulated activity until I began to feel the eyes of Trude's parents upon me. I did not have to spend the night on a sack of straw in the attic and enjoyed wonderful meals of which at the time only the self-sufficient in the country were capable. Trude and I skilfully hid our secret from her parents. Shortly before midday on the second day I finished tuning the piano. Mother Kraus was sent for from the village tavern to try it out. Both piano owners promised to recommend my work. Over the next few nights I crept by to visit Trude regularly and was so well fed that I no longer had to queue at the field kitchen.

A few days later I borrowed a bicycle and pedalled to the picturesque fishing village of Greetsiel on the coast. The landlady of the village tavern at Pilsum had recommended me most warmly to the pastor there. He and I became close at once, for his only son had been flak gunner on *U-843*. This Monsoon-boat had been mined only a few hours out of Kiel after making the home run. His son survived. After the meal the parson led me into the church where he proved himself an excellent organist. When he entrusted me with tuning the church organ, I was happy to quickly dispel his initial reservations as to my technical ability.

Over lunch next day the pastor surprised me by being better informed about our Monsoon-boats than we were ourselves. 'Our son and eleven others survived on *U-843*. Far fewer could be saved from other boats, and from most of them nobody. The balance is dreadful. Of the forty-five boats in the Indian Ocean, thirty-four are considered sunk: on the way there, on the way back or around the so-called Happy Islands, of which you know one. Only *U-188* and one other boat came back safely. Some of the men may have been taken prisoner or remain in the hands of the Japanese, who are fighting on. Until the present the loss rate is 76 per cent! A record harvest of death, greater than in any other theatre of war. My wife and I are so thankful to God that our son was spared.'

'Pastor, from where do you get these statistics?'

He shrugged his shoulders slightly: 'Young man, I am well known to a highly-placed naval officer at Kiel.'

I stayed at Greetsiel for three days. I enjoyed the job and after that the pastor recommended me to some of his colleagues. After taking my leave, I returned the bicycle to Pilsum and five days later, well supported by Trude's rations, left by train for Emden. In the late afternoon I entered the Wasserburg Hinte country house after strolling the extensive estate. Here in the Burg during years past I was to have tuned a rather neglected grand piano.

The tall and very gaunt baron and his simply dressed but elegant wife greeted me with courtesy. Even before I could begin my work the couple invited me to sit at a table covered with a white cloth. The small room was at ground level. The baron explained: 'At the moment our house, including our large living room, is occupied by refugees.' With these words he offered me a seat at the round oak table with a view over the park with its old trees.

When an old female cook placed the meal on the table with pride and a smile, my surprise did not escape the baroness for she asked me, 'Herr Staller, when did you last have haunch of venison?'

'I am sorry, Baroness, but for the life of me I cannot remember!'

Her husband explained: 'An English major accompanies me on my rounds since we are not allowed to shoot at the moment. Our guest hunter always displays his great generosity and allows us more than sufficient from his bag. He is more interested in trophies, and so the game goes to feed our hungry refugee women and children. My wife and I are alone and don't need very much for ourselves.' He was silent for a moment and I saw him suck on the grey moustache at his upper lip. 'You see, our son fell at Kharkov as a panzer officer.'

He scarcely seemed to notice my sincerely expressed condolences for he continued immediately: 'How did you get through the turmoil of the war years?' Initially rather hesitant, I recounted some of the more important events of my voyages but both of them wanted to know more and plied me with questions. When I mentioned my short adventure aboard the defective old boat, the Baron nodded in agreement and spoke reflectively and more to himself: 'Every sacrifice is only justified if it serves a good cause. Senseless sacrifices on the other hand – no matter how heroic they seem – are madness. You probably had very level-headed comrades aboard.' He gave me a friendly but examining look and surprised me by asking: 'Were you disappointed when the war ended for you because of the diesel malfunction?'

Despite my slight doubts I decided to answer honestly: 'On the contrary, Baron; I have been carrying light baggage for months.'

'And what does that mean?'

'That I have long since tossed overboard everything that was cumbersome in this war, namely all ballast by way of feelings. On the last voyage of *U-188*, but also after it, nothing could shake me any more.'

He rose abruptly and I also stood. The baron seemed slightly uneasy as he laid a hand on my shoulder in a fatherly gesture: 'Herr Staller, you should not speak so. You are very young and have your life before you. Cynicism is the enemy of life. You must have ideals!'

'What ideals should one have then?' I was slightly taken aback myself at the frosty tone of my voice. He seemed to consider, then said rather imploringly: 'Believe me, there are still ideals, if you can distinguish them from falsities. It is very difficult for me, after all the madness you have been forced to endure, to find the words which are not mere clichés. One must never lose belief in the good in people, in the good in the world, or else everything will sink into chaos.'

'But we are now in dreadful chaos!'

The baron went to the window, looked at the refugee children playing outside and replied without turning round, 'I don't disagree, Herr Staller. It does have the advantage though that we are finally rid of the Brown rulers, let us hope for ever! You are one of the very few of your branch of service who has survived the madness. But what use are healthy bones if you are not capable of building a new Germany and a more peaceful world? You have a fine trade! Can you not preserve the belief in the old steadfast ideals of humanity?'

Now he turned, glanced briefly at his wife and probably saw my perplexed expression when I responded: 'Of course, Herr Baron.'

'In the First World War I was a company commander, and I know exactly what I am saying. There was then as there is today something worse than a mortal wound, namely the spiritual destruction of the human being. On the bridge of your U-boat you saw proud ships go down with their crews and in Germany people standing by the wreckage of all they possessed. They lost their friends for no recognisable sensible reason. Millions of Germans had to pledge their lives, many of these were not convinced of the necessity for the conflict. Of the suffering which this war brought to other peoples I do not need to speak. We are no longer able to change that. Therefore we need the determination to build a new and better world. And you should contribute to it.'

Only the pastor at Grafing had ever spoken to me so insistently when he advised me upon leaving school in 1937 to learn the trade of organ builder. Now I stood in the presence of this man who stared at me almost pleadingly. His eyes seem to be struggling with me more than his words. I wondered why this man seemed to have such a great interest in me. Slightly rattled I replied, 'Thank you, Herr Baron. Shall I start now and look at your grand piano?'

As if freed, we both began to laugh. With a wave of his arm he said, 'No, first of all come for a walk with me. The grand piano will still be here in the morning. My wife is not in the mood for finger exercises today.' He looked at his wife who shook her head with a smile. Shortly after that we strolled through the freshly cultivated fields and extensive pasture grazed by Friesian cattle. For the first time I noticed that my host had a walking stick and limped slightly. He saw my glance and said scornfully, 'That is my small memento of war so that I should not lightly forget the glorious days of 1914 to 1918. Herr Staller, I did not want to say it in the presence of my wife, but you remind me very much of my son even if Arthur was taller and rather more broad-shouldered than yourself.'

That night I slept in the British officer's folding camp-bed in the small living room, eagerly tuned the grand piano the next morning, and after taking my leave of the baroness in the early afternoon I spent a short while with the baron in the park. He gave me an almost friendly slap on the shoulder: 'Our Germany is at the moment totally freed of all glitter and golden banners. For the moment it is just something bleeding. I believe that it will become more miserable and poverty-stricken. It will require courage for the Germany of tomorrow to come alive. It will not be easy for you and other young people.' I almost saw my own father in him as the fully composed old gentleman looked at me with benevolent eyes and added softly, 'That all has to pass so that we Germans can finally find ourselves again.

A Government which has no virtues can never work for the benefit of a people.' He shook my hand with a firm grip. 'Farewell, young man! May you arrive home safe and soon! Build good church organs so that your life finally has meaning!'.

The next day I awoke on the straw sack in my attic, climbed down the ladder into the workshop of the old master cartwright and helped him lift a very heavy spoked wheel up to the loading surface of a big harvest-wagon. I had no work for several days. The sun rose and set over East Frisia as over everywhere in this world. I was often obliged to join the long queue at the field kitchen and assuage my hunger with cooked broad beans. Trude often came to me at night bringing food. The Reichsmark was long since worthless, and I felt happiest when I could travel for food and a small reward restoring organs or pianos.

At the end of June I was in Jever, dusted off and tuned an organ and spent several days with the pianos of various families. In a tavern on the edge of town, overrun with refugees, I found makeshift lodgings. The proprietor had returned in very poor health from Russian captivity. I learned from him what it meant to fall into Soviet hands. When I compared the sufferings of these men to mine, I felt more than happy to be where I was and despite my lack of freedom considered myself a lucky dog.

I received opportunities for work right through that summer of 1945 and could generally avoid the broad beans. At the end of August I went daily with many other comrades to Pilsum for collection on the airfield at the former German aerodrome at Wittmund. For days rumours had been circulating stubbornly that we were to be released from there.

Chapter Twelve

Released, Recaptured, Escaped

A s I climbed up with my sea bag into the back of a Canadian Army lorry I was only too ready to believe in this release story, and trembled with glee. The chain-link gate at the entrance to the aerodrome stood wide open and was unguarded. The lorry drove past empty hangars and barrack huts. Young men in mainly Kriegsmarine or Luftwaffe uniforms waited to the left and right. Some of them waved to people they knew. I searched for familiar faces and then saw Hermann Mair. The engine-room petty officer also noticed me and gesticulated with both arms. Minutes later we embraced, overcome by our feelings. He was the son of the tavern proprietress in Gries-Strasse at Grafing and was known at home as 'Grieswirtshermann'. 'Man, Toni, so you survived as well!'

'As you see, the sharks rejected me for being too bony!'

'I can't say that for myself. I would say, ill weeds grow apace and fat always floats! We two were simply not on the list to die, even though two minesweepers sunk under my arse!'

He told me that he had gone into the drink twice, but came up each time. 'When I saw my canoe sink the second time and I was hanging there in the water in my lifejacket, the Tommies fished me out and took me to their island. I have been here two days waiting for release.'

We were standing in front of the hangar in which we had placed our seabags on freshly laid straw and full of expectation watched a military lorry draw up carrying a fresh intake. Hermann seized my arm and then we both bawled across the courtyard, 'Schorsch! Franz!'

Within a short while, Franz Pfeilschifter came running up to us in his Luftwaffe paratrooper uniform. He pointed back over his shoulder and shouted with a laugh, 'The Navy is of course the slowest again. When the Rauscher Schorch gets here with his seabag then we shall actually be four Grafingers! I cannot believe it!' Just behind him we heard Schorsch' voice: 'I expected to see the Northern Lights, but never again your faces!' How great was our joy! Until late in the night we exchanged experiences and often asked ourselves if our home town of Grafing, not far from Munich, had been destroyed by bombing.

Over the next few days the Swabians were released together with men from the eastern provinces of Germany unable to return home and invited to go to Swabia. Finally it was our turn. On 31 August 1945 at sunset a long goods train bearing former Kriegsmarine, but also Army and Luftwaffe men, rolled out of Bremerhaven for the south. During the long journey through the mild summer night none of us thought of escaping. Why should we? We were on the way home!

'Why do you think armed Canadians are travelling with us in the passenger coach at the tail?' said Schorch Rauscher, standing near me at the wide open sliding door. He expressed what everybody was thinking.

Hermann Mair recalled: 'Before we left I saw those guys carrying a great heap of provisions into their coach. Maybe they have to guard us at Munich main station before they can let us journey farther with our release certificates.'

We laughed and never considered why returners-home needed to be guarded, stared out happily and at peace over the moonlit landscape and alternately tried to get some sleep. Our joy at returning home was troubled, however, whenever we rolled by black-rusted ruins or slowed through stations bombed beyond recognition. The train made only three longish stops when the Canadians gave us to understand that we were at liberty to answer our calls of nature in the fields.

Approaching Munich our goods train began to move more slowly for no obvious reason. Pfeilschifter stood next to me. We watched as men ahead of and behind our wagon used the opportunity to jump out of the train. Some waved to us and even to the Canadian guards. Nothing happened. 'They're right, Why take the long detour to Munich when you live in the neighbourhood? Toni, it's a good sign. It won't be long before we've done it too.'

The train was rerouted, steamed through Munich's southern station at a fast pace then slowed when passing the ruins of the eastern station. We wondered where we were being taken. Soon we four Grafingers stood at the wagon door very unsettled, looking out at our beautiful home town between hills and woods as the train roared past it. 'Damn it!' yelled Pfeilschifter, 'Why is this chap up front driving this loco so fast? We could have jumped off nicely just there!'

Towards midday on 1 September we came to a stop inside the former military aerodrome at Mietraching near Bad Aibling to be surrounded by Americans with 'MP' painted in white on their helmets and pointing their weapons at us. Minute by minute we became quieter and more distrustful. Not far from our wagon an American officer was seated below a sunshade in conversation with our Canadian transport officer. Finally they seemed to have come to an agreement. The Canadian rejoined his men in the coach at the tail of the train. Then he leaned out of the window and waved both arms as a signal to the driver to start off.

At Rosenheim station we stopped close by another prisoner transport. We were surrounded by American troops again. Nobody was allowed to leave the train. Behind me I heard some conversation with the prisoners in the other train and kept my eye on an American close by. An aged railway worker came along the side of our train tapping the wheels and couplings with a hammer. As he approached I heard my colleagues call across, 'What is this circus? What do the Americans want of us? The British have released us.' Suddenly I shrank back as I heard the reply, 'They are giving us over to the French. Probably to work in their coal mines.'

Amongst all this confusion of voices I heard Grieswirtshermann call out, 'I've got paper, can anyone lend me a pencil for a moment?' I never saw who helped him out, but Hermann then told me, 'Toni, place yourself so that that nervous gum-chewing hero out there can't see me.' I turned my back to the American and saw Hermann write with a stump of pencil 'We are four Grafingers. Please put the signals at Oberelkhofen to "STOP" We want to get out!'

Let's hope that works, I thought. I sat at the door dangling my feet with my back to Hermann, bent close to the wagon floor. The

American didn't like this and gave me an unmistakable hand-signal that he wanted me completely inside the wagon and waved his machine-pistol at me to emphasise the point. Out of the corner of my eye I saw the old railwayman slip Hermann's slip of paper into the pocket of his oil-smeared trousers and then step up his pace. Meanwhile I tried to give the impression of unwillingly obeying the American's order. I stood up slowly and squeezed Hermann's arm. 'Let's hope that the Canadians play along like they did the last time if they see us jump out at Elkofen.'

'It's all the same to me!' Pfeilschifter's voice sounded determined in the extreme. 'There is no way I'm going to pass through Grafing a second time.'

'Nor I,' the other three Grafingers assured him. Our paratrooper looked around with a challenging expression. 'Boys! Wherever we happen to stop . . . even though it might fall away very steeply down the side of an embankment . . . we must jump out come what may. We know the district and I'd rather break my legs than work in a French coal mine.'

While still in Rosenheim we positioned ourselves with our packs at the door of the wagon facing our direction of travel. I heard a couple of voices join in. 'Let me near the door. I want to try it!'

The goods train raced at high speed through the scenery so familiar to us, roared through Assling and as it neared Elkhorn we became increasingly more worked up. 'Did the old guy at Rosenheim fail to get the message?' Schorsch Rausch shouted in agitation. We were standing at the door, tense and in the paratrooper pose. At last the train brakes screeched and squealed and we reached for a secure handhold. Paratrooper Franz Pfeilschifter sprang out at once with his rucksack, Hermann Mair followed him. Schorsch and I threw out our seabags and jumped almost together from the train now proceeding at not much more than walking pace. It was a double section of track in this sector which ran along the edge of a wood about ten metres above the Attel Valley. We curled ourselves into a ball for the roll down the slope. A few bushes impeded a more rapid descent. Once we got to flat ground I lay briefly without moving before looking up at the goods train, now gaining speed with its human cargo. As I watched, more men were jumping from the train.

'Will the Canadians ignore them?' I wondered. Through the twigs of a bush I kept my eyes on the last coach until finally it disappeared from sight through the woods.

At that moment I heard Hermann say, 'Franz, that bit of a jump wasn't so bad. We can all still stand, even if we didn't roll as elegantly as you!' By way of reply the paratrooper yodelled his pleasure. We began to laugh with our release of tension, only Schorsch remarked with a disapproving tone: 'I wonder if the Canadians woke up meanwhile? They must have seen us! Anyway, at least they didn't open fire!'

Hermann Mair told him, 'Without any doubt they saw us. Those fine Canadian boys just simply let us run for it.' I added, 'We were very lucky to have had them!'

We saw a couple of figures disappearing into the nearby woods. We rejoiced, shouldered our baggage then strode through a freshly-mown meadow along the wood's edge. It was sunset, and below trees of pine and fir we followed the narrow path past the railway buildings at Oberelkhofen station before heading downhill along a narrow gravelled road. Below lay a proper highway with cat's eyes blinking in the evening sun. Beyond the few houses of Unterelkhofen village, at last we saw towering before us the red slated roof and tower of the castle visible through the thick abundance of the leaves of old oak, maple and chestnut trees. This was the seat of the aristocratic Rechberg family. So we were almost home! Even if we could hardly credit it ourselves, all four of us had made it. Each of us had one way or another survived this accursed war!

Probably the others were just as excited as I when we saw the landlord at the door of the Tower Inn. He was looking towards us with curiosity. Schorsch Rauscher laughed: 'Just look! Paule of the Pullover! The old landlord still has it, but see how it now hangs from his shoulders like an old flour sack!'

'That's right,' I said, 'He hasn't been as well fed as before the war!'

Now he came alive. 'Come in, come in! No returners-home pass me by without drinking their fill. Come, I invite you!'

'We really want to go home', Pfeilschifter and I said almost simultaneously and had to laugh. Pullover Paule replied in wounded tones, 'Your people have waited for you for so long, what do a couple more minutes matter? So, what's it to be?'

Resisting slightly, we followed the old man into the parlour. To start off he provided a long-winded explanation as to why he could only serve watered-down beer. Meanwhile we settled down on a wooden bench below the dark beams of the ceiling. We were the only drinkers. Through a window in the thick outer wall of the inn I looked up to the castle, almost hidden by the foliage of the old trees. I reflected. None of us early returners-home – and to judge by what Paule said only very few had come home so far – had received more than a single letter from home during the last few months. The post was not yet up and running again. Therefore I asked the landlord if all was well in Grafing.

'Certainly! Not much happened here; there was no fighting. Four weeks ago there was a collision at Oberelkhofen when a train loaded with American tanks crashed into a waiting train. All the goods wagons of the latter were crammed with returners from western Germany. There were many dead, including two Americans. A couple of the bodies were laid to rest up there in a newly-created cemetery. The two dead Americans were flown home. And by the way, Toni! Your father has been home three weeks! He told me how he escaped from the Russians!'

I jumped up in excitement and shouted, 'That can't be true!'

'Of course! Or have I ever lied to you?' Pullover Paule seemed only to take offence briefly and then rose waving his arms to silence the questions of the others. 'Each one in turn. Therefore, Toni; your household is now complete once more. In many other families a son, or several, or the father fell or is missing. You will hear that for yourself.' He looked at us and I saw that Franz Pfeilschifter was staring impatiently and expectantly at the eyes of the landlord when he began, 'Franz, I have not heard anything bad from your family, nor from that of the Grieswirts nor from the Rauschers.' A great stone fell from the hearts of us all.

Pullover Paule seemed to be truly glad at our surprising return home. Obviously we were curious to hear how it had all finished and so he was pleased to complete the story: 'The Americans arrived on 1 May. There was snow on the ground even on that day. They sent us a penal unit, apparently the Americans have penal companies. Anyway, this fighting unit was neither too friendly towards us nor too hateful. After all we now know about the concentration camps we wonder that they didn't handle us more harshly. In Grafing they turned a blind eye to Polish, Russian and even French forced labourers looting for three days.

'Wines, liqueurs, schnapps and champagne had been stored in the Schusser cellars for a Munich hotel. Their management thought that their stocks of alcohol would be safer against the bombing in our town. After the boozing the former forced labourers were too drunk to do much looting but there were said to have been some rapes, but I cannot say that for certain.'

Our mugs had been emptied long since and I was desperate to get home. Therefore it was with relief that I saw Franz Pfeilschifter rise and thank our host with a friendly slap on the shoulders: 'Thank you Paule. But now we must be off home.' We others thanked him too, and he left us with 'My best regards to your parents.'

We went from Unterelkhofen to the outskirts of Grafing town in almost record time. Here Franz Pfeilschifter took his leave of us and set off across the meadow to the converted gymnastics hall where his parents lived and ran a restaurant. Then, shortly before we reached Gries-Strasse I saw my sister Anneliese cycling towards us. I shouted her name so loudly that my voice cracked. She braked to a halt in front of us, dropped her bicycle and fell with a sob into my arms. 'Oh my God, Toni. We all thought you had had to go on another boat and must be dead!' I held my sister gently with my hands on her shoulders and pushed her back a little see how she had grown. 'You're a big girl now, Annaliese,' I exclaimed.

'And pretty too!' Grieswirtshermann added with a broad grin, 'Annaliese, we got through it too, don't you think we have earned a kiss too? Pfeilschifter Franz taught us how to bale out from a moving train. Ill weeds grow apace!' Laughing at his own local humour he took Rauscher's arm and dragged him away. 'Come on, Schorsch! Soon we'll be home for our own welcome!'

I was alone with Annaliese for a few moments and read her thoughts when she looked at my seabag. I guessed that she was hoping for more packs of cigarettes, but I had to disappoint her. She

181

looked slightly embarrassed at my suggestion. 'We've got very few left from your last leave. They always come in useful when we're short of food.'

Annaliese ran ahead of me up the steps to our small flat and shouted, 'Toni's back!' Soon I was embraced in the small kitchen by my parents and the other two sisters. It was a very emotional scene. My mother couldn't stop crying. As before I had the strange sensation after having lived through a period of great danger and now being lifted up in the claws of an eagle to be brought to calmer regions. I was home at last. During this endless reunion which I wanted to go on for ever I made the conscious effort to free my mind of the fear of death and the horror which I had had to live through. Not to forget them but to gather new strength, for in that moment I had a feeling that I must not be weak in future. When things began to calm down I saw my maternal grandmother sitting quietly at the table. 'Grandma! Are you also living with us?'

'Yes, Toni, I'm in your room.'

'It's not important, Toni, we'll find space for you,' my father said, slapping me on the back. He had always had the knack of hiding his true feelings behind an ever-present cheerfulness. We sat together happily in our small kitchen until the early hours.

Next morning, when I went dressed in my leather shorts to the municipal offices to report my return, my presentiment of the previous day was confirmed, namely that I was going to need all my mental strength from now on. A number of acquaintances shook my hand in a friendly manner, but as they did so several times I detected a latent reproach. As a U-boat man – 'You were an elite corps!' – apparently I shared in the responsibility for Germany being divided up into four zones between the victors, and even the smallest villages overflowing with refugees and those driven from their home provinces. I heard things such as: 'Toni! Now we have an almost insoluble problem! Don't you think so too?' Though outwardly unconcerned, I asked myself, 'Is it a crime if a soldier fought for his country; no, was obliged to do so? Where could I have hidden out for years in order to escape the draft? I only volunteered in order to avoid the accursed compulsory Work Service'.

Naturally I knew long before that in our country ravaged by war,

ood rationing had had to be introduced because of the numbers of
refugees forced into our much-reduced territory. When in his stuffy
office municipal officer Huber gave me my ration book and I stared
at the coupons which had to be presented when purchasing food I
was horrified: 50 grams of meat per week – less than two ounces!.
My mother had promised to put roast pork on the table for my 22nd
birthday in three weeks' time: from where was it to be obtained if not
stolen? Then I recalled that though they had used up my packs of
cigarettes long ago, in Yugoslavia my father had organised a large
parcel of Greek cigarettes with which my mother could barter.

Down in the street I was accosted by the mother of one of my
friends. She took my hand and began to cry: 'Toni! Our Fritz no
longer believed in victory, but he had to fight in Berlin in the last
weeks of the war and sacrificed his life. Toni, you were a volunteer.
Did you believe in the end in holding out for the miracle weapon?'

'No. Like many others towards the end I just tried to get through it
alive.'

'No? And yet you volunteered for the Kriegsmarine?'

I shrugged my shoulders in resignation, for I was already getting
sick of having to continually justify myself.

When I got back to our kitchen, which smelled of boiled roots, my
father seemed to guess the cause of my depression. 'Toni! We are at
the bottom of the pit. For that reason from now on it can only go
upwards. Don't pay it any attention if somebody thinks you ought to
be accused of something. I too was often asked why I was home
already. There are many trees as upright as a candle, but only a few
upright people. You and I can find it amusing that nobody here was
ever a Nazi. You and I of all people, we both were? I refuse to discuss
it any more.'

I told my father that despite what he said, it still depressed me. The
farther I went from Bavaria, the more beautiful had been my picture
of it and its people. 'And now this!' He sat smiling at the kitchen table
as though he had given the subject a great deal of thought. 'The times
are changing. Maybe also people. What then, Toni? You have known
my position since you were a child. In March 1932 I had to swear
both yourself and Annaliese to absolute secrecy about a drive in the
car of my friend in Neuötting. You were still small children when we

183

scattered anti-Nazi pamphlets in the village street. But I have to admit, nobody suspected then what the future really had in store for us.' The memory of that story was still clear in my mind. 'Toni! The violence of Nazi rule and its consequences brought many to realisation for the first time when it was already too late. In my opinion the people overseas reacted much too late. But my boy, the suffering and misfortune which failed to break us can only make us stronger even though it now forces us to justify ourselves. Yet . . . even the occupying Power here, the Americans, only became the great advocates of human rights after they had almost exterminated the Indians in their own huge lands and put the survivors into reservations. Not to mention slavery.'

I assured my father that I understood what he was saying, and asked him how I could have refused to serve.

'The point is, Toni, that I did my duty as a conscripted soldier against my better conscience in order not to be put up against the wall by convinced Party followers. In the last months of the war it was often difficult for me. But you have to look at the other side too. They had to obey orders and their bomber crews devastated our towns and cities. I am not an academic but I do maintain that nails should not be made from good steel nor good people turned into soldiers. Nevertheless it was done in the name of the people on both sides. One of my company commanders, with whom I had a very good relationship, taught me in a quiet hour Abraham Lincoln's statement: "You can fool all of the people some of the time, and some of the people all of the time, but not all of the people all of the time.' It is something I have taken to heart.'

My father's words were balm for my wounded soul, and I also remembered the parting words which the Baron von Hinte had spoken to me as I left East Frisia. Having regained my composure told my father of my intention to restart work organ making and wanted to see if the firm of Siemann in Munich was still in business. He replied that I should travel there to find out, but that if not I could tune pianos in Grafing in exchange for food. 'Reichsmarks won't buy anything now. Bakers, butchers and everyone else have to take them when they are offered with ration coupons. They all want to barter even the farmers.'

'OK, why should it be any different here to North Germany?'

Next day I stood in shock before a charred mountain of rubble from which everything of value had long been cleared: nothing remained of the formerly so proud organ-building firm of Siemann. A narrow path had been shovelled clear between the walls either side of Karl-Strasse. A haggardly elderly woman was passing by dragging two buckets of bricks. In reply to my enquiry she told me that the Siemann family had died in the cellar of their house and now one of their employees had started up the business again in a shed somewhere on the land. I carried her buckets to the ruins close by, where she lived in a cellar.

Walking home I stopped briefly before the rubble which marked my former workplace and decided to make a bare living working as I had done in East Frisia. Any shortfall would be made up by mother's root-soup and the remnants of father's cigarettes. Still wrathful at my reception, but yet full of hope and a revived joy of living I thought 'Don't let them get the better of you, Toni, sooner or later you will build organs again, perhaps even as an independent business. Over the last few years plenty of these instruments have been destroyed. Others could not be cared for during the war and have gone to seed. Somebody must do something about it!'

Back home I was surprised by the news that my father and I, and other returners-home, plus a number of youths and even middle-aged men, had been ordered by the US military authorities to attend at the Ebersberger Forest for a two- to three-week period of labour. There would be a small piece-rate payment in Reichsmarks. If we failed to report punctually on the following Monday our ration cards would be withdrawn. I asked my father what he thought we would be doing in the forest.

'The Americans want to do their French brothers-in-arms a good turn. We are to cut down trees for pit props in some mining gallery or other in France and load them up on a by-road for haulage.'

'That doesn't sound much fun, but at least it's better than actually being down some French coal mine fitting them.'

My father laughed. 'Every cloud has a silver lining, Toni.'

The Grafing municipal administration had provided everybody involved in the tree-felling with a textiles purchase permit for work overalls – without this permit no clothing of this nature could be bought. Thus we were all dressed uniformly in blue overalls.

After three weeks' hacking, the bald patches in the wood gave it a sad look. It bristled with countless stumps, but not a single branch or splinter had been left behind. The whole wood looked as though it had been swept clean, everywhere old men, women and children collected up precious tinder and firewood for the approaching first winter of peace. Many even dug up tree stumps. These foragers loaded up wheelbarrows or small carts before pushing or towing them for miles to dwellings or refugee camps. The most pitiful sight of all was the women and children who had fled the Russians and whose hunger could be seen in their eyes. We could do nothing to alleviate their obvious distress, but from their plight we realised that despite our own hunger pangs and calloused hands we had it comparatively good. My heart also bled for all the sound trees which we had had to fell.

On the last day of the forced labour contract I returned to the Grafing lorry together with my father tired, hungry and smeared with resin. Hermann Mair approached me to ask if I would be going to a dance at a tavern known as 'The Dirty Handkerchief'. These dances were notorious and I told him I would be delighted to attend on another occasion, 'I've got to clean and tune the piano at the Post tavern on Markt Platz. You know that our liberators have taken over the bar parlour as their club room. Perhaps this job might pay off.'

'Toni, I shall wish it for you. Don't let these brothers fob you off too cheaply.'

When I removed the wooden cover protecting the piano chords that early evening, a tall, slim Texan with a narrow moustache and steely grey eyes was watching my every move. I was standing bent over the instrument and looked at him with my head down. 'Are you worried I might be planting a little bomb for Saissrainer's best piece? He looked at me without understanding, glanced at his watch and made hand signs that I should get on with the main job. I worked at the tuning with great concentration, silently and unhurriedly, ignoring his presence. Later the club room filled quickly with noisy GI's who took their places on chairs and benches. Many of them rested their brown laced-boots on the table and leant back in relaxation. It was a good thing that I had started the job early, for I could not have done the tuning with the racket they were making.

A well-fed Afro-American watched me with curiosity from a nearby chair while eating a ham roll. He must have noticed me drooling for he got up, wandered over to the counter and returned with a tin of cola and another ham roll which he pressed into my hand. I forced myself to eat and drink slowly. As soon as I had finished the Texan was there again ordering me to get on with it. A few routine procedures and the piano was ready to play. 'Ready!' I reported casually.

At once the Texan took over the swivel chair at the keyboard, touched a few keys and listened intently. After that he swept into masterly jazz. The crowded club room fell silent to hear him. After a few minutes he stopped abruptly and in his hard eyes I saw something approaching recognition of my work. I rubbed my forefinger and thumb together near his face. His expression darkened and behind me I heard the black American laugh. Slowly and hesitantly he took an almost full pack of Chesterfields from the breast pocket of his brown uniform jacket, knocked out a single cigarette and offered it to me while pointing to the exit. Calm outwardly but raging inside I snatched the whole pack, turned and made for the door. For a few seconds total silence reigned in the parlour bar, and then suddenly all the Americans began laughing. A young GI followed me out into the deserted Markt Platz and with a few kind words pressed an unopened pack of Camels into my hand, said something I failed to understand and then went back to the club house.

Once home I laid my earnings with pride on the kitchen table: 'A bit more hard currency for the house! Every day a piano tuned in an American club room and we would soon be out of the woods.'

Over the next few weeks I cycled out seeking work as a piano tuner. Because of my lack of adequate tools I had to extend my radius of search ever farther afield. In late autumn with my father and sisters, we helped two farmers at the potato harvest. In those days harvesting machines were unknown, we had to unearth each precious tuber by hand. As a member of the provincial sickness insurance fund my father knew many farmers and was held by them in high esteem.

187

This worked to our advantage as harvesters and clampers. Our total income came to about 30 hundredweight of potatoes which we stored in teacher Kleiner's cellar. We were very pleased with ourselves and had become virtuosos at survival.

About the same time the family Pfeilschifter left Grafing and Herr Leo Steinfeld took the lease on the gymnastics hall. He was a very experienced cattle dealer and Jewish. From the day of his arrival the thing he had in common with the youth of Grafing was joy in having survived. He brought an orchestra from Munich whose members he had chosen himself and they played on the gymnastics stage for the dining/dance floor. Behind the stage was a lively market in buy and sell. As neither I nor my new girlfriend Elfriede from the Sudetenland were attracted to this much we went there mostly only as guests.

One lively evening at table Leo Steinfeld did suggest that I should try to enjoy life more and make up for the lost years, but I told him I only had eyes for Elfriede. Despite our love for each other Elfriede and I were not able to marry for several years. There were several reasons for this: living space was strictly limited because of the refugee overspillage, and despite the support of my fiancée and my father's assistance, it was difficult to gain a foothold in my trade. Finally though I did succeed. After overcoming many obstacles I set up my own independent firm as organ maker. The deepest feelings of pleasure continue to overwhelm me whenever I hear one of my organs playing in a church.

Chapter Thirteen

Epilogue

The former *U-188* E-room petty officer Gottlieb Baumann from Darmstadt was the first of us to organise an annual U-boat Veterans Reunion. It was initially poorly attended for lack of addresses to write to. At Whitsun 1953 I had been married to Elfriede for three years and, with doubts and very mixed feelings, brought her with me to my first reunion at Höchst in the Odenwald. The hearty greetings accorded me upon my arrival exceeded all my expectations. Once again Gottlieb Baumann hit the nail on the head as he shook hands with Heigl and myself: 'What do you reckon then? Our two rascals have turned up and even brought their wives. And rightly so. One cannot enjoy himself so much at being one of the survivors if he is alone!' We talked, and as we did so the dreadful memories were resurrected. As we thought back at the pointless sacrifices made by the many young men on both sides who disappeared without trace below the waves of the world's oceans, it came home to us what indescribable good luck those of us who served aboard *U-188* had had. Our former officers Meenen and Benetschik, former Chief Petty Officers Korn and Schulz and we others could hardly grasp the fact that our boat had survived whilst the majority of the others had gone down. Only now, sitting before full wine glasses, did it become clear what stress and strain had been inflicted upon us in that boat for weeks and months. Elfriede listened in silence. Only once did she ask me, 'But Toni, why didn't you tell me all this before? It must have been terrible.' Other wives seemed to feel the same.

In 1980 it fell to me to arrange the reunion for us former *U-188* men and their wives at the Hotel Fletzinger, Wasserburg am Inn. By then of course we were all long settled in our civilian occupations and one of the veterans was even the master of a merchant ship. Without exception we were all happy to be civilians and a couple of the members had become 'freedom fighters'. My trade, organ maker, which requires skill, an appreciation of music and a certain degree of architectural-artistic intuitional grasp, was understood by few of the former U-boat men. As we stood in the workrooms of my organ-building firm following an excursion to Bad Wiessee, I was inundated with numerous questions. 'Toni, we thought you were a real screwball then and used to ask ourselves, what type of living one would expect from making organs? Apparently the answer would be, a good one! Have you done all this by yourself, built it all up without outside assistance?'

In the parochial church of St Sebastian in the neighbouring district of Ebersberg, Franz Mlnarschik gave an organ recital. The inner workings of the organ had been made by myself and my assistants from new without changing the exterior of the instrument. Herr Mlnarschik taught music at Grafing High School and was a connoisseur of the organ. My former shipmates listened deeply moved as the nave of the church was flooded by the various loud and softer tones. In the end I was filled with the greatest satisfaction that now even the last sceptics amongst my former comrades-in-arms seemed convinced that organ building was a trade with a claim to being a life's work. That made me very happy.

On 28 February 1998 Herr Meenen wrote to all surviving crewmen of *U-188* in a letter repeated here partly verbatim, partly in words to the effect of those written in extracts

At Christmas 1995 my English pen-friend Norman Gibson, our former 'enemy', surprised me with the enclosed memorial booklet. Gibson was aboard the *Fort Buckingham*, the ship sunk by *U-188* in the Indian Ocean in January 1944. He authored the book 'Survivors' with the help of a journalist friend (Binning) and articles contributed by P. A. Ricklidge and the German radio officer A. Moer. Ricklidge sailed on the *Fort La Maune*, which we sank a few days after the *Fort Buckingham*, while Moer was aboard the *Charlotte Schliemann*, prevented from refuelling us because she had been sunk by the Royal Navy in the southern Indian Ocean. This

Epilogue

book depicts without any resentment and with British fairness the sufferings of both the British and German shipwrecked. The 1943/1944 operation of *U-188* as set out in the War Diary is practically the framework. In short, it was written for us survivors to remember, in memory of the many dead of both sides who fell in service, and above all as a warning to our children never to allow such a catastrophe to occur again . . .

Below the photographs of Gibson and Rucklidge at the conclusion of the British book is written:

Seafarers may perhaps be garrulous, but they have little left over for literature. Therefore many stories of the sea have never been committed to paper. A small collection of personal experiences from the Second World War has been assembled here for later generations to read. The reader will gain from the collection the insight that many stories will never be told because the survivors of shipwrecks ultimately went down, were lost, without leaving behind a trace of themselves as the result of exposure, exhaustion or storm.

Translator's Note

Relating to The Events of 9–11 April 1943 as Recounted in Chapter 4

O n 9 April 1943, *U-188* was some 500 sea miles south of the tip of Greenland when she came across westbound Convoy ON 176 consisting of forty-eight ships. This convoy had sailed with a strong warship escort from Liverpool for New York on 21 March 1943. Lüdden kept in distant visual contact, regularly informing U-boat Command of the convoy's position, speed and bearing while waiting for other boats to arrive.

That same day, HMS *Beverley*,[1] a destroyer escort, collided with the freighter *Cairnvalona*. As a result her anti-submarine detection gear and degaussing equipment were knocked out. Although ordered by the convoy commander to put into Nova Scotia to repair, the commander of HMS *Beverley* insisted on remaining with the convoy, although the destroyer was now not very useful as a convoy escort.

In the early hours of 11 April by when no reinforcements were reported to hand, Lüdden decided to attack the convoy alone. In the *U-188* War Diary[2] he noted the Sea State as 2 – a light breeze with calm rippled waves, crests glassy but not breaking, wave height less than four inches. The wind was coming from the SSW, moonlight, little cloud and strong Northern Lights providing clear visibility and a good view of the convoy.

It was a surfaced attack, Lüdden being on the bridge with the

1. Geoffrey Blewett, *HMS Beverley – A Town Afloat (1940-1943)* (Alan Twiddle, 1998) and my grateful acknowledgement to contributor Nick Woods for his information.
2. My thanks to Capt. Jerry Mason USN (ret'd), http://www.uboatarchive.net for making available the six pages of the *U-188* War Diary for 11 April 1943.

watchkeeping officer and two lookouts. He was seated at the UZV, a binocular torpedo sight. The data from this instrument was passed to the control room below for the firing angle to be computed.

At 0549 hrs Lüdden fired two torpedoes at a tanker. The first hit, the second kept running. He fired two more at freighters; these third and fourth torpedoes and the second one all ran for between 118 and 131 seconds, and all hit and sank the destroyer HMS *Beverley* at the rear of the convoy and of whose presence Lüdden had not been aware.

The tanker described by Lüdden was in his estimation of about 8,000 gross tons. At 1,500 metres it completely filled his UZV and so he had an excellent view of it. It had masts forward and midships, a thin funnel astern and he noted that the stern section of the tanker seemed unusually long. The *U-188* War Diary states: 'After 94 seconds, torpedo hit on tanker at rear third. Tall white explosive column rose up from seat of impact. Tanker buckled at rear section and sank by the stern after 45 seconds.' In this world, an empty 8,000-ton tanker would normally take far longer than 45 seconds to go down.

The section of the War Diary between 0552 and 0559 hrs is absent or censored, but from Staller's account we know that *U-188* next came across 'a straggler'. This was another peculiar-looking ship, a freighter 'with superstructure running along its length' as Lüdden described it in his summary of the sinking at 0559 hrs.

U-188 was chasing the convoy, and Staller was on lookout astern, and so he was surprised when the freighter passed the boat heading away from the convoy. The first torpedo struck the forecastle. 'While passing us slowly at 2,000 metres', lookout Anton Staller wrote, 'the second torpedo struck the freighter astern. Aside from the magnifying effect of the glow of the shipboard fire, I thought this ship looked *gigantic* . . . ' No wonder it did with all that superstructure running from stem to stern. The burning stern 'reared up again' and the 5,000-ton freighter 'bow heavy, began to sink'. Staller stated that there seemed to be an internal explosion and then 'a cloud of white steam' which led both himself and Lüdden to conclude that this had been 'the boilers exploding'. As with the tanker no crew or survivors were seen, and like the tanker, the freighter sank almost at once at 0559 hrs.

U-188 gave chase to the convoy for a few minutes but then had to dive to effect urgent repairs. In a signal to U-boat Command at 1705 hrs (FT 1612/11/882), Lüdden stated that 'from 0550 hr quadrant AJ 9661 sank two steamers of 5,000 tons and one tanker of 8,000 tons.' One of the 'steamers' was the destroyer HMS *Beverley*, and the matter of the other two was resolved as follows.

U-188 was the only U-boat to have fired torpedoes at this convoy or in this general sea area on 11 April 1943. Therefore the three torpedoes fired by Lüdden at other targets were deemed officially to have sunk HMS *Beverley* since no other ship was hit.

Convoy ON 176 sailed from Liverpool composed of forty-nine merchant ships, the names of all of which are known. *Lancastrian Prince* was sunk on 12 April 1943 by *U-404*. The other forty-eight ships all sailed again in later convoys. Therefore no merchant ship was lost from the convoy on 11 April. Yet both the unidentified tanker and freighter _were not only hit by torpedoes aimed at those two ships specifically but they were also seen to sink by Lüdden and his bridge watch_. Here is the crucial point which distinguishes this mystery from all others. Two ships were sunk but no ships were lost.

Neither of the two ships issued an SSS message on the distress frequency stating the ship's name as required by Admiralty instructions. Nobody was ever seen aboard either ship, or attempted to get the boats away. Neither the rescue ship *Melrose Abbey* nor any of the warship escorts were detailed to search for survivors of either of two merchant ships alleged to have been sunk on 11 April. The German wireless monitoring service 'B-Dienst' never intercepted any signals traffic mentioning the sinking of any ship from Convoy ON 176 on 11 April 1943 except the destroyer HMS *Beverley*.

Upon their arrival at Lorient, Lüdden and the *U-188* crew members involved would have been subjected to intense questioning by the BdU Staff to establish what lay behind the two claimed but evidently imaginary sinkings. The fact that Lüdden continued to command the boat afterwards makes it clear that his account, no matter how fantastic it might seem, was accepted.

Kapitänleutnant Lüdden was eventually awarded the Knight's Cross in 1944 for sinking 50,000 tons of shipping in the Gulf of Aden area. Though credited with sinking HMS *Beverley*, a veil of silence was drawn over the other claims. As far as U-boat Command was concerned, these two merchant ships never existed, and the matter was forgotten.

The marine insurers Lloyd's of London have an immense quantity of material going back 300 years regarding the sightings of ghost ships at sea. The most famous case is certainly *The Flying Dutchman*. Admiral Dönitz stated that in 1942 several U-boat logs had entries recording the sighting of this phantom ship off the Cape of Good Hope. The most significant case of all, explained below, may throw light on what a ghost ship actually is, and may also explain the effects seen by Lüdden and his lookouts including Anton Staller aboard *U-188*.

On 5 January 1931, the Norwegian 6,000-ton freighter *Tricolor* left Colombo, Ceylon (modern Sri Lanka) deeply laden for Yokohama with general cargo and chemicals, some of which were loaded on deck. The P&O mail liner *Naldera*[3] reported that she came across *Tricolor* five miles offshore near Barberyn listing heavily with flames shooting up above her mastheads. *Naldera* stood by and watched *Tricolor* explode and sink at 1515 hrs. Six of the crew were lost when the ship went down. Weather was sunny and clear, visibility seven sea miles.

On the sixth anniversary of the *Tricolor* tragedy, 5 January 1937, the Indian-flag cargo ship *Khosrou*, 4043 tons, of the Bombay and Persian Steam Navigation Company and bound for Calcutta was proceeding off Colombo at five knots in rain and mist. Every two minutes the ship's master gave a blast on the fog horn. When he heard the sound of another ship's siren he stopped his engines and drifted, listening. The fog horns of the two ships continued to resound until the second ship suddenly appeared out of the mists astern.

The pilot Robinson and the ship's master logged a 6,000-ton motor ship about a cable's distance (600 feet) away. She passed the *Khosrou* in plain sight. The name *Tricolor* could be read on the ship's hull through binoculars. The ship appeared abandoned with nobody at the helm or on the bridge. The *Tricolor* then disappeared again into the mists. After no more than five minutes the mist lifted to provide

---

3. *The Argus* (Melbourne, Victoria), 19 January 1931, p.10.

visibility extending for seven miles. The *Tricolor* was nowhere to be seen but could not have sailed seven miles in five minutes.[4]

Tricolor was a typical ghost ship circulating near the location of her watery grave where she had sunk in 1931, and now she appeared, apparently abandoned, six years later to the day. Three pertinent facts are known about this ghost ship: (i) she knew that it was the sixth anniversary of her sinking; (ii) she knew that it was misty and (iii) she indicated her *awareness of the presence* of the *Khosrou* by replying to the *Khosrou*'s fog horn.

Until now it has been the belief that the nature of a ghost ship cannot be known, that it is an image of the original ship woven in some mysterious way into the fabric of the seascape where it came to grief, condemned to repeat the event endlessly. True to form the ghost ship *Tricolor* knew that it was the anniversary of the sinking. Unlike the day when the real *Tricolor* sank, it was misty and the ghost ship *Tricolor* knew that she should use her siren. When she heard the fog horn of the *Khosrou*, a ship in the 1937 present, she replied and gave the game away.

The most likely explanation would seem to be that a ghost ship is simply a maritime version of a UFO,[5] unsubstantial but able to perform marvels. Accordingly, at the scene of the naval tragedy of 11 April 1943, the ghost tanker and ghost freighter made themselves invisible to the convoy and placed themselves in a position where they knew that Siegfried Lüdden would inevitably choose to fire at them, and the theatre of 'being torpedoed and sunk' was then played out.

---

4. Fritz Leingber, *Los Fantasmas* (Barcelona, 2003), pp. 89–90.
5. E.g. 'The entities identified as ghosts and UFOs etc. are all plasma forms from the counterpart Earth': a theory expounded in several books such as *Our Invisible Bodies* (2006) and *Dark Plasma Theory* (2008) by the American plasma physicist Jay Alfred, also on-line.